D1559706

Fieldwork Dilemmas

Fieldwork Dilemmas

Anthropologists in Postsocialist States

Edited by

Hermine G. De Soto
and
Nora Dudwick

THE UNIVERSITY OF WISCONSIN PRESS

The University of Wisconsin Press
2537 Daniels Street
Madison, Wisconsin 53718

3 Henrietta Street
London WC2E 8LU, England

5   4   3   2   1

Printed in the United States of America

Library of Congress Cataloging-in-Publication Data
Fieldwork dilemmas: anthropologists in postsocialist states /
   edited by Hermine G. De Soto and Nora Dudwick.
      262 pp.   cm.
      Includes bibliographical references and index.
      ISBN 0-299-16370-9 (cloth: alk. paper)
      ISBN 0-299-16374-1 (pbk.: alk. paper)
      1. Ethnology—Europe, Eastern—Field work.
   2. Ethnology—Former Soviet republics—Field work.
   3. Ethnology—Field work.   4. Europe, Eastern—Social conditions.
   5. Former Soviet republics—Social conditions.
   I. De Soto, Hermine G.   II. Dudwick, Nora.   III. Title.
      GN585.E852 F54   2000
      305.8′00947—dc21   00-008600

To Ida, Sultana, Igor, and Ari, for their patience
and support during the editing of this volume
Nora Dudwick

To the life of Ana Maria Gruél-Steidle, my mother
Hermine G. De Soto

Contents

Foreword: Ethnography and Postsocialism   ix
Nancy Ries

Introduction   3
Nora Dudwick and Hermine G. De Soto

**Part 1. Fieldwork in Disintegrating and Reintegrating Nations
    and States**   9

1. Postsocialism and the Fieldwork of War   13
    Nora Dudwick

2. Would the Real Nationalists Please Step Forward:
    Destructive Narration in Macedonia   31
    K. S. Brown

3. Telling Stories of Serbia: Native and Other Dilemmas
    on the Edge of Chaos   49
    Marko Živković

Part 2. Fieldworkers in the Postsocialist Field   69

4. Crossing Western Boundaries: How East Berlin Women
    Observed Women Researchers from the West after
    Socialism, 1991–1992   73
    Hermine G. De Soto

5. Ethnographic Encounters in Post-Soviet Kyrgyzstan:
    Dilemmas of Gender, Poverty, and the Cold War   100
    Kathleen Kuehnast

6. When Text Becomes Field: Fieldwork in
    "Transitional" Societies   119
    Igor Barsegian

7. Fieldwork and the "Doctoring" of National Identities
in Arctic Siberia   130
David G. Anderson

**Part 3. Negotiating Personal Relationships in the
Postsocialist Field**   149

8. Intruder in Uzbekistan: Walking the Line between
Community Needs and Anthropological Desiderata   153
Russell Zanca

9. Mixed Devotions: Religion, Friendship, and Fieldwork
in Postsocialist Eastern Germany   172
Daphne Berdahl

10. Researcher, Advocate, Friend: An American Fieldworker
among Balkan Roma, 1980–1996   195
Carol Silverman

Afterword: Intimations from an Uncertain Place   219
Michael Herzfeld

Contributors   239
Index   244

Foreword
Ethnography and Postsocialism

The manifold and often strikingly paradoxical transformations which have occurred in the societies of eastern Europe and the former Soviet Union with the collapse of state socialism present ethnography with numerous and arguably unique challenges—empirical, theoretical, logistical, method-ological, representational, and ethical. In contexts where the relationships between state and citizen have been massively and rapidly reconfigured, where revolutionary ideologies have been delegitimized (to be replaced with an assortment of new convictions, from manic capitalism to activist na-tionalism), where class, interethnic, and even gender relations have been radically transformed, where economies have disintegrated and entire life-ways have evaporated, established ethnographic frameworks may seem in-adequate to the descriptive task at hand. Yet ethnographers in postsocialist states feel an obligation to try to record the particular patterns social dis-orientation takes and to outline some of its comparative features. This is an important task: collectively, ethnographers have the power to deconstruct the dominant discourse of "transition" (see Barsegian, this volume).

The anthropologists writing for this volume have been actively engaged in fieldwork in socialist and postsocialist societies within the past decade and often over extended periods of time. From the point of view of social science, they have thus been privileged witnesses to radical sociocultural transformations and have faced the descriptive challenge (and opportunity) of conveying the complexities of their informants' changing life-scapes and relating these to structural transformations. But the more compelling issues for anthropologists who have experienced the passage from late socialism into postsocialism—the issues which form the heart of this volume—exist in the borderlands between the personal, the professional, and the political.

Each of the chapters in this volume poses questions about anthropolog-ical positionings in the field and in the practices of representation. As De Soto puts it in her chapter, reflexive anthropology requires that we ponder seriously "how one bridges the gap between oneself and the people one studies" and that we consider whether or not the knowledge we gain from fieldwork in postsocialist societies—the very knowledge on which we build our careers—"will help to reduce social inequalities, social injustices, and many other forms of human rights violations." At the very least, this means that ethnographers must actively dialogue with people, and not merely speak for them, regarding the difficult question of how people live and what the future may hold for them (Anderson, this volume). As part of our ethnographic exchanges, one of the most important things we can do (in postsocialist societies as elsewhere) is to reveal the degree to which and ways in which people wield their own individual and collective agency—despite unpredictability, loss, conflict, and structural change—agency which may, as Anthony Giddens suggests in *The Constitution of Society* (1984), have significant (although only partly visible) impact on structure itself. This may entail sharing with our interlocutors whatever tools we may possess to mount their own critiques of the new colonizations they are enduring, colonizations which may include our very presence among them.

Each of the ethnographers represented here has vital stories to tell of the kinds of mistakes and gains to be made in the painstaking endeavor of maintaining the interpersonal relationships crucial to participatory inquiries. Their accounts argue for the importance of humanistic engagement with our informants and their communities despite the cost in terms of the analytical objectives and theoretical commitments we may bring into the field. Some of these authors face the political and personal dilemma of how to represent ideological positions or constructions of history with which they may disagree (see Brown; and Živković); some face the challenge of trying to "catch" something of local reality before it vanishes or transforms itself while they experience the discomfiture which many citizens of postsocialist states now chronically live with—the lack of a sense that even the nearest future is predictable or that the contours of society are articulable (see Kuehnast). Some find viable a position where other possible positions intersect (see Zanca; Berdahl; and Silverman), yet locating such a position may be an extremely tricky but crucial ethnographic quandary where politics are concerned: Dudwick finds a position which at least partly mediates contradictory moral demands, although it is clear that this is no easy resting place but instead is one which must be constantly renegotiated in the process of continuing fieldwork and writing.

As Katherine Verdery, among other scholars, has emphasized in her *What Was Socialism? And What Comes Next?* (1996, p. 4), the Cold War was "a cognitive organization of the world" (for various treatments of this point see especially Kuehnast; Anderson; Barsegian; and Zanca, all in this volume), which shaped mutual perceptions and practices in a multitude of far-reaching ways. Ethnographers go to postsocialist societies armed with all kinds of nearly unexaminable perceptions, mythic categories, and competitive stances and encounter there people similarly equipped. "Disarmament" in the field is a long, circuitous, and often painful experience of undoing deeply hidden expectations, tripping over multiple levels of contradiction, and letting go of cherished theoretical implements. As a collective effort, the accounts in this volume compose an essential roadmap for others engaged in fieldwork in postsocialist societies or, for that matter, in any society undergoing rapid and multiple changes.

NANCY RIES

Fieldwork Dilemmas

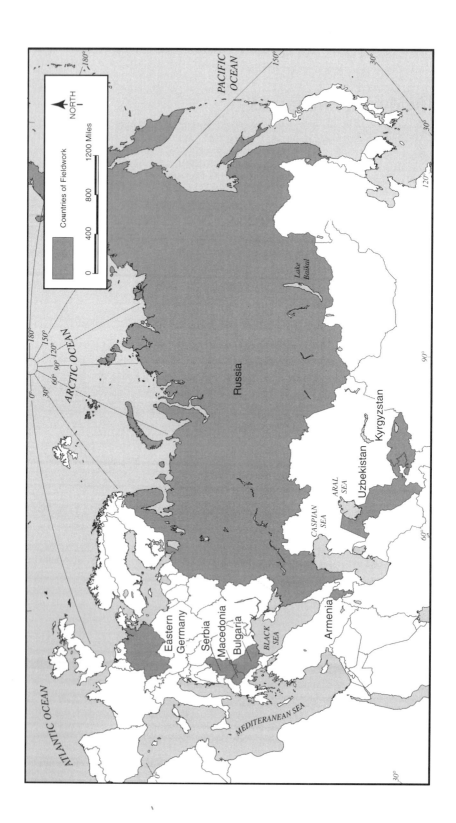

Introduction

Nora Dudwick and Hermine G. De Soto

This volume is the first to examine systematically the postsocialist field and the special issues it raises for ethnographic fieldworkers as they document the rebuilding of states, political and economic dislocations, plummeting living standards, new emerging gender inequities, and ethnic and nationalist violence. It offers firsthand accounts of the ethical and practical fieldwork dilemmas which confront anthropologists working in rapidly changing societies, many of which only recently opened up to foreign ethnographers. This volume should be of particular interest to anthropologists concerned with fieldwork issues and students examining these issues as part of a course of study in anthropology or other social sciences. Because of the focus on field research in eastern Europe and the former Soviet Union, this volume is also relevant to Europeanist ethnographers, sociologists who use ethnographic field methods, and scholars and students in other social science disciplines—particularly political science—specializing in this geographic area.

In this collection, fieldworkers returning from Armenia, Bulgaria, eastern Germany, Kyrgyzstan, Macedonia, Russia, Serbia, and Uzbekistan analyze the ethical and pragmatic challenges they encountered during the "Second Great Transformation" in eastern Europe and the former Soviet Union (Verdery 1997: 716). The range of fieldwork sites presents the great diversity among postsocialist societies while raising questions about the

3

definitions and boundaries of postsocialism. Some chapters are written by anthropologists who started fieldwork during the socialist period; others, by younger researchers who started after the socialist collapse. The younger anthropologists confronted a field situation in turmoil, with little guidance from senior colleagues. They worked out for themselves the ethical, practical, and theoretical issues involved in researching painful simultaneous transformations of polity, economy, society, and culture.

All the chapters, however, document in one way or another the struggle the fieldworkers encountered as they sought to reconcile previous experiences and positions—including ideologized Cold War values—with new human experiences and to avoid succumbing to new postsocialist stereotypes about socialism, "the West," "transition," and "civil society." At the same time, the discussions are deeply relevant to the classic themes of anthropology. As Katherine Verdery points out, "The anthropology of Eastern Europe [and postsocialism] offers a beginning, as it takes on a job other anthropologists have done for decades: describing the penetration of capital into noncapitalist ways of organizing the world" (1997: 716).

The principle organizing theme of this collection, however, concerns the specificity of the fieldwork dilemmas that postsocialist society raises for the ethnographer. One of the reasons for this specificity lies in a shared socialist past that continues to play a decisive role in the everyday life, social relationships, and cultural practices of postsocialist societies. The socialist state significantly penetrated personal lives, creating a strong resistance in the form of sharp polarization between publicly espoused ideology and privately held beliefs; between official economies of shortage and flourishing "second economies"; between public values of modest egalitarianism and private values of material acquisition and display. To varying degrees, personal relations in socialist societies were based on strong demarcations between trusted "insiders" and distrusted "outsiders."

These important continuities notwithstanding, the postsocialist world confronts even fieldworkers with experience in socialist societies with a new field and a dramatically different set of problems. In contrast with the stability or "stagnancy" of socialism, citizens of postsocialist countries now find themselves confronting a rapidly mutating "past" and an unpredictable future. They understand that they are going through some kind of transition—although even this has become a contested concept—but they have no clear sense of where they are headed. They feel shock and indignation at the sudden and extreme decline in their economic and symbolic status, or what Bruce Grant (personal communication) has called "the Third Worlding" of the former Soviet Bloc. They have become deeply and disquietingly aware of the malleability of culture, power, history, states, and state borders.

The collection takes up a range of fieldwork issues. Several ethnographers analyze the influence of Cold War images on their field relationships, the ways in which both they and their informants came to understand how these highly ideologized stereotypes had mediated their perceptions of each other. They explore how the particular history of Cold War relations shapes the significance of being a native or a Western anthropologist, particularly when local people view the West either with unrealistic hope or with bitter disappointment. They also examine the penetration of Western, particularly American, consumerist images and their influence on changing concepts of self, gender, insider, and outsider.

The complex and delicate aspects of establishing and maintaining field relationships in the postsocialist field are a concern that runs through the collection. Several authors explore the many ways in which the postsocialist context of formerly closed and isolated societies has influenced the development of friendship and trust. The material misery, insecurity about the immediate future, and sense of national humiliation that people in the field are now experiencing raise ongoing personal and professional dilemmas for fieldworkers. Interested in reconciling professional detachment with humanistic concerns, several fieldworkers explore the complex relationships between scholarship and advocacy, detachment and empathy. Focusing on the postsocialist task of rebuilding nations and states, fieldworkers pose the question of whether researchers are likely to be manipulated for political or ideological ends when informants are struggling to reshape social, national, and state identities. Several chapters explore the feminist dilemma. They examine how the East–West divide between capitalist and socialist, and now postsocialist, societies created unconscious Cold War habits of objectifying and distancing oneself from "the other" that now interfere with the ability to understand and interpret the experience of postsocialist women.

Many anthropologists have confronted the sometimes gratifying, sometimes intimidating realization of how closely our informants follow and react to our work. In this collection, fieldworkers acknowledge the troubling awareness that, whether or not they intend it, writing the ethnography of postsocialism often becomes a political and constitutive act. In *When They Read What We Write,* a 1993 collection edited by Caroline Brettell, anthropologists initiated an important discussion about the implications of carrying out fieldwork in societies where we cannot escape critical scrutiny, reflection, and commentary on our work. Anthropologists of socialism have also discussed their concern about the moral and ethical implications of their work (Sampson and Kideckel 1989; Kideckel 1997a, b; Beck 1993; Hann 1987, 1993). The accounts in this book engage in this ongoing debate about the complex entanglements of fieldwork with theory, epistemology, ideology, belief, and politics.

All the contributions address the importance of negotiation between fieldworker and field as well as the way in which fieldworkers must continually reposition themselves personally and professionally during fieldwork. Despite overlap and continuity among chapters, however, we have organized them in three sections, each of which highlights one or more subthemes. In part 1, Nora Dudwick, Keith Brown, and Marko Živković document the sharp ethnic tensions and organized violence in communities which have either experienced or still fear the disintegrating impact of war. Such circumstances provide very limited spaces in which fieldworkers can negotiate. Fieldwork under these conditions, where literal survival may become an issue for informants, often forces the fieldworker to take sides, although the act of taking sides itself can be fraught with moral and even physical dangers. The authors in part 2—Hermine De Soto, Kathleen Kuehnast, Igor Barsegian, and David Anderson—raise the complicated issue of negotiating field relationships in the radically unequal power context, in which the Western ethnographer becomes the symbolic bearer of Western authority and Cold War victory. In part 3, Russell Zanca, Daphne Berdahl, and Carol Silverman focus more on interpersonal spaces and the way in which fieldworkers reposition themselves professionally, personally, and emotionally in relation to the various individuals they encounter in the field.

Respect for the confidentiality of informants and the integrity of cultures is basic to fieldwork ethics. Yet, as we document in this volume, the potential impact of ethnographic representation on the field community, as well as its potential for appropriation and manipulation by factions inside or outside the community, forces fieldworkers to find new ways of carrying out research and to reexamine their professional and personal stances. Issues of confidentiality and representation—the uses to which one's text may be put—particularly arise in contexts of revolutionary transformation, acute ethnic and racial conflict, and war. This collection presents detailed images of everyday life as the context for examining the theoretical implications of ethical issues raised by fieldwork during the Second Great Transformation in eastern Europe and the former Soviet Union (Verdery 1997: 716). We hope it will stimulate interest in further research and debate about the moral and human dilemmas raised by fieldwork. The accounts in this collection demonstrate that, given the instability of these societies and peoples' active searches for new models, fieldworkers, as representatives of the ideals and fears associated with the hegemonic West, must confront the fact that their texts will themselves become resources in ongoing struggles to rebuild society.

This volume emerged out of a feeling, shared by all the authors, that there was something peculiarly postsocialist about the inevitable complexity of fieldwork relationships we were experiencing. (Early versions of some of the chapters were presented at a panel session, "Human Dilemmas of Doing Fieldwork in Disintegrating Postsocialist Societies," which we organized for the 93d annual meeting of the American Anthropological Association.) Putting the volume together has been illuminating for the editors, and we hope for the other authors as well, for we have encountered in each other's chapters sudden insights that make sense of some particularly confusing, troublesome, or undigested episode from our own fieldwork.

That this volume has come together is the product of many people's hard work; in many ways, *Fieldwork Dilemmas* is the result of collaborative efforts among reviewers, editors, and contributors. We would like to thank the contributors for revising their chapters several times—often on the run while engaged in fieldwork—in response to different reviews, and for their careful cross-referencing of each other's work.

We wanted the book to read as a coherent, thematic whole—a collective statement on how fieldworkers attempt to make sense of field sites in east-central Europe, Russia, and Central Asia that are in radical transformation—rather than simply a set of accounts sharing a subject or an approach. The contributors' willingness to take into account each other's insights and research has been as intellectually challenging as it has been practically complex: communicating between and within continents by way of telephone, express delivery, postal service, electronic mail, and fax. Such activities also created unforeseen delays and chaotic moments that were cheerfully balanced by our families and friends. We want especially to thank David J. De Soto, Igor Barsegian, Ariel Dudwick, Ida Dudwick, Kathleen Kuehnast, Mary Jo Heck, and Eileen Ewing for their endurance, emotional support, and tolerance.

Throughout the editing of this book we received generous advice on how to improve each chapter and the collection as a whole. We are particularly grateful to Nancy Ries and Michael Herzfeld, who took time from busy schedules to read the entire manuscript and produce illuminating and thought-provoking works that frame the volume. We have been fortunate in our reviewers, Caroline Brettell, Bruce Grant, and Andris Skreija, all of whom are particularly equipped to review this work: Caroline Brettell, on the basis of her pathbreaking collection that opened up the discussion of what it is like to write about subjects who will read and react to one's analysis; Bruce Grant, because of his own extensive fieldwork in Russia, which has revealed from the inside the kind of dilemmas dealt with in these chapters; Andris Skreija, because of his deep familiarity with and many years of research in the former Soviet Union. We must also thank one anonymous reader who also offered many valuable suggestions for revision. Mary Jo Heck helped us to edit earlier versions of the chapters, but coming from the

8   Introduction

completely different discipline of the English language and literature, she
has been much more than an editor. She has also helped us, with her insights
and comparative perspective, to conceptualize the volume as a whole.
Robin Whitaker provided a meticulous reading and polish.

Finally, we feel uniquely fortunate that Rosalie Robertson, formerly of
the University of Wisconsin Press, was the one to shepherd us through the
early stages of publication. We have benefited from her own anthropological background and her insight into the aims of the volume, and we thank
her for her generous assistance and patience.

References

Beck, S. 1993. The struggle for space and the development of civil society in Roma-
    nia, June 1990. In H. G. De Soto and D. G. Anderson, eds., *The curtain rises: Re-
    thinking culture, ideology and the state in eastern Europe,* 232–266. Atlantic High-
    lands, N.J.: Humanities Press International, Inc.
Brettell, C., ed. 1993. *When they read what we write: The politics of ethnography.*
    Westport, Conn.: Bergin and Garvey.
Hann, C. M. 1987. The politics of anthropology in socialist eastern Europe. In
    A. Jackson, ed., *Anthropology at home,* 139–153. ASA Monographs 25. London
    and New York: Tavistock Publications.
Hann, C. M. 1993. After communism: Reflections on East European anthropology
    and the "transition." *Social Anthropology* 3: 229–249.
Herzfeld, M. 1997. Theorizing Europe: Persuasive paradoxes. In Provocations of
    European ethnology. *American Anthropologist* 99 (4): 713–730.
Kideckel, D. 1997a. Utter otherness: Western anthropology and East European po-
    litical economy. In Sue Parman, ed., *Europe in the anthropological imagination,*
    134–147. New York: Prentice Hall.
Kideckel, D. 1997b. Autoethnography as political resistance: A case from socialist
    Romania. In Deborah Reed-Danahay, ed., *Auto/ethnography: Rewriting the self
    and the social,* 47–70. Oxford: Berg Academic Publishers.
Sampson, S. L., and D. Kideckel. 1989. Anthropologists going into the cold: Re-
    search in the age of mutually assured destruction. In P. R. Turner and D. Pitt,
    eds., *The anthropology of war and peace: Perspectives on the nuclear age,* 160–173.
    Westport, Conn.: Bergin and Garvey.
Verdery, K. 1997. The "new" eastern Europe in an anthropology of Europe. In
    Provocations of European ethnology. *American Anthropologist* 99 (4): 713–730.

PART 1

FIELDWORK IN DISINTEGRATING AND REINTEGRATING NATIONS AND STATES

The Renegotiation of Borders and Boundaries

In the postsocialist world, serious civil and ethnic conflicts have accompanied redefinitions of societies and cultures, rebuilding of nations and states, and reconfigurations of power alignments. These conflicts sometimes force ethnographers to choose between loyalty to friends and notions of academic honesty, between partisanship and neutrality. Dudwick's chapter traces the evolution of a research relationship from the emergence of a national and democratic movement in Soviet Armenia, as nationalism and violence on both sides of the border led to armed conflict between Armenians and Azerbaijanis. Dudwick further examines the nature of the "research bargain" and the difficulties of balancing professional, pragmatic, and personal relationships in the unstable fieldwork situations that characterize postsocialist societies in conflict. According to both the mythology of the discipline and the reality of this intense experience, doing ethnographic fieldwork entails feelings of empathy that often develop into a strong sense of identification. The stronger the sense of empathy and identification, the more betrayed all parties feel when they rediscover their differences. The postsocialist field raises many issues of grave historical wrongs that need to be explored openly. Yet, as Dudwick writes, ethnographic analysis of these issues can itself become a powerful political act with public and personal consequences, because native anthropologists and foreign anthropologists face different risks and responsibilities.

Brown, working in the post-Yugoslav field of Macedonia, poses questions about the roles and responsibilities of anthropologists and the place for respect and sensitivity when "people have got history wrong." This question is particularly salient when people's "certainties" can be labeled nationalism and argued to create an atmosphere of violence. Initially, he felt supported by Handler's (1988) perspective—that opprobrium is the cost when one conducts effective research rather than acting as apologist for the ways of others. Yet in Macedonia, Brown concludes, people's investment in a particular version of history is not about personal prestige or ideology, but about stability, family life, and their children's future. In effect, his position is a response to the question of what to do when the mythologies we deconstruct turn out to be the glue our subjects use to keep their strained societies from fragmenting into war.

As a Serb who grew up in Yugoslavia but trained as an ethnographer in the West, Živković is both an insider and an outsider. As he tries to deconstruct the complexities of Serbia at war, Živković disavows attempts to search for what "was really, really happening." Instead, he concentrates on the stories that Serbs tell themselves (and others) about themselves. Exploring these stories, Živković argues, helps one discover more durable

11

discourses about identity and social reality during a situation of "radical uncertainty." Živković notes the advantages of being an insider: others did not see him as a potential broker or useful advocate from the powerful West. Rather, he is able to use his insights as an insider to explore issues of epistemology and representation, both morally complex issues in a world where even representation, as a form of evaluation and criticism, can have serious consequences.

1

Postsocialism and the Fieldwork of War

Nora Dudwick

Inaugurating Fieldwork in a Fragmenting Field

In 1987, I began my fieldwork in what was then the Soviet Union. Attracted to this last great frontier of ethnography, I applied for and received a nine-month fellowship from IREX (International Research and Exchanges Board, a scholarly organization which offered grants and arranged research visits and visas to the Soviet Union and eastern Europe) to conduct research on the construction and negotiation of Russian and "Soviet" identities among Russian youth. My introduction to the field, however, took a rather unanticipated twist, which itself reveals something of the field context. Shortly before my departure to Moscow, where I had planned to do my research, the Soviet Ministry of Higher Education, responsible for finding placements for IREX fellows, informed me that because no places were left at the highly sought-after Moscow State University, they had placed me instead at Yerevan State University, in Armenia.

In 1987, it would have been next to impossible to remain in the Soviet Union as an unaffiliated—hence, dangerously unsupervised—scholar. I therefore went to Yerevan, but with the intention of trying to change my placement back to Russia. Events in Armenia soon overtook me, however, and before I knew it, the emerging nationalist movement had become the topic of my dissertation-to-be.[1]

I subsequently spent two academic years and two summers conducting research in Soviet Armenia. In 1991, however, my "field" changed dramatically. No longer part of a large and seemingly powerful state, Armenia had become a tiny country involved in an undeclared war with another now-independent fragment of the former Soviet state. The physical landscape remained the same, but the political, economic, and social landscape had dramatically altered,[2] affecting every aspect of daily life. Our difficulties as fieldworkers in grasping the meaning and implications of these drastic transformations parallel and reflect the bewilderment of those who must live through these changes every day. These transformations have also altered relationships of trust and friendship established over many years, while our acquaintances reshape their social and cultural identities in unanticipated ways and fight to maintain a normal physical existence in the midst of economic state collapse. In the course of their efforts to reconstitute their lives, we, too, may feel instrumentalized—as purveyors of goods, services, and contacts with the West or as allies for political projects we may dislike. At the same time, while we pursue our own research agendas, we may feel we are exploiting our subjects' misery by responding to it as part of an intellectual problem or by distancing ourselves from it in our role as "voyeuristic spectators of plays in which others suffer or attain happiness as actors" (Koepping 1994: 24).

Working in the postsocialist field raises critical issues of trust and loyalty. These were complex matters in socialist societies. The dissonance between official ideologies and private beliefs, between public postures and private practices, raised constant questions about motives, conspiracies, loyalties, and betrayals, minefields through which the fieldworker had to find a path. The field was both dichotomized and highly polarized—state versus society; government versus citizen; Soviets versus Westerners—forcing participants to take sides. This polarization also characterizes the postsocialist field. Indeed, one of the most frequent admonitions I heard in Armenia during the heady days of mass collective actions was, "Those who aren't with us are against us."

How can we, as fieldworkers, maintain our moral and intellectual compass in the face of such rapid and unexpected transformations, in a field rife with hostile antagonisms? In his discussion of research relationships, Peter Loizos refers to the Faustian contract anthropologists make with their informants. In return for being studied, for offering food and drink, information, friendship, and moral support, our informants expect us to serve them until they release us (Loizos 1994). Leaving aside the practical assistance we may or may not be willing and/or able to render informants, I see the moral dilemma raised by the Faustian contract as follows: In our written work, do we strive to convey the subjective world of our informants, to represent it in a way which they recognize, or do we strive to deconstruct the values by which our informants live (Handler 1993: 73; see also Živković, this volume)?

When we deconstruct deeply held beliefs about ethnic or national superiority that are an essential part of how people think about their community, or when we question the sacred narratives of historical suffering used to justify aggression, our informants may perceive us as betraying them by rejecting their vision of the world after accepting the benefits of the Faustian bargain. For as Jaffe suggests, a degree of advocacy appears to be "one of the unspoken conditions" of participation among individuals who have a political agenda (1993: 56).

In this chapter, I explore some of the ethical and human dilemmas that confronted me after I found myself in a fragmenting field, bewildered to find myself simultaneously the subject of interest, suspicion, and high expectations. Because so few Westerners were present in Armenia, particularly in 1987 and 1988, I found myself thrust into the role of the "authoritative" interpreter of Armenian events to the West. This unexpected role forced me to confront issues of trust and betrayal, loyalty to my friends and acquaintances versus loyalty to abstract political ideals and notions of professionalism, because I realized my words or silences might be used in ways I had never intended, and could also critically affect my ability to continue my work.

Fieldwork during Perestroika

Having spent several academic years studying the Russian language, culture, and history in preparation for carrying out research in Russia, I was completely unprepared for Armenia. As far as Armenian history, language, and culture were concerned, I was virtually a tabula rasa. In one sense, my innocence was an advantage: I had no specific preconceptions about Armenians or "Armenianness" to interfere with the task of understanding Armenian (as opposed to Soviet) culture through the perceptions of my informants. How and what my informants chose to introduce to me as Armenian shaped my own notions of what it meant to grow up in Armenia, and the accidental nature of my entry into Armenian society convinced me of my own neutrality when this society began to polarize and fragment. At the same time, my initially benign acceptance of Soviet culture (a long-standing personal reaction to what Barsegian, in this volume, refers to as Western social sciences' demonization of the communist world) also gave me the impression that my approach to my field was less intrinsically Western and American than I now, in retrospect, understand it to have been.

In February 1988, when the demonstrations and an identifiable movement began, I had spent five months among people who combined warmth and hospitality with a great curiosity about someone who was not only from the West but also lacked even semifamiliarity as a diaspora Armenian. Our reciprocal interests and needs brought us together. When my only light bulb burned out and I had squeezed out the last of my Pepsodent, it was my new friends who replaced these deficit goods. When I became ill, it was my friends who delivered mustard plasters, rosehip jelly, and mulberry brandy, guaranteed to cure most ills. They provided information and insights, introduced me to useful and interesting people, and willingly helped me with my exploration of Armenian society and culture.

We also shared numerous aggravations. I listened sympathetically to their bitter complaints about the endless number of forms they had to fill out, certificates they had to line up for, and officials and doctors they had to bribe in order to rent an apartment, receive medical treatment, or obtain ordinary household goods. Like them, I spent hours prowling the meagerly supplied shops for basic necessities, visiting the university Department for Relations with Foreigners week after week, waiting endlessly in offices to talk with officials who were usually "out" or "engaged" before I could sort out the most trivial of problems connected with travel, housing, and visas. Like my friends, I dealt with rude and aggressive authorities who summoned me to their offices to berate me for violating rules, in my case, for spending nights away from my dormitory and traveling to other cities without authorization. When the kinds of encounters I found offensive, as an American with a strong sense of "her rights," coincided with those that angered my acquaintances, I ceased to examine critically the meaning of their dissatisfaction, and I imputed to it the same content as my own (see Barsegian, this volume, on mutual East–West perceptions). Common annoyances and occasional outrage bound us together—at least in my own eyes—in a shared culture of criticism and protest.

Researching a Nationalist Movement

In February 1988, large demonstrations began in Armenia and in Nagorno-Karabagh, a small autonomous *oblast* located in Azerbaijan. In the intoxicating atmosphere produced by Gorbachev's call for perestroika and *glasnost,* Armenian activists took up an old cause, that of the unification of Armenia and Nagorno-Karabagh, with its 70 percent Armenian population. The "Karabagh movement" united people with a vast array of dissatisfactions. The nationalist wing of the movement called for the rectification of what its members depicted as Stalin's injustice—the arbitrary separation of a single Armenian people and territory into two parts; the democratic wing condemned government corruption and called for a free press and social justice. Although only a small core of activists took a leading role, the movement and its demands resonated through the larger society, where dissatisfactions were rife and where Gorbachev's reforms had reduced the fear of expressing them.

My subjective sense of a bond of understanding intensified during the course of the demonstrations. Victor Turner (1969) writes lyrically of "communitas," when certain rituals create in participants an intense affective bond which temporarily replaces the sense of hierarchy and difference. For many participants, both Armenians and outsiders such as myself, the demonstrations were just such a ritual. The demonstrations began on a bone-chilling Saturday afternoon in February 1988, when several hundred people gathered in front of Yerevan's opera theater in response to a summons by activists to show their support for Armenians who were striking in Nagorno-Karabagh. As each day passed without sanctions from the authorities, people gathered at the opera in increasing numbers to listen to news and exhortations from a variety of professional and amateur historians (economists, writers, poets, and scientists). Their presentations on the ancient and recent histories of Karabagh, reasons for its separation from Armenia, and the oppression experienced by the Karabagh Armenians at the hands of "Turks" (Azerbaijanis) came together in a convincing and moving narrative of Armenian oppression and resistance. Together, orators and audience participated in the reconstruction of Armenian national identity.[3]

Parallel with this reconstruction, a series of dramatic confrontations pitted Communist authorities, who denied, belittled, or tried to deflect issues of national conflict, against the demonstrators, whose hoots, whistles, and boos of contempt appeared to erupt from years of resentful and fearful silence toward the power of the state. Speakers presented the issues as black and white: Karabagh Armenians experienced ethnic discrimination; the Azerbaijani government unfairly oppressed them; Communist Party authorities treated Armenian citizens without regard or respect; Armenians yearned for democratic freedoms and an end to hypocrisy and corruption. Ethnic and political issues fused in such a way as to provide something for everyone, to create a feeling of shared grievances and goals among people who had very different perspectives and agendas.[4]

At the end of February, news reached Armenia that in the depressed Azerbaijani city of Sumgait, large crowds of Azerbaijanis had attacked Armenians with vicious, improvised weapons, destroying their homes and property in the process. Official figures (never accepted by Armenians) claimed that 32 people, including 26 Armenians, had died. The three-day continuation of the rampage without the intervention of Azerbaijani police or the Soviet troops stationed nearby convinced many Armenians that the

Azerbaijani and Soviet KGB had actively provoked the violence to frighten Armenian separatists in Nagorno-Karabagh. Under the impress of these violent events, the impact of which was amplified by taped interviews of hysterical refugees who had sought asylum in Armenia, I interpreted this Manichaean scheme of innocent and reasonable Armenians confronting armed, aggressive adversaries as a description of fact rather than as a stereotyped representation of reality.[5]

Since coming to Armenia, I had based my understanding of Armenian culture on a set of Armenian self-representations that had been profoundly shaped by collective memories of the state-organized violence in the Ottoman Empire between 1915 and 1918. While the conflict with Azerbaijan escalated, self-representations of Armenians as an ancient, cultivated, and Christian people increasingly dominated the movement discourse, and the image of victim became increasingly foregrounded.

Victimhood, however, depends on the existence of an aggressor. Many of my informants saw the aggressor as the Azerbaijani people, as a whole or in part, or the Azerbaijani leadership, or a combination of these two elements. The reasons they proposed for the violence ranged from genetically or culturally programmed savagery, expansionism, and nationalism to the ignorance of the uneducated population misled by their mullahs and politicians and provoked by anti-democratic, anti-Armenian elements in the Kremlin. Trained as an anthropologist to interpret ethnic differences as constructed rather than inborn, I nevertheless lacked sufficient detachment to question either this fundamental presentation of the facts or the assertion that the line between victims and aggressors, in the present case, corresponded to the line between distinct ethnic and national communities. I had slipped into the "disciplinary mainstream" of those anthropologists of nationalism that Richard Handler has criticized as "unabashedly romantic, buying into the ethnic self-definition of the people he or she studies" (Handler 1993: 74). Perhaps like many ethnographers new to their field, I was entranced by the differences between the field and my own society—the intensity and vitality of relationships and the intense politicization of daily life—and I felt as if I were defending the rights of the underdog.

In June 1988, I left Armenia for the United States, armed with stacks of *samizdat* (a Russian term, also used in Armenian speech, short for "self-published materials") and published materials about the history of Armenian–Azerbaijani relations and dozens of interviews with political activists. My fieldnotes were filled with records of my conversations with acquaintances and friends, virtually all of whom supported the unification of Nagorno-Karabagh and Armenia for one or a combination of reasons. I spent the next months digesting and organizing these materials. Even after reading material which represented Azerbaijani claims, I concluded that the desire of the Karabagh Armenians to join Armenia was based on reasonable demographic, legal, and political arguments. In retrospect, it is clear that my lack of detachment caused me to miss the forest for the trees, to accept the premise that the conflict was one which admitted a "correct" as opposed to an "incorrect" solution, and to succumb to the temptation to find out (as Živković, this volume, puts it) what had "really, really" happened rather than to pull back and analyze the very premises and terms of the conflict.

The Development of Armed Violence

In November 1988, interethnic violence again erupted in Azerbaijan and spread throughout both republics, resulting in a mass population exchange. In January 1990, a final pogrom forced the large and prosperous Armenian community living in Baku to flee Azerbaijan. By 1991, the 450,000 Armenians living in Azerbaijan (excluding those in Nagorno-Karabagh) had fled to Armenia or other Soviet republics, and the 160,000 largely rural Azerbaijani inhabitants of Armenia had fled to Azerbaijan. Meanwhile, the recently formed Azerbaijani Popular Front had organized an effective road and rail blockade of Nagorno-Karabagh and of Armenia, which had previously received 85 percent of its fuel and supplies through Azerbaijan.

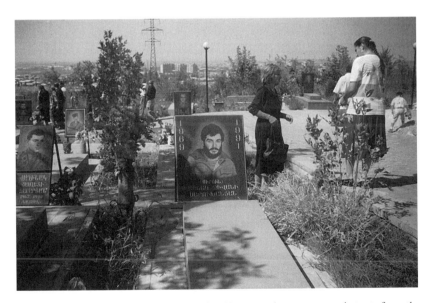

Mourners at Yerablur Cemetery, overlooking Yerevan, where many combatants from the Nagorno-Karabagh war are buried, 1995 (Photograph by Nora Dudwick)

Sharing a meal with members of the Armenian army and former combatants in Nagorno-Karabagh, 1995 (Photograph by Gayane Shagoyan)

The conflict gradually transformed from a succession of brutal but disorganized confrontations between poorly armed villagers to a war between increasingly well-organized militias, sometimes involving Soviet troops and armaments. In 1991, Soviet troops aided specially appointed Azerbaijani police in deporting Armenians living in the Shahumian region, contiguous with Nagorno-Karabagh. By 1992, a nascent Armenian military regime in Nagorno-Karabagh had wielded competing local militias into a quasi-professional army. By 1993, Karabagh forces broke the blockade of Nagorno-Karabagh by establishing a broad land corridor linking the region to Armenia. They also created a wide buffer zone around Nagorno-Karabagh, thoroughly and deliberately looting and destroying Azerbaijani villages and towns, including those which had served as strategic posts for bombing Nagorno-Karabagh's capital and its airport. As the Karabagh forces expanded into Azerbaijani territory outside Nagorno-Karabagh, they displaced approximately three-quarters of a million Azerbaijanis, some of whom fled to Iran.[6]

Meanwhile, I had learned more about the long history of Armenian–Azerbaijani hostilities and the Azerbaijanis' own narrative of victimization. The main events of this narrative frequently inverted Armenian accounts.

Thus, while Armenians remember May 1918, when Muslims killed thousands of Armenians, Azerbaijanis recall the "March Days" of 1917, which began in Baku when Bolshevik and Armenian forces slaughtered thousands of Muslims (the name "Azerbaijani" was not yet current) and for which the May events were a form of revenge. Azerbaijanis further recall the efforts of the independent Armenian republic of 1918–1920 to "cleanse" their territory of Muslims and the role of General Andranik, a national hero in Armenia, in expelling Muslims from Zangezur, a contested border region now in Armenia.[7] The cleansing of Azerbaijanis from Armenia inverted the Armenian narrative about the loss of Nagorno-Karabagh and Nakhichevan (another contested region, now administered by Azerbaijan) and the destruction of the city of Shushi,[8] an important center of Armenian (but also Azerbaijani) culture in pre-Soviet times. Armenian accusations that Azerbaijani discrimination encouraged the exodus of Armenians from Nagorno-Karabagh were matched by Azerbaijani complaints about the forced resettlement of Azerbaijanis from Armenia to Azerbaijan in 1949.

In private conversations, I heard disquieting stories about the 1988 deportation of Azerbaijanis from Armenia, which suggested that this had not taken place in the restrained manner Armenians had initially described. I learned more about the pre-1988 tensions between Armenians and Azerbaijanis and about the visible contempt and disdain with which Armenians often regarded their Azerbaijani neighbors. Stories of hostage-taking, torture, and even ritual killings became rife on both sides. The Armenian narrative of victimhood, however, was unable to keep up with these developments; each time I returned to Armenia, I discovered a greater disjunction between admissions of violence committed and the ideological form in which the violence was presented.

Writing about Violence

Accusations flying on both sides of the border about grievous wrongs committed by the "enemy" confronted me with the problem of how an ethnographer should respond to political violence. Political violence, of course, is not a monolithic phenomenon. Some cases involve very unequal situations of domination and oppression by a powerful state, as South African apartheid did; others involve radical or terrorist groups that are ostensibly aligned against what they perceive as an oppressive state apparatus but that also victimize ordinary citizens, such as the Shining Path in Peru. How one interprets the violence can determine one's stance and to what extent one can or should unambiguously align himself or herself with one of the parties. The well-meaning anthropologist with a concern for human rights can

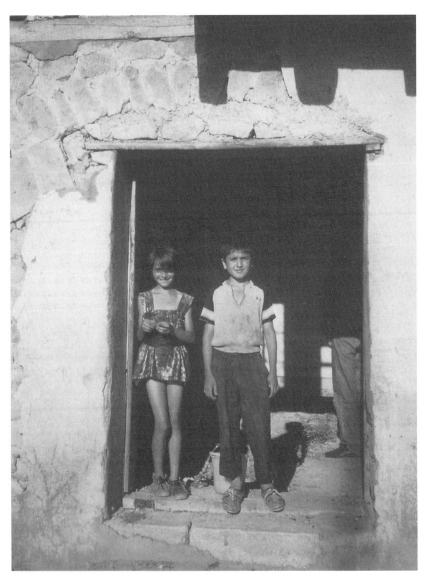

Armenian children in Shushi, 1995 (Photograph by Nora Dudwick)

seriously misinterpret the field. In presenting such an example from Guatemala, Stoll describes how human rights activists operating on a "simplistic 'army versus the people' paradigm" tried to protect peasants against army repression but blundered into what was really an old land dispute between different groups of Mayan peasants (Stoll 1994: 3). In effect, the activists' own stereotypical schemes of "innocent" victims blinded them to the complexities of the actual situation and even reduced their ability to influence events positively. Although this example focuses on human rights activists, I consider it relevant to the case under discussion, for although anthropological analysis may not be intended as a form of activism, once it is written for a readership, the parties to the conflict it analyzes will most likely appropriate it if it supports their claims. Ethnographers of war and violence must therefore accept that their work and their words can have real and grave consequences for the people they study.

When I began research in Armenia, there may have been ethnic tensions on the banal level of local brawls, petty prejudice, and barbed racial jokes, but ethnic stereotypes were not so heavily ideologized. In fact, Azerbaijanis appeared to live in Armenia almost outside Armenian consciousness. Armenian self-representations were constructed out of experiences of the past, rather than drawn particularly from the present, and were focused on victimhood. Having conscientiously listened to this narrative of the past from my informants, I found it all too easy to fit events into this model of victims and aggressors when Armenian separatist demands spiraled into wholesale violence. Of course, there *were* victims—all those who had suffered death, injuries, and terrible losses—but the strength of the Armenian stereotype obscured the extent to which victims were to be found on both sides.

In 1995, I conducted interviews with Armenians from different regions of the country to determine the different motivations and trajectories which had pulled them into the conflict. I discovered a diversity of attitudes and a level of involvement in the violence which contradicted prevailing and "official" depictions of the violence as primarily defensive. The stories recounted by men who had participated in the war, either in border defense units or as volunteers in the Karabagh forces, exposed the sharp gap between public and private discussions about the war. If speaking publicly, Armenians represented their own complicity as a natural, if regrettable, reaction to unbearable provocation; privately, my informants were willing to admit that many Armenians had used the war as an escape from difficult private life, as a means of aggrandizement, or as an outlet for violence and brutality entirely unconnected with the conflict. Even in unofficial conversations, however, those interlocutors who made such admissions were often heavily and angrily criticized.

Negotiating the "Research Bargain"

More than one anthropologist has commented on the fragility and ambiguity of research relationships. Regarding the controversy which greeted Arthur Vidich's study of a small New York town, Brettell noted, "It was apparent that the method of participant-observation itself, whereby an outsider becomes an insider, a stranger becomes a friend, and confidences become data, was not fully understood . . ." (Brettell 1993a: 11). Even when informants claim to want an "outside view," they rarely consider "the possibility that this point of view might contradict their own" (Glazier 1993: 41). This possibility was brought home to me during a field visit when an old friend introduced me to his acquaintance as an anthropologist who had written a dissertation on Karabagh, "proving that it was Armenian." The social context did not encourage an elaborate rebuttal, but I wondered to what extent my friend, a bright man with a deep sense of irony, believed his own words. If his understanding had been formed by my earlier, uncritical reception of Armenian representations, did this mean I should make a clear announcement to him and others regarding my current skepticism? Would this end both friendship and access to information, both facts and attitudes?

Peter Loizos (1994) has argued that to the extent anthropologists base their research relationships on nonjudgmental friendship or "negotiated trust," they risk the loss of both if they disagree with informants or cease to be a "reliable advocate" of their cause. In my own case, for example, I now realize that my foreigner status, not only as an American but as ethnically non-Armenian, initially provoked speculations that I was everything from a CIA to a Mossad agent. Over time, my outsider status became blurred by familiarity and friendship. I worried that despite self-conscious efforts during my first period of research to warn acquaintances that anything they told me might end up in print, they did not fully understand the nature of the "research bargain" (Howard Becker's term, cited by Brettell 1993a: 11).

Moreover, as an anthropologist of Armenia, I did not have the usual recourse of escaping from the field and from my informants. I soon found out that my work was informally but constantly monitored through the transnational networks of kinship and friendship which link Armenia with its large North American diaspora. Comments from acquaintances in Armenia about papers I had delivered to small university audiences in America no longer come as a surprise. When one's subjects are not only literate but also acutely interested in how they are represented to the rest of the world, the anthropologist ends up writing for—and inevitably finds herself or himself pressed to address—competing or potentially hostile audiences. In my case, in addition to my professional colleagues in the West, these overlapping audiences include my "subjects" and a large, engaged diaspora, as well as Azerbaijani colleagues.

Although none of our audiences are monolithic, some opinions more than others dominate public discourse and confront the anthropologist most directly. Furthermore, our ability to work depends on establishing positive official and informal contacts in the field. In a polarized situation, it is easy to fall unwittingly into the role of spokesperson for a particular point of view and avoid outspoken skepticism regarding the very authorities or organizations upon whose good offices continued professional access depends.

The knowledge that my words will be judged according to often conflicting criteria forces me to consider how far I can or should identify personally or professionally with these different communities. To the extent my views concurred with official or mainstream Armenian self-representations, I could remain confident of obtaining the necessary official invitations and visas. I could also rely on the personal and professional support of diaspora organizations and individuals. As one of the few American anthropologists working in Armenia who had witnessed the birth of the Karabagh movement and presented a sympathetic reading of Armenian aspirations, I earned an initial popularity with Armenian colleagues in the United States. As a result, I was frequently invited to speak at Armenian-organized conferences, especially on topics related to the Nagorno-Karabagh conflict. Diaspora organizations funded one trip to Armenia and attendance at several conferences and offered generous informal assistance. This assistance was offered without any hint of conditionality, but I have always been aware that a relationship exists between my expressed views and my professional possibilities.

Over the years, friends and acquaintances in Armenia and the United States have trusted me with information that contradicts the predominant official Armenian self-representation as an innocent, much sinned-against people and is potentially damaging to this public representation, especially outside Armenia. For a country involved in an undeclared war, it has been important politically and economically to downplay that involvement in order not to jeopardize international goodwill or assistance. The confidences I have received thus raise acute issues of friendship, trust, and betrayal. If I use this information in my work, am I violating my part of the research bargain from the viewpoint of those I studied, who depend on me to guard this dangerous private knowledge from potentially hostile audiences? To what extent have I endangered my friendships with people who, as insiders, experience and feel deeply about the conflict in ways which I cannot share? And how can I balance my responsibility to maintain their trust with my own ethical abhorrence of war and violence and the fear that my silence may contribute to its prolongation?

Making Critical Choices

The ambiguities of establishing and maintaining a balance among personal, professional, and pragmatic relationships in the field characterize fieldwork everywhere. Given the violence that has accompanied political transformation in many postsocialist states, however, fieldworkers who began their research during the stable 1980s now find themselves grappling with tensions between long-established relationships of empathy, friendship, and loyalty on the one hand and, on the other, a sense of impotence, disillusionment, and even anger at being "duped" when old friends reappear in the guise of aggressors rather than victims or when resistance transforms into ethnic and nationalist violence. These transformations force us to rethink our own analyses, stereotypes, biases, and sympathies. More important, they confront us with critical ethical choices.

At the same time, I had to consider yet another aspect of the research relationship—my status as a foreign anthropologist. As Živković reminds us (in this volume), native anthropologists do not always have a better grasp of events. Indeed, as Barsegian notes (in this volume), they may sometimes feel uncomfortably like voyeurs when they observe their society with a detachment of which their "subjects" remain innocently unaware. Research relationships depend in a complex way on the relationship between the fieldworker and the field, and it is probably impossible to allocate clearly the levels of access, knowledge, and responsibilities between native and foreign anthropologists. Yet disagreements, particularly in highly polarized wartime situations, clearly entail more serious consequences for the native, or near-native, anthropologist. He or she may be able to establish relationships of trust more easily but may have more to lose by appearing to be a traitor.

Peter Loizos, a near-native anthropologist who entered the society from which his own father had come, encountered this problem when he refused to subscribe to the Greek Cypriot version of their conflict with Turkish Cypriots (1994: 49). As for native anthropologists, Maya Povrzanovič, a Croatian anthropologist, argues that because war is literally a matter of life and death for them, their work will always be seen as "blatantly partial." Readers will place greater trust in foreign anthropologists, who are able to write without this emotional burden (1993: 125). At the same time, she acknowledges that foreign anthropologists risk losing their credibility should they fail to walk the tightrope and come to seem too partisan.

Given our ability to abandon our fields, the risks entailed in the task of

representing and interpreting violence may seem less acute for foreign anthropologists. Yet to the extent that foreign anthropologists become participants, we, too, carry burdens of obligation, trapped by the Faustian contract in webs of friendship, reciprocal obligation, and trust, which make us
fearful of betraying one or another person or principle. How can we fulfill
these obligations? One solution is to recall that multiple perspectives exist,
even in the most apparently polarized situation. In trying to grasp whether
there are essential differences in thinking and feeling between us and them,
we often do not see the differences between *them* and them.

Notes

Many institutions and individuals have made possible the fieldwork described in this
chapter, as well as the possibility to reflect and write on it. Here I would like to express my gratitude to the International Research and Exchanges Board, which
funded my first nine months of fieldwork in Armenia, and to the Harry Frank
Guggenheim Foundation, which funded the postdoctoral research grant on the cultural construction of violence and death in the Nagorno-Karabagh war. The Institute for European, Russian and Eurasian Studies of George Washington University
generously provided an office, facilities, and informal collegial support for much of
the period during which this chapter and book were in preparation. I also wish to
thank those colleagues who were kind enough to read and comment on earlier
drafts of this chapter. They include Igor Barsegian, Caroline Brettell, Hermine De
Soto, Bruce Grant, Mary Jo Heck, Kathleen Kuehnast, Peter Loizos, and Maja
Povrzanovič, as well as a reader for the book who chose to remain anonymous. Most
of all, I must express my gratitude to my Armenian friends, colleagues, and acquaintances for their friendship, assistance, and forbearance over the years.

    1. This experience was my first introduction to the highly controlled conditions
and level of supervision which Soviet officials imposed on foreign scholars, as well
as these officials' disregard for regional, cultural, and social differentiation within
the Soviet state. Perhaps not surprisingly, it predisposed me to respond quite sympathetically when Armenians complained about Russian and/or Soviet indifference
to their claims.
    2. What makes the postsocialist field particularly "postsocialist" is a complex is-
sue. I suggest that one of its special qualities is the fact that Western anthropologists,
no matter what their political orientation, nevertheless approached the socialist and
postsocialist field with a set of stereotypes strongly conditioned by Cold War rhetoric. Particularly in the Soviet Union, where we established relationships with
people whose multiple and overlapping ethnic, religious, linguistic, and/or regional
identities intersected with their identity as citizens of a centralized state, it was
tempting to interpret the advocacy of national languages, religions, and traditions
as a form of resistance toward a totalizing, homogenizing, and oppressive state. I

also consider that the existence and shape of the many ethnic conflicts which have emerged in the wake of the Soviet collapse owe much to the rigid controls the state exercised in public and private life. These controls, in my view, impeded the development of functioning mechanisms for resolving tensions between ethnic and other kinds of social groups. At the same time, the intense ideologization of Soviet society hindered development of a pluralistic, self-critical discourse and encouraged a dichotomization of the world into friends and enemies.

3. Without being clearly aware of it at the time, I was in fact observing the process whereby people construct history through a complex of memory, recovery, and invention (Lewis 1975). In Armenia, a long historical and literary tradition of narratives about martyrdom and suffering shaped the emerging narrative, in a process Hayden White (1987) has analyzed in his studies of narrative.

4. The Karabagh movement, as this movement became known, is the focus of my dissertation (Dudwick 1994), as well as several articles (1989, 1995, 1996). Mark Malkasian (1996), also present during this first tumultuous year, provides fascinating coverage of the personalities and events. Levon Abrahamian (1990a, b), an extraordinarily insightful anthropologist and patient and generous friend, provides some unique insights into the movement.

5. I am not questioning the events in Sumgait, which have been extensively documented by Shahmuratian (1990), among others. I am not so ready to accept Armenian interpretations of the events, however, because as far as I know, it has never been clearly ascertained which persons, parties, or organs of local or central government were responsible for instigating the violence and/or failing to respond to it promptly.

6. For an account of atrocities on both sides, see the Human Rights Watch (1994).

7. These events have been addressed by many historians, among others, Richard Hovhannisian (1971), Ronald Grigor Suny (1993), and Ter Minassian (1984). Robert Cullen (1991), a journalist, has commented with ironic perceptiveness on the reciprocal nature of the recriminations between Armenians and Azerbaijanis.

8. Even the spelling of this city forces the analyst to take sides: "Shushi" is the Armenian name for this historic town; "Shusha" is the Azerbaijani name.

References

Abrahamian, L. 1990a. Archaic ritual and theater: From the ceremonial glade to Theater Square. *Soviet Anthropology and Archeology* 29 (2): 45–69.

Abrahamian, L. 1990b. The Karabagh movement as viewed by an anthropologist. *Armenian Review* 43 (2–3): 67–80.

Brettell, C. B. 1993a. Introduction: Fieldwork, text, and audience. In Caroline B. Brettell, ed., *When they read what we write: The politics of ethnography*, 1–24. Westport, Conn.: Bergin and Garvey.

Brettell, C. B., ed. 1993b. *When they read what we write: The politics of ethnography.* Westport, Conn.: Bergin and Garvey.

Brettell, C. B. 1993c. Whose history is it? Selection and representation in the creation of a text. In C. B. Brettell, ed., *When they read what we write: The politics of ethnography,* 93–105. Westport, Conn.: Bergin and Garvey.

Cullen, R. 1991. A reporter at large (Armenia and Azerbaijan): Roots. *New Yorker,* April 15, 55–76.

Dudwick, N. 1989. The Karabagh movement: An old scenario gets rewritten. *Armenian Review* 42 (3): 63–70.

Dudwick, N. 1994. Memory, identity and politics in Armenia. Ph.D. dissertation, University of Pennsylvania.

Dudwick, N. 1995. The cultural construction of political violence in Armenia and Azerbaijan. *Problems of Post-Communism* 42 (4): 18–23.

Dudwick, N. 1996. Nagorno-Karabagh and the politics of sovereignty. In Ronald Suny, ed., *Transcaucasia, nationalism and social change: Essays on the history of Armenia, Azerbaijan, and Georgia,* 427–440. Ann Arbor: University of Michigan Press.

Glazier, S. 1993. Responses to the anthropologist: When the spiritual Baptists of Trinidad read what I write about them. In C. B. Brettell, ed., *When they read what we write: The politics of ethnography,* 38–48. Westport, Conn.: Bergin and Garvey.

Handler, R. 1993. Fieldwork in Quebec, scholarly reviews, and anthropological dialogues. In C. B. Brettell, ed., *When they read what we write: The politics of ethnography,* 67–74. Westport, Conn.: Bergin and Garvey.

Herzfeld, M. 1987. *Anthropology through the looking-glass: Critical ethnography in the margins of Europe.* New York: Cambridge University Press.

Hovannisian, Richard G. 1971. *The Republic of Armenia.* Vol. 1: *The first year, 1918–1919.* Berkeley: University of California Press.

Human Rights Watch. 1994. *Azerbaijan: Seven years of conflict in Nagorno-Karabagh.* New York.

Jaffe, A. 1993. Involvement, detachment and representation in Corsica. In C. B. Brettell, ed., *When they read what we write: The politics of ethnography,* 51–66. Westport, Conn.: Bergin and Garvey.

Koepping, K-P. 1994. Ethics in ethnographic practice: Contextual pluralism and solidarity of research partners. *Anthropological Journal on European Cultures* 3 (2): 21–38.

Lewis, Bernard. 1975. *History: Remembered, recovered, invented.* Princeton, N.J.: Princeton University Press.

Loizos, P. 1987. Intercommunal killing in Cyprus. *Man* (n.s.) 23: 639–653.

Loizos, P. 1994. Confessions of a vampire anthropologist. *Anthropological Journal on European Cultures* 3 (2): 39–53.

Malkasian, Mark. 1996. *"Gha-ra-bagh!" The emergence of the national democratic movement in Armenia.* Detroit: Wayne State University Press.

Povrzanović, M. 1993. Ethnography of a war: Croatia 1991–92. *Anthropology of East Europe Review,* Special Issue, 11 (1–2): 117–126.

Shahmuratian, S. 1990. *The Sumgait tragedy: Eyewitness accounts.* New Rochelle: Aristide Caratzas; Cambridge: Zoryan Institute.

Stoll, D. 1994. Guatemala: Solidarity activists head for trouble. Unpublished manuscript, in author's possession.

Suny, R. G. 1993. *Looking toward Ararat: Armenia in modern history.* Bloomington: Indiana University Press.

Ter Minassian, A. 1984. *La République d'Arménie:* Brussels: Éditions Complexe.

Turner, V. 1969. *The ritual process.* Chicago: Aldine.

White, H. 1987. *The content of the form: Narrative discourse and historical representation.* Baltimore: Johns Hopkins University Press.

2

Would the Real Nationalists Please Step Forward
Destructive Narration in Macedonia

K. S. Brown

This chapter, like others in this book, is in some sense based on "meta-data"—notes and queries concerning the complex relationships among people, objects of study, and forms of knowledge that the practice of anthropological fieldwork generates. The personal salience of these issues was compounded by the context in which I conducted research for my doctoral dissertation between March 1992 and October 1993. I was attached to the Institute for National History in Skopje, in the Republic of Macedonia, through an academic exchange scheme between Britain and Yugoslavia. By the time I reached Skopje, though, the Republic of Macedonia was no longer a part of Yugoslavia, but had joined the former republics of Slovenia, Croatia, and Bosnia-Herzegovina in declaring itself autonomous and sovereign. However, in the Macedonian case, international recognition was withheld. This was in part because of neighbors' objections to the use of the name "Macedonia" to denote the new state and in part because of fears that recognition might precipitate conflict of the type that was occurring in Bosnia.

In the period when I lived there, then, Macedonia was in the process of a rapid and far-reaching transition which touched its inhabitants' lives in myriad ways. Much of what Macedonia's inhabitants experienced at that time was common to other postsocialist states: massive inflation, economic reforms which made the private sector more lucrative than formerly secure state employment, and a seemingly catastrophic loss of national status on the world stage.[1] The rapid changes in economic and political conditions bred uncertainty regarding the future and a mixture of nostalgia and bitterness toward the socialist past. For Macedonians, too, the specter of violent communal conflict within what had been their country loomed large. Although the Yugoslav Army withdrew peacefully from its Macedonian bases in 1992, and the country escaped the horrors of the wars of 1991–1993, the existence of different ethnic groups within the republic remained a potential resource that nationalist politicians could exploit.

In this state of suspension, once-Yugoslav Macedonians found their claims of constituting a viable political community challenged in a way that their former fellow citizens had not. What came under particularly close scrutiny were those accounts of national origin and activism produced during the Yugoslav period. It was my own interest in pre-Yugoslav Macedonian history that brought me to Skopje, fortuitously, at the very time that such history became charged with the weight of present claims and future aspirations. In such an environment, I set out to research and write a dissertation with the title "Of Meanings and Memories: The National Imagination in Macedonia." It was the subtitle, in particular, that caught the attention of those who had a considerable stake in national reality.

The aspect of postsocialism in Macedonia on which this chapter focuses is this particular concern with a disputed past. Macedonians face a particular legitimation crisis in the post-Yugoslav world, because so much of the apparatus of state was put in place only during the post–World War II period, which has been so widely dismissed as Tito's invention. Included in this apparatus of state was a historical profession whose mission was to narrate the history of the Macedonian nation. What, now, are Macedonians to make of a past which was only documented within Yugoslavia, according to historiographical doctrines now easily dismissed in a broader forum as the product of socialist ideology? I would consider this the dilemma that faces Macedonians, and the conversations recorded below demonstrate two responses to it.

In each case, my own dilemma is also foregrounded. The certainties with which these people confront the past can easily be labeled as nationalism and argued as creating an atmosphere in which violence and those who preach it may succeed. What is the role or responsibility of an anthropologist who enters such an arena? What place is left for respect and sensitivity when, for the anthropologist, people have got history wrong? Simultaneously, though, in a situation where "historical truth" is so sanctified yet people are creatively reshaping the past, what are the effects of the anthropologist's decision to highlight their inventiveness? I offer here concrete illustrations of situations that raised these questions and an account of my own attempts to handle them. In common with others faced by contributors to this volume, the dilemmas have epistemological and moral dimensions (see especially Dudwick; and Živković, both in this volume). And like all good dilemmas, they have no straightforward solutions.

Anthropological Background

The problems that I have briefly described above are not new ones. They could be argued to be variants of the old one of "cultural relativism." The ground of this debate has by now been well worked, a staple of introductory studies of anthropology. Most frequently the issues chosen to be highlighted are those in which individual rights are sacrificed to societal priorities and those in which prompt consideration of whether or not "individual rights" can be considered a universal good. That said, when the issue is one like that of female circumcision, in which individuals are asked to endure pain and suffer long-term effects as a result of traditional practices, it has become acceptable to look askance at the practices.

Taking issue with the way in which a group of people think about their collective past might seem less urgent. But the ease with which what is referred to as nationalism creates conflict and suffering on a broad scale, as demonstrated in the breakup of Yugoslavia, has made anthropologists leery of embracing or encouraging the kind of approaches to history that are considered to promote the policies of governments which pursue homogeneity within their frontiers. In recent years scholars from a number of disciplines have sought to demonstrate the significance of the sociohistorical context in shaping such historical discourses in eastern and southeastern Europe without relying on commonsense distinctions of "truth" and "falsehood" (Hayden 1993, 1996; Lass 1988; Simmonds-Duke 1987; Verdery 1990, 1994; Watson 1994). Old distinctions nonetheless die hard. Simplified visions of socialist society and nationalist frenzy have enjoyed a particular vogue in journalistic and street-corner accounts of recent events in Yugoslavia. Commentators in the West have been ready to charge native scholars of the Balkans as subjective and tendentious, and their compatriots as being in the grip of false consciousness, when they show attachment to some particular version of the past. Indeed, the criticism extends from this to imply that such attachments themselves have direct and dangerous effects in the present.[2]

A good example of a historical narrative that arouses such a set of strong reactions is that of the battle of Kosovo in the context of Serbian national history. Commemorated in oral epic and occupying center stage in Serbian medieval history, the battle marked the last stand of a Serbian army against a larger Ottoman force and ushered in Ottoman rule that lasted until the nineteenth century.

The battlefield lies in a region where Albanians now constitute a majority and have consistently sought greater autonomy. In the late 1980s it was the site of a speech by Slobodan Milošević in which he first deployed the populism that became his trademark and which has come to be identified as ethnic nationalism. In part as a result of subsequent events in which Milošević has clearly been implicated, the narrative of the battle of Kosovo is now all but taboo outside Serbia. To suggest that one finds inspiration in the narrative, or that one is stirred by the heroism of the principal actors, is to label oneself a Serbian nationalist or sympathizer. Conversely, within many Serbian circles, attempts to complicate the narrative by suggesting that the battle cannot be explained as "Serbs defending Christendom," or that it tells us more about internecine quarrels than about Serbian unity, mark one as anti-Serbian in the present as well. When a historical event is appropriated, its meaning becomes a problem, and any interpretation becomes an act of political intervention.

The example of Kosovo is given in part because it may be familiar to readers. In their chapters in this volume, Barsegian and Dudwick also stress the interconnection of particular historical narratives and present political movements. In Macedonia, the southernmost republic of the former Yugoslavia, it could be argued that history represents a similar rallying point for people, and it was that dimension of history that prompted my research in the first place. In particular, my interest was focused on the importance of events in August 1903 in Kruševo, a mountain town in southwestern Macedonia. In the course of my research and in writing my dissertation, I argued that Kruševo has gained its importance from the way in which its fate in that year—when it was a key site in an uprising, known as the Ilinden revolution, and was then destroyed by fire and sacking—can be read as mirroring that of Macedonia as a whole in the twentieth century.[3]

That was and remains my analytical position, which I reached after extensive archival and field research. However, in this chapter I want to reflect on two encounters with Macedonians that I had while en route to this conclusion, encounters in which I had to confront real-world consequences of that position. The two exchanges took place in 1993, the first in February, the latter in September. I have chosen to base my analyses here on verbatim citations from my field diaries of the time; therefore, some introduction and justification are required.

Although the two entries were made only six months apart, they represent very different styles. The first describes an interaction between myself and two historians at the Institute for National History, one a friend and colleague, the other a senior figure. In the case of this encounter, I have given their full names here. They have engaged directly in what was called a *polemika* in the Macedonian press, prompted by the events described here

(Bitoski 1993a, b, c; Donev 1993). To seek to conceal their identities would, I consider, be inappropriate to the public positions that they hold. By contrast, in the original journal entry describing the second encounter, I used only the first letters of people's forenames. I have chosen to preserve that convention here and say more about it in the preamble to that citation.

The first excerpt contains no explicit reflection on the possible interpretations of the interaction I had with the two historians. It strikes me now as the work of someone with clear ideas about his own importance. This second entry includes the inflections and influences that I thought noteworthy at the time of writing. My awareness of them was undoubtedly in part a consequence of greater communicative competence and greater confidence in my ability to interpret the nuances of conversational practice. This might seem like a straightforward celebration of the value of fieldwork. I hope to demonstrate, though, that such confidence is paradoxically accompanied by a greater mistrust of any singular and authoritative interpretation of social phenomena, including one's own. This reflexive effect, in the course of which I came to reassess my easy assumptions about the location of nationalism, is what the following analysis sets out to demonstrate.

Situation 1: A Dispute with an Expert

In February 1993, I was reading at my desk in the office I shared with Jovance Donev, a historian at the Institute for National History, in Skopje. I had been in Skopje for almost a year and was more or less fluent in the language—fluent enough, at any rate, to engage in a continuous ironic commentary on the world and Macedonia's place in it with my office mate. Jovance—often called by the diminutive familiar form of his name, Jovan—had been appointed as my local mentor and was on the brink of finishing his doctorate; we had decided to collaborate on a paper, which we had submitted to a conference. A senior member of the institute, Krste Bitoski, came into the office, and the following is what I wrote down at the time.

Krste Bitoski just came into the office to ask about our article. Jovance referenced me a couple of times and told him the title and the general idea; how history was used; gave the example that the Kruševo Republic was called a socialist republic (I wonder why he chose that example). Bitoski asked where the title came from. Jovance shrugged, gave a vague gesture. Krste: "Change it, why don't you? It's a hundred year anniversary. Some document, or something between the wars, with Ilinden." Jovance: "We thought this would be more interesting." Krste: "Be that as it may; find something else more . . ." He finished the sentence with that. I broke in: "More what, exactly?" He [Krste] turned, didn't respond; I was out of line. Jovance took over. "We'll talk about it, Keith and me, we'll find something more . . ."

I then asked if we could be told what the criteria were exactly that we should be following. He [Krste] mentioned in the discussion that this was a celebration, also. When Jovance finally said something about an 1870s Russian document, he [Krste] was satisfied, got up, left.

There are a number of ways to make sense of what was going on here. One might, for example, regard the tension as arising from Zanca's "processual paradox," which he suggests pervades any interaction between young Western interlopers and eastern European experts in devalued scientific methods (Zanca, this volume). But the key point was that my office mate and I were planning to write a paper which challenged certain of the conventional and consensual points in Macedonian history, as determined by the professionals of the national institute. The institute was set up in the late 1940s, along with a panoply of other state-funded institutions, with the aim of promoting the distinctiveness of the Macedonian people and their struggle for freedom according to the best principles laid out by Lenin's writings on the national question. Its staff, composed of professional historians with no teaching commitments, have sent out volley after volley of scholarly works on a relatively narrow range of topics. A majority of the researchers have always focused on the war of national liberation of 1941–1944 and the involvement of the Macedonian people and their communist party with the greater efforts of Tito and his *partizani.*

The next largest group have written on the period of activism at the turn of the century, when organizations were set up to liberate the region of Macedonia from Ottoman rule. According to the work of the institute, the culmination of these revolutionary activities was the Ilinden uprising of 1903, an armed insurrection in the course of which pitched battles were fought between insurgents and Ottoman forces and a number of towns were taken over briefly by the rebels. Their most celebrated achievement was the seizure of Kruševo, a town roughly 25 miles northwest of modern Bitola, which was the major administrative center of the Monastir region in the Ottoman period. At the time of the rising in 1903, Kruševo was a wealthy market town of substantial stone-built houses with a population over 10,000. Its wealth came not from agriculture—it was high in the mountains—but from trade, overseas earnings, and livestock-keeping. It had been settled by Vlach-speaking refugees from the larger metropolis of Moschopolis, destroyed in the early nineteenth century. A majority of these refugees considered themselves Hellenes (Greeks). By the turn of the century it was also home to a large Slav-speaking minority, mostly craftsmen and hired laborers, who were referred to by the dominant population as Bulgars.[4]

Members of both groups, who constituted separate religious communities, were active in the Internal Macedonian Revolutionary Organization, which had been formed in 1893 in Thessalonica (Perry 1988). When this organization planned an armed insurrection against the Ottoman authorities, it decided to make Kruševo and its small Ottoman garrison a primary target. Accordingly, on the night of August 1, a force of around 800 men surrounded the town, and in the course of the following morning they succeeded in burning the barracks and gaining control of the whole town. The insurgents shot a small number of townsfolk as spies and then, in cooperation with townspeople, set up some kind of provisional government. After several days (the sources differ on how many) the insurgents withdrew in the face of overwhelming Ottoman forces, which then bombarded and sacked the helpless town.

Two Kruševo natives were centrally involved in the action. Nikola Karev, from the community known as Bulgars, was the local representative to the central committee of the organization and was the military commander of the insurgent forces; Pitu Guli, a Vlach-speaker considered to be a Hellene, was the leader of the local *cheta,* or insurgent band. His was the only force to engage the Ottoman forces directly, and Guli himself was killed in a defensive battle on the road approximately five miles outside Kruševo.

All this is common knowledge in Macedonia. But the above description, in the uncertainty of its language, would offend. For what I have described as a provisional government is recorded in Macedonian history books as a republic—not only as that but as the first republic of the Balkans, with Karev as president and a manifesto proclaimed before its citizens. And what I have described as a defensive battle is in Macedonian historiography the last stand of the rebels, who were faithful to the slogan of the rising, which was "Freedom or death!" and which were the last words of Pitu Guli. By their respective associations, Nikola Karev and Pitu Guli occupy treasured places, as state-maker and as patriot, in the history of a republic whose borders and language were formalized only after 1944.[5]

Our paper, as planned and ultimately written in the middle of a sweltering Skopje summer, took issue with all of this. We pointed out that the first text that exists of the so-called Kruševo Manifesto was in fact from a play written in the 1920s. There it appears, not as a statement of ideals read to an enthusiastic audience, but as a letter sent to neighboring Turkish villages, to urge them not to join Ottoman forces and attack the town. We also noted that references to a republic being formed appeared only after World War II. None of the three main contemporary sources alludes to more than some temporary form of government. Finally, we suggested that Pitu Guli's battle was not a defense of the town and that its prominence in postwar celebration was in part a product of Guli's not having been closely associated with Bulgaria compared with other leaders who were. He was a Macedonian hero by default, in the absence of others (Donev and Brown 1993).

A hint of what we had planned was clear in the title that we had proposed for the paper: "One History, Many Meanings." It was probably that, and the reputation that my colleague had earned for arguing with his seniors in the institute over the interpretation of sources, that brought Dr. Bitoski to our door. The point that Jovance made to him—that in postwar sources, the republic is referred to by whatever the contemporary term for the republic was—was a perfect example which supported our central argument: that the past, far from occupying independent and inviolable status, keeps time with the present.

To most Western scholars, certainly since Edward Carr's *What Is History?* (1969), this would be an unexceptionable point. But a majority of the Macedonian historians in the institute in 1993 still considered history as a social science, composed of hard facts. Theoretical debate has not been the sharpest within the academy; emphasis, throughout the Yugoslav period, was laid on establishing what has happened along the road to the socialist present. The historical profession was held to have shared in the march forward, and its elder statesmen were revered. Thus our suggestion that history is rewritten by each generation was deeply offensive to senior members of the institute, who saw themselves as carrying a torch which illuminated the truth.

This, at any rate, was how I perceived the old guard, and Bitoski seemed to me to be their spokesman. Here, in my view, was a member of the *nomenklatura* anxious to protect the edifice constructed over the years by his profession. An additional dimension of this view was my belief, fueled by some rumors that I chose to heed, that the institute had been staffed not by the best historians but by men willing to toe the party line. So this kind of reaction, in 1993, was to me the last gasp of a worn-out set of ideologues, either frightened by the advent of what I thought of as the truth or so enmeshed in their own useful fictions that they had come to believe them. This intervention left me only more determined to pursue my own brand of what, following Richard Handler (1985), I would term "destructive narration," emphasizing the contingencies and ambiguities in the telling of history and thereby destabilizing any single version. Bringing into play a dogged literalism, I cast myself as the standard-bearer of the new paradigm for Macedonian history. All this was the immediate cause of the querulousness and sense of righteous indignation evident in the tone of my original journal entry.

Regarding this fragment again, though, I note that Bitoski was not concerned with the issue of what we were going to say so much as with the status of the symposium that we planned to attend. It was, he stressed, to be a "celebration." Again, it is easy to take a dismissive approach to such a sentiment and suggest that such events are the hallmark of regimes at once self-congratulatory and clearly deeply insecure about the past. But the phenomenon is not confined to the so-called obsessive Balkans. As recently as the summer of 1995, a storm erupted over the planned "Enola Gay" exhibit at the Smithsonian Institution in Washington, D.C., to mark the 50th anniversary of the end of World War II. The Smithsonian proposed to document the context in which the United States had deployed atomic weapons and, in particular, to question whether or not the dropping of the second atomic bomb on Nagasaki was justified. A storm of protest arose from veterans' groups and also emanated from the newly right-wing Congress, where it was suggested that left-wing revisionists had got hold of museums.[6]

With this perspective in mind, then, Bitoski's intervention looks rather different. He was not protecting his cohort so much as pointing out that "popular" history may have different priorities from what we thought we were doing. A similar message was delivered by other members of the profession when we finally did give the paper at a symposium in Kruševo. Colleagues suggested that there was no fundamental ideological problem with the paper. As far as they were concerned it was wrong, but it did present a case for a professional discussion of methodologies. To present it in the more public forum that we did, though, was inappropriate.

In some sense, then, this "expert" response by Bitoski was not nearly as malign as I presented it at the time. It was, certainly, an objection to the substantive content of what we planned to discuss. This I took at the time as his principal point of contention. But he was far more concerned with the impact that our choice of venue for our paper might have. In particular, it might be said that Bitoski's intervention represents an awareness of audience and consequences that I, in my enthusiasm, did not see so clearly.

Postfield Reflections: Where Methodology Meets Ideology

Since returning from the field, I have read several pieces which might have alerted me to the dangers I could encounter when trying to put my ideas before an audience of Macedonian readers. The richest source of such data is Caroline Brettell's edited volume *When They Read What We Write* (1993a). Two pieces in particular, that by Brettell herself and that by Richard Handler, stand out.

Brettell's chapter (1993b) focuses on her research on the history of French Canadians in Illinois and the role that a charismatic individual, Charles Chiniquy, played in their settlement there. She describes the fallout from a public address she gave about Chiniquy, whose reputation had been that of saintly founder but who turned out, from her research, to have had more human dimensions. In the question and answer session that followed her lecture, she had attempted to make some comparisons which might clarify some of what she was saying. She then found her words quoted out of context, and she encountered some hostility from former colleagues in the community. Brettell identifies her predicament as resulting from the mix of audiences; was the talk, after all, supposed to fit the genre of celebratory homage or that of scholarly investigation? The problems she describes are reminiscent of those of the Smithsonian Institution in the "Enola Gay" case.

With the publication of his book *Nationalism and the Politics of Culture in Quebec* (1988), Richard Handler faced a slightly different set of objections. In his case he stressed that Quebecois culture was performed self-consciously rather more than it was practiced unconsciously. This was in line with his general argument that culture itself, while claiming "natural" quality, is always and everywhere in the process of manufacture. His chapter in Brettell's edited volume deals with the academic responses of Quebecois scholars to his book (Handler 1993). A key dimension of their criticism, as he reports it, was that he as a U.S. citizen was criticizing or discounting the authenticity of Quebecois culture. As an outsider from a larger state, his interventions were considered an extension of political oppression by that state. The clash was not so much about the content of the past as about Handler's discussion of the people involved in the past's representation and about the politics of power difference that this discussion helped to further.

In his 1993 contribution to Brettell's edited volume, Handler considers the implications of his own plight for anthropologists more generally. He defends his position by stating that the opprobrium may be regrettable, but it is the cost of conducting effective research. In such contexts, where particular issues arouse violent sentiments, to seek to avoid them by softening one's tone is, in his view, to patronize the people whose culture and country one is studying. The alternative to the kind of no-holds-barred, take-offense-if-you-will approach that he takes is, in Handler's view at least, to surrender any kind of authority and become anodyne apologist for the ways of others.

In different ways, then—Brettell in her practice, Handler consciously—both these anthropologists came face to face with the potential adversarial quality of writing about other people's pasts. In both cases, by presenting versions of events that did not mesh with those prevalent, the anthropologists found themselves cast as unsympathetic or hostile other, and met corresponding and strong reactions to their work.

In a slightly different setting, James Clifford has described the plight of the expert witnesses in a case regarding Mashpee identity. As Clifford (1988: 322) points out, in the courtroom there is no room for the kind of opinion so beloved of academic writing: "An adversary system of justice, the need to make a clear case to counterbalance an opposing one, discourages opinions of a 'yes, but,' 'it depends on how you look at it' kind. Experts on the stand were required to answer the question: Is there a tribe in Mashpee? Yes or no?" For Brettell, all her research was compressed by her audience into an answer to the question, Was Charles Chiniquy a saint? For Handler, the question is, Is Quebec culture genuine? In each case, the courtroom atmosphere was not one that the scholar chose, but one that he or she found himself or herself cast into. Although anthropologists can choose the questions that they research, it is difficult to control the questions that others may put to them.

This is nowhere more the case, perhaps, than in Macedonia today. Indeed, the Mashpee parallel is apt: as Clifford reports, the Mashpee were asked to define themselves as tribe, which meant first providing some definition for *tribe* itself—a word with commonsense reference that becomes much more slippery when one attempts to refine it. *Nation*—or the Slavic term that is sometimes translated in that way, *narod*—has similar properties. It is in trying to obtain for themselves from the world community recognition as a nation, or *narod,* and thus as a sovereign self-governed state that the former Yugoslavs of Macedonia have found themselves, as it were, in the courtroom. Although an early judicial committee recommended that their application for recognition be accepted, it was not. The republic has spent several uneasy years being treated as a "quasi-state" (Jackson 1990), eager for scraps of legitimacy from different governments around the world. As late as 1996, though, they marched in the parade at Atlanta, not under *M,* where they would place themselves, but under *F* for "former"—the name used in dealings with the United Nations, until Greek objections were ironed out.[7]

In such a situation, it is no wonder that anthropologists and historians find themselves pressed to provide answers to questions which are not necessarily their own. Indeed, a setting like this, where a small nation is ultimately struggling for its right to be recognized, makes one feel that the questions one has chosen to explore are idle and irrelevant. This, it should be noted, was not the tone adopted by Bitoski. Indeed, the more I reflect on his intervention, the more courteous and understated I realize his approach was. But where this world-setting became a part of the foreground is in the second encounter I wish to describe.

Situation 2: An Encounter with Two Believers

In August 1993, I was sitting in a bar in Kruševo. I had just been at a round-table symposium, as coauthor of the paper which we had been advised not to write but which we had written anyway and then presented. I had been based in the town for four months, mostly interviewing elderly people to find out about the history of the town. I was having a lively exchange with various people in the town about my ways of interpreting history when we were joined by a young couple, one of whom had gone out of his way to help me with my research. He made some comments about the past and the use of historical documents, and then the conversation went on. Again, I wrote a record of what was said. As noted above, I preserve the use of pseudonyms in this case. These are not the words of professional spokespeople, and this distinction justifies to me what appears to be a double-standard in naming practices. The presence of ellipses and parentheses here is in sharp contrast with the attempted transparency of the first entry and is itself, perhaps, demonstration of greater nuance in my responses.

C—— and wife (A——) then went on. The republic: of course it was a republic. A—— cited old people, now dead, who had remembered Karev delivering the manifesto on Gumenja (or did she say from the Greek school, or did she say from a house balcony, which was the way it was in the film? I think the last, which surely shows the way things get lost once they start getting celebrated). She also said, "It's all very well to have the ideals you have (about the open society, debate, etc.) but the narod here is behind, it isn't ready for that. And it's easy for you (there was an economic twist to all of this) in America to think and write all this, but we're stuck here." Our whole conversation finished with the observation: We have obligations, whereas the young *gospodin* [monsieur] is free—a reference to their kids, waiting at home.

Although clearly suspicious of it, Bitoski had never engaged with the substance of what we planned, in part because we were vague about it. A——, though, did. She pointed out that the existence of a manifesto is suggested by the oral record. In another conversation I had with her husband, he put the same point differently: even if no one in 1903 actually used the term *republic,* giving it *de jure* status, it was nonetheless present in all but name. It therefore had *de facto* status. In the very choice of language, he appeared to recall Clifford's point, that the legal record may omit much of what actually happened. What this encounter revealed, then, as well as what occurred in all sorts of other settings, was an abiding conviction that in 1903, in Kruševo, something significant did happen. By demanding the kind of proof I did, I was guilty of overliteralism, of conducting a misdirected search for the concrete.

However, what was more striking about A——'s reaction was not this starting point but the direction that her comments took afterwards. For she effectively suggested that my interest in the past of Kruševo was a product of leisure and advantage. This was a reaction to my claims, at various points, that what was needed was an open discussion of sources and motives of the people celebrated in Macedonian history. Her point, as it appears here, was simple: not now, not here.

This was, of course, also the reaction of Bitoski. However, where he confined the arena of appropriateness to a symposium whose purpose was to commemorate rather than to interrogate the past, A——'s objections widened that arena considerably. The invocation of America, in particular, made the international dimensions of Macedonian history apparent. Throughout the period in which I was living in Macedonia, recognition remained just around the corner. Fighting had broken out in Bosnia only a few weeks before my arrival in March 1992, and people had still been in a state of shock. For those who had visited Bosnia in better days, they knew that the different confessional groups lived so closely together that any separation of the alliances that had been made in the Yugoslav period would be painful and protracted. While Macedonia remained unrecognized and economic conditions worsened, it was easy for people to believe that the unthinkable could happen there too, and people could find themselves divided.

A——'s argument of the untimeliness of my interest in former divisions was as much about the present as the past, as she acknowledged. Suppose, she said in another conversation, you find out that Vlach and Macedonian were opposed then, as we know they were before World War II: doesn't that just build up and justify antagonism in the present? And then what happens between a Vlach husband and a Macedonian wife? And what happens to their children? This set of questions, reflecting as it did her own personal circumstances, reflected a personal family fear. Her investment in the history of Kruševo in 1903 as a multiconfessional place of cooperation between former groups thus mirrored, at the most personal level of all, the state-building project of the Macedonian government in the Yugoslav period.

Being confronted in this way with an individual whose investment in a version of history is not about personal prestige or ideological outlook is humbling and unsettling. Ultimately, what is at stake for this woman is the future of her marriage and the lives of her children. Where I saw a cover-up or a distortion of the full picture of the past, she saw a blueprint for the kind of relations that should exist and that she has dedicated her adult life to perpetuating. And where I had been able to see myself as a voice of the enlightened future, disrupter of the old guard's monopoly on history, she saw me as a selfish, self-obsessed, and self-important foreigner, oblivious to the present and future implications of my own concern with the past.

Ideology Revisited

This table-turning is perhaps a good place to end this discussion. For what the two encounters taught me is the difficulty of talking about a single nationalist culture of history in Macedonia—and perhaps, by extension, in any postsocialist society. For the nationalism that disrupts people's lives most immediately in Macedonia and elsewhere does not spring ready-formed from its inhabitants, but involves a much broader context. A major part of that context is a world order which, for all its pleas for multicultur-alism and tolerance, was constructed on a model which presumed the ulti-mate desirability of the nation-state. Nationalism, then, does not inhere in local versions of the past; what I hope these situations demonstrate is the extent to which those versions are responses to an agenda for postsocialist Europe that has, thus far, created only states where groups have made clear and unambiguous claims to cultural longevity. Even where groups and their leaders, as in the case of Serbia, are vilified, their claims to independent po-litical existence are recognized.

The interlocutors I have described here share certain views of the Mace-donian past. More precisely, though, and more saliently, they express con-sensus on the limits within which complex histories, in a politicized world, should be put on display. Although couched in the idiom of historical truth, their concerns are primarily with the potential political consequences of broadcasting or publicizing uncertainty before a world audience. For it could be argued that the real force of nationalism lies in the demands made by a world community of nation-states, that any people who wish to join should organize themselves and their pasts in a recognizably national way. In this sense, Macedonians—or at least some of them—force us to question our easy generalizations about nationalism in the Balkans. My conversa-tions with Macedonians certainly had that effect on me. For with their faith in what might appear to be myths of intercommunity cooperation, they ar-gue for a chance to build their world on a different model from the one that we tend to project into their lives. In seeking to deconstruct the bases of such different models, we may unwittingly serve the very cause we think we are opposing. Paradoxically, then, it is not a post-Yugoslav Macedonian, but the eagerly destructive anthropologist, who is the nationalist in the story.

Notes

The research on which this chapter is based was assisted by a grant from the Joint Committee on Western Europe of the American Council of Learned Societies and the Social Science Research Council, with funds provided by the Ford and Mellon Foundations. I would like to thank Matti Bunzl, Victor Friedman, Gabe Lyon, Shel-ley Stephenson, George Stocking, and Marko Živković for their reactions to and comments on earlier versions, and the book's reviewers for their constructive sug-gestions. I would also like to thank Nora Dudwick and Hermine De Soto for their editorial input and endurance.

1. This last point might appear odd to make regarding Macedonia, given the considerable global attention that the recognition issue attracted. This notoriety, though, was considered by Macedonians a poor replacement for the high status formerly enjoyed by Yugoslavia as a leading light in the nonaligned movement.

2. As a point of clarification, I do not consider that nationalism (a way of thinking about the world) and ethnic cleansing (a practice which calls into question the humanity of its practitioners and denies humanity to its victims) are equivalent or vary directly. I do believe that both are built on a double standard revolving around a set of paradoxes well described by Morgenthau (1957). The easy collapse of concern with identity and extreme behavior, though, is a rhetorical move that I am challenging here. One of the most prominent producers of this view is the journalist Robert Kaplan, whose best-selling *Balkan Ghosts* (1993) is alleged to have directly influenced White House policy in the year of its publication (Drew 1994). In the chapter dealing with Macedonia, Kaplan presents a picture of the earnestness of politicians, propagandists, and professional historians in the three countries of Greece, Bulgaria, and Yugoslavia, each of whom assured him that they were telling the truth and that all he would hear elsewhere would be lies. Kaplan is at pains to point out how absurd he found all of this certainty and also to link it to extremism and violence. Kaplan's book has been critically reviewed by Cooper (1993) and Malcolm (1993).

3. Some mention of the 1903 uprising, Kruševo's importance, and subsequent celebrations in the republic is made by Danforth (1995), Poulton (1995), and Schwartz (1996), all of whom broadly follow the description of the Macedonian revolutionary organizations provided by Perry (1988). Those anthropologists who have focused more on Greek Macedonia (Agelopoulos 1994; Cowan 1997; Karakasidou 1997; Vereni, n.d.) have tended to report less significance for the events of 1903 than for those of the subsequent period of 1904–1908, commemorated within Greece as the "Macedonian Struggle" (Dakin [1966] 1993).

4. The destruction of Moschopolis, which, if it were in existence today, would be in modern Albania, is attributed to the actions of Ali Pasha, a renegade Ottoman official who carved out his own fiefdom and played host to Lord Byron. His headquarters were in Ioánnina in what is now northwestern Greece, and he was nicknamed the Lion of Ioánnina. The names "Greek" and "Bulgar" in the nineteenth century have been argued by some to denote class rather than national or ethnic identity, whereas others build claims to modern national territory on the frequent deployment of these names in sources throughout the nineteenth century (Stoianovich 1960; Vermeulen 1984; Brown 1995a, esp. chap. 3).

5. ASNOM, the Anti-fascist Council for the National Liberation of Macedonia, met on August 2, 1944, a date referred to throughout the Yugoslav period and afterwards as the second Ilinden (Brown 1995b).

6. The exhibit took its name from that of the airplane, which was at the heart of the display, and the dispute was widely reported in the U.S. media. In an editorial in the *Philadelphia Inquirer* on February 1, 1995, the secretary of the Smithsonian was quoted as admitting that the basic error was an attempt to "couple a historical treatment of the use of atomic weapons with the fiftieth anniversary of the end of the

war." This particular editorial was scathing in regard to what the impossibility of the combination revealed about American resistance to "sincere and open historical inquiry."

7. *Narod* was a technical term in the Yugoslav constitution, in which a sharp line was drawn between the Slavic groups that were constituent peoples of the federation and those other groups that were considered as "nationalities," or *narodnosti*—ethnic groups that had a named state outside Yugoslavia. An excellent discussion of the politics of status involved in these terms' usage in Bosnia is given by Bringa (1995: 12–36). In post-Yugoslav Macedonia, although the constitution stresses the equality of all citizens, vestiges of the Yugoslav system remain. While Macedonians constitute a narod, other groups are minorities, *maltsinstva,* or are even still referred to as narodnosti (Victor Friedman, personal communication). A key debate within the republic is over Albanian demands to be recognized as a narod, equal as a collective to Macedonia. The central significance of narod in postwar Yugoslavia is laid out by Hayden (1996).

References

Agelopoulos, G. 1994. Cultures and politics in rural Greek Macedonia. Unpublished Ph.D. thesis, Cambridge University.

Bitoski, K. 1993a. Obvinenija bez argumenti. *Puls* (September 3): 22.

Bitoski, K. 1993b. Istorijata kako selektor. *Puls* (September 10): 21.

Bitoski, K. 1993c. Arogancijata na avtorot na "nesoborlivite" vistini. *Puls* (October 1): 21.

Brettell, C., ed. 1993a. *When they read what we write: The politics of ethnography.* Westport, Conn.: Bergin and Garvey.

Brettell, C. 1993b. Whose history is it? Selection and representation in the creation of a text. In C. Brettell, ed., *When they read what we write: The politics of ethnography,* 93–105. Westport, Conn.: Bergin and Garvey.

Bringa, Tone. 1995. *Being Muslim the Bosnian way: Identity and community in a central Bosnian village.* Princeton, N.J.: Princeton University Press.

Brown, K. S. 1995a. Of meanings and memories: The national imagination in Macedonia. Unpublished Ph.D. dissertation, University of Chicago.

Brown, K. S. 1995b. The oldest profession: Macedonian historiography in the post-Yugoslav world. Paper presented at the American Association for the Advancement of Slavic Studies Convention, Washington, D.C.

Carr, E. H. 1969. *What is history?* London: Macmillan.

Clifford, J. 1988. Identity in Mashpee. In *The predicament of culture: Twentieth century ethnography, literature and art,* 277–346. Cambridge, Mass.: Harvard University Press.

Cooper, H. 1993. Review of "Balkan ghosts." *Slavic Review* 52 (3): 592–593.

Cowan, J. 1997. Idioms of belonging: Polyglot articulations of local identity in a Greek Macedonian town. In P. Mackridge and E. Yannakakis, eds., *Ourselves and others: The development of a Greek Macedonian cultural identity since 1912.* Oxford and New York: Berg.

Dakin, D. [1966] 1993. *The Greek struggle in Macedonia 1897–1913.* Thessalonica: Institute for Balkan Studies.

Danforth, L. 1995. *The Macedonian conflict: Ethnic nationalism in a transnational world.* Princeton, N.J.: Princeton University Press.

Donev, J. 1993. Imperijata go vrakja udarot. *Puls* (September 17): 21.

Donev, J., and K. Brown. 1993. Mechkina usloga na Mechkin kamen. *Puls* (August 20): 21.

Drew, E. 1994. *On the edge: The Clinton presidency.* New York: Simon and Schuster.

Handler, R. 1985. On dialogue and destructive analysis: Problems in narrating nationalism and ethnicity. *Journal of Anthropological Research* 41 (2): 171–182.

Handler, R. 1988. *Nationalism and the politics of culture in Quebec.* Madison: University of Wisconsin Press.

Handler, R. 1993. Fieldwork in Quebec, scholarly reviews, and anthropological dialogues. In C. Brettell, ed., *When they read what we write: The politics of ethnography,* 67–74. Westport, Conn.: Bergin and Garvey.

Hayden, R. 1993. The triumph of chauvinistic nationalisms in Yugoslavia: Bleak implications for anthropology. *Anthropology of East Europe Review,* Special Issue: *War among the Yugoslavs* 11 (1 & 2): 72–78.

Hayden, R. 1996. Imagined communities and real victims: Self-determination and ethnic cleansing in Yugoslavia. *American Ethnologist* 23 (4): 783–801.

Jackson, R. 1990. *Quasi-states: Sovereignty, international relations and the third world.* Cambridge: Cambridge University Press.

Kaplan, R. 1993. *Balkan ghosts: A journey through history.* New York: St. Martin's Press.

Karakasidou, A. 1997. *Fields of wheat, hills of blood: Passages to nationhood in Greek Macedonia 1870–1990.* Chicago: University of Chicago Press.

Lass, A. 1988. Romantic documents and political monuments: The meaning-fulfillment of history in 19th-century Czech nationalism. *American Ethnologist* 15 (3): 456–471.

Malcolm, N. 1993. Seeing ghosts. *National Interest* 32: 83–88.

Morgenthau, H. J. 1957. The paradoxes of nationalism. *Yale Review* 46 (4): 481–496.

Perry, D. 1988. *The politics of terror: The Macedonian revolutionary movements, 1893–1903.* Durham, N.C.: Duke University Press.

Poulton, H. 1995. *Who are the Macedonians?* Indianapolis and Bloomington: Indiana University Press.

Schwartz, J. 1996. *Pieces of mosaic: An essay on the making of Makedonija.* Hojbjerg, Denmark: Intervention Press.

Simmonds-Duke, E. M. 1987. Was the peasant uprising a revolution? The meaning of a struggle over the past. *Eastern European Politics and Societies* 1 (2): 187–224.

Stoianovich, T. 1960. The conquering Balkan orthodox merchant. *Journal of Economic History* 20: 234–313.

Verdery, K. 1990. The production and defense of "the Romanian Nation," 1900 to World War II. In R. G. Fox, ed., *Nationalist ideologies and the production of national cultures,* 81–111. American Ethnological Society Monographs No. 2. Washington, D.C.: American Anthropological Association.

Verdery, K. 1994. From parent-state to family patriarchs: Gender and nation in contemporary eastern Europe. *East European Politics and Societies,* Special Issue: *Gender and Nation* 8 (2): 225–255.

Vereni, P. No date. Os Ellin Makedonas: National identity between history and memory in Western Greek Macedonia. Unpublished MS, in the author's possession.

Vermeulen, H. 1984. Greek cultural dominance among the Orthodox population of Macedonia during the last period of Ottoman rule. In A. Blok and H. Driessen, eds., *Cultural dominance in the Mediterranean area,* 225–255. Nijmegen: Centrale Reprogafie.

Watson, R. S., ed. 1994. *Memory, history and opposition under state socialism.* Santa Fe, N.M.: School of American Research Press.

3

Telling Stories of Serbia
Native and Other Dilemmas on the Edge of Chaos

Marko Živković

In the summer of 1991, when war broke out in Yugoslavia, I was taking an intensive Japanese language course in Ann Arbor, Michigan. It was my second year as a graduate student in the University of Chicago anthropology department, and I was getting ready to do fieldwork in Japan. Born and raised in Belgrade, I became a Japanophile during my high school years, and having studied Japanese along with clinical psychology at the University of Belgrade (where I got my B.A.), I was finally about to realize a 15-year-old dream of going to Japan through the circuitous route of cultural anthropology. What I considered home, however, was rapidly disintegrating, and the war was gaining in intensity as it spread from Slovenia to Croatia and finally to Bosnia in the following year. Still carried by the momentum of my interest in Japan, I spent the 1992–1993 academic year studying Japanese in Yokohama, but midway through I decided to switch my area of research from Japan to Yugoslavia.

I returned to Belgrade in the summer of 1993 for two weeks, for another two weeks in the winter of 1993–1994, and again for two months later in 1994. I hardened to the unsettling experience of moving between the "inverted worlds" of Belgrade and Chicago and finally went for a six-month stretch of fieldwork beginning in February of 1995, followed by two-month stays in 1996 and 1997. I had no external funding for any of these trips, and

I stayed with my parents in Belgrade, carrying the "native anthropologist" role to its logical extreme.[1]

In this chapter I deal with problems posed by doing fieldwork as a native ethnographer in a situation where nationalist mobilization intersected with an ambiguous transition from communism amidst the turmoil of war and disintegration of the common state. In Serbia and, more specifically, in Belgrade, these circumstances combined in a way that presented me with a number of epistemological, methodological, and ethical dilemmas.

As a native, however, I rarely encountered the problems that usually face fieldworkers perceived as outsiders belonging to more powerful countries. I was thus not approached as a potential broker who might speak out on behalf of some domestic cause to those who matter (the West, the United States . . .), nor was I perceived as somebody who could "open doors to the presumed riches of the West" (see Kuehnast, this volume). People knew that I had been living in the United States, and a few times I was jokingly called a spy, but this was a far cry from the experiences reported by Russell Zanca in this volume. I do not mean to underestimate the pervasive paranoia that gripped Serbia at the time I did my fieldwork there; it is only that I myself was spared suspicion.

Although temptations were not lacking, I resisted being drawn into particular political groups or coopted into political agendas and did not engage in any overt political activities while in the field. To refuse to take a position in a highly politicized society such as present-day Serbia, however, could itself be seen as a political or ethical choice—an issue I address later.

Thus the primary dilemmas I faced were either epistemological-methodological (what is important to know? what is knowable? how does one get to know it? etc.) or had to do with representing a group (a nation, a people, a society) to several potential audiences in a world where representation can and does have quite real consequences. In this chapter I show how these dilemmas led me to focus on the social life of stories Serbs tell themselves (and others) about themselves.

How to Deal with Rapid Change

One of my major problems was how to deal with what I came to call the opacity of social reality. The rapid change and general turmoil of Serbia in the aftermath of Yugoslav disintegration made social reality confusing to such an extent that many natives felt it to be as opaque to them as to any outside observer. One of the best native social commentators, Stojan Cerović, expressed this paradox succinctly in his commentary on the July 1995 United Nations hostage crisis: "Sometimes it is of great advantage to be a foreign correspondent. When you don't understand something, you think that it is because you are not from here and not initiated into the mysterious customs of this exotic country. But how could we, who are from here, how could we confess that we don't understand what is happening here any better than if we suddenly found ourselves in the midst of Kazakhstan?" (Cerović 1995: 6).

The ability of almost everyone in Serbia at that time to figure out the social landscape was severely impaired. That landscape was populated by government ministers, directors of big firms, regional bosses, Socialist Party functionaries, generals, prophets and pundits, influential writers, opposition leaders, police chiefs, criminal-warlord "businessmen," and the State Security Service. How much power, influence, and autonomy all these actors and institutions actually had was far from clear, yet it was important to try to figure them out in a world in which nothing seemed to be stable, rational, or what it was supposed to be. As Eric Gordy has observed: "By rotating its cast of ideological surrogates through the musical chairs of power, the regime protects itself from its own positions and actions. Rarely speaking or otherwise appearing in public, Slobodan Milošević can rightly claim that he never advocated nationalist or any other positions. In fact, every major political move of his regime has been announced, defended, and removed from the agenda by surrogates" (Gordy 1996: 121).

Most people oscillated between two positions. There was, on the one hand, a widespread awareness that all power indeed ultimately flowed from Milošević and that he was the only one who shuffled the deck of Serbian politics. On the other hand, the regime largely succeeded in transferring the responsibility for the disastrous results of its rule—disintegration of the common state, reduction of Serbia to pariah status, one of the highest hyperinflations ever recorded, and a lost war—onto either foreign powers or a cast of internal "enemies."

A piece of urban folklore, a "story truer than true," that I heard from several independent sources offers an excellent illustration of this situation: After a series of brutal killings of postmen delivering pensions in 1991 and 1992, it was arranged that pensioners would gather in a designated room of their apartment complex or at the nearest community center and wait for a postman escorted by police to distribute their pensions. The story had it that they would grumble to the postman, asking why it had taken so long, why the payday was so irregular, why the pension was so miserable, and so on. The obviously opposition-minded postman would tell them: "Ask Milošević." At that they would get angry and start telling him that Milošević was not to blame, that it was the opposition instead who was to blame for everything.

The person who reported this story would be outraged—how could the pensioners be so blind? Elementary logic should have told them that the

Serbian opposition, whose impotence they were daily witnessing on television, could not be responsible for the disappearance of the pension funds. The opposition hadn't been able to push a single law past the Socialist majority in the Parliament, so how could it influence such a centralized institution as pension funds? It should have been obvious to the pensioners who the actual masters of the state purse were and thus who was responsible for their misery.

Yet the theory promoted by the regime media as early as spring 1991 still held sway in 1995 when I collected this story. This was the implausible theory that the damage done to the center of Belgrade during the March 1991 opposition demonstrations was to blame for the depletion of pension funds. The opposition destroyed Belgrade, this theory held, so the money's gone.

The logical contradiction, however, can be seen here only by the distanced observer who can afford the luxury of a synoptic view. For those submerged in day-to-day living, information was so scant and so contradictory that they were forced to resort to convoluted conspiracy theories whose logic tolerates the most glaring contradictions. My predicament was that, like most people in Serbia, I had no way of knowing what was happening behind closed doors and in the corridors of power, and yet the cataclysmic events made it urgent to know what was going on while it was still happening. Under the conditions of perpetual emergency that had obtained in Serbia since at least 1991, rumors and conspiracy theories tended to proliferate, and the ethnographer was faced with the issue of how to deal with them. Should one despair that reality and truth seemed beyond grasp, or should one make the most of the situation? Faced with the situation where events were slipping away and would not stay still for me to make up my mind, I decided to give up the ambition of finding out what was *really, really* happening and instead collect as many examples as I could of narrative genres ranging from everyday talk and urban folklore through social commentary to studies produced by Belgrade social science institutes. After all, other social scientists, both domestic and foreign, were already busy reconstructing the events of the last 10 or so years, and the bibliography of serious works on "why Yugoslavia disintegrated" was rapidly growing (see, for instance, Cohen 1992, 1993; Glenny 1992; Ramet 1992; Woodward 1995). I wanted to offer something that would meaningfully complement existing scholarship rather than duplicate it and that would bring an anthropological, culturally sensitive angle to a field dominated by political science–type analysis.

Stories Serbs Tell Themselves (and Others) about Themselves

In rumors, urban legends, everyday talk, popular songs, newspaper columns, television debates, and parliamentary speeches I came to discern recurring motifs that were ultimately organized into a finite set of narratives, or what I came to call stories Serbs tell themselves (and others) about themselves. Where a fund of narratives is shared by a community, often a single phrase or image is enough not only to invoke a "story" but also to impart a particular twist to it.

Relating these stories, I suggest, is a good way to capture the atmosphere of the moment, for their proliferation was one of the symptoms of, as well as a significant way of coping with, a situation of radical upheaval and uncertainty. Thus, at the most immediate level, presenting the stories that well up at such times might contribute to the phenomenology of living under conditions of instability, breakdown of established norms, and general lack of moral compass.

Second, the stories not only fulfill the epistemological role of "making sense" out of an opaque, turbulent social reality for those caught up in it; they have pragmatic consequences as well. Social actors (individuals and groups variously situated within the socioeconomic structure) also use them to maneuver for the most advantageous position within the Serbian "quality space" (Fernandez 1986b). My presentation of these stories, particularly those told in the public domain, would moreover have the advantage of offering a sense of the "complex spectrum of political agendas" (Grant 1993: 17).

Finally, the most prominent stories are usually not products just of the moment. They index other stories Serbs have been telling themselves for a much longer period. These stories have their genealogies; they point to and reverberate with "durable yet changing discourse[s]" that have "repeatedly reemerged in historically disparate political circumstances" (Gal 1991: 441); they follow certain routes, use certain imagery, involve certain typical characters, themes, plots, and clusters of images formed, I would suggest, at the confluence of local history and European "geopolitical imaginings."[2]

Elsewhere, I analyze some of the themes, characters, and images that make up the stories Serbs have been telling themselves and others since the mid-1980s, such as the Turkish Taint (Živković 1995) and Byzantine Revival (Živković 1998b), Violent Highlanders vs. Peaceful Lowlanders (Živković 1997a), and the Identification with Jews (Živković 1994) or with Gypsies (Živković 1997b).[3] Here, I would like to focus on the most prominent types of narratives that try to make sense of the highly ambiguous present in terms of Serbia's communist legacy.

How to Deal with "Postsocialism"

When it comes to the "postsocialist syndrome," I was faced with a defi-
ciency in my native knowledge. Although I had lived in socialist Yugoslavia
for 28 years, I found it problematic to take myself as a native informant, for
it was clear that one's experience of socialism depends to a great extent on
one's generation as well as on what stratum, class, or circle one belongs to.
I belong to a generation of people who grew up during the "golden 1970s
and 1980s," when it was possible, especially if you were a carefree student,
to enjoy the good sides of Yugoslav socialism and largely ignore the rest.

Socialist regimes often seemed to breed a particularly strong sense of
living in parallel worlds—on the one hand, a world of official dogma, slogans, and parades; on the other, the intimate, private world of kitchen talk,
dachas, and meanderings of everyday life. Everyday reality often starkly
contradicted official dogma, yet the majority of people living in such systems managed to adjust and even consider their lives quite normal (even
though from the standpoint of strict logical consistency, they would seem
to be living in bad faith). Depending on the country and period, the world
of official communist ideology was more or less rigid, and it tended to en-
croach upon the private world of everyday life to a lesser or greater extent.
Yugoslav socialism migrated from a typical Stalinist model in its earlier
stages (1940s and 1950s) to a system in which the encroachment of ideology into everyday life was arguably felt less than in any other "people's
democracy."

Though evaluations of the socialist era vary depending on one's generation, situation, and personal experience, I would argue that for all the
wealth of personal idiosyncrasies, stories about the communist legacy in
Serbia can be usefully classified into three main types. The first two types
could be characterized as resentment versus nostalgia, while the third presents a more complex argument about "living in bearable evil." Perhaps the
best example of the resentment story is one told by Slavenka Drakulić.

Grandma's Cupboards, or On Bitterness and Nostalgia

Drakulić concludes her book on everyday life under communism, *How We
Survived Communism and Even Laughed,* by cataloguing the contents of her
grandmother's cupboard. In the 1970s, while her grandmother was in the
hospital, Drakulić's mother took the opportunity to clean her cupboards
and drawers of "trash." One cupboard, Drakulić writes, "was full of neatly
stored detergent that had turned almost to stone, bottles of rancid oil, several kilos of sugar, flour, and coffee, some packages of tea, biscuits, pasta,
cans of tomato paste, beans, and even a kilo or two of salt, in spite of the

fact that nobody remembers a shortage of that." Those cupboards and drawers, she concludes, "looked like a museum of communist shortages," showing "not only how we survived communism, but why communism failed. . . . collecting was a necessity, because deep down nobody believed in a system that was continuously unable to provide for its citizens' basic needs for forty years or more" (Drakulić 1993: 189).

Drakulić's book was intended as a native's account not only of everyday life in Yugoslavia but also of the "trivia of daily living" in the whole of communist eastern Europe. It is a bitter account dominated by images of decrepit buildings and rubbish in the streets, crowded apartments, unreliable cars, sickly children, boring jobs, poor-quality food, suspicion, deceit, and apathy. The distinctions between her Yugoslav experience and the experiences of women elsewhere in eastern Europe were often blurred. Visiting these countries, she wrote, felt "very much like revisiting my own past— shortages, the distinctive odors, the shabby clothing. After all, we had all long suffered under the same ideology" (Drakulić 1993: xiv).

While, as another native, I could corroborate most of her descriptions of the minutiae of everyday life in Yugoslavia, I found that I did not endorse the flavor, the twist, or the interpretation Drakulić put on them. A very popular Belgrade writer, Momo Kapor, for instance, made a name for himself in the 1970s and 1980s as a collector of everyday trivia perhaps best epitomized by the term *grandma's cupboards.* The contents of these cupboards were probably identical to the contents of Drakulić's grandmother's, but Momo Kapor's detailed catalogues carry a quite distinct flavor. They are suffused by intimacy and hues of cozy nostalgia and are definitely not marshaled as evidence of "communist shortages." That my own memories of such everyday trivia are much more in accord with Kapor's than with Drakulić's doesn't mean that her interpretation is invalid or not widely shared, but it points to the diversity of ways in which so-called communist everyday life was experienced in Yugoslavia.

Everyday life in socialist Yugoslavia necessitated a repertoire of tactics for obtaining scarce goods and services that would strike a citizen of a more rationally organized Western democracy as circuitous. Having friends or friends of friends strategically distributed through banks, post offices, various bureaucracies, and, perhaps most important, hospitals was valuable capital that enabled one to cut corners, jump long lines, and, in general, make one's everyday life easier.

These everyday poachings and little tricks constituted a socially accepted way of life in Yugoslavia and were a part of a widespread ethos. To trick the system was a matter of honor, and skilled practitioners unashamedly bragged about their clever schemes. To rely on personal connections in procuring hard-to-get goods and services, to do one's own private business on company time, or to embezzle anything from nails from your factory to paper clips from your office are practices familiar to anyone who lived under state socialism. There was a sense of solidarity in having to make do in that manner and a corresponding disdain for those who were too straight. Admittedly, at least since the late 1960s, that kind of practice in Yugoslavia assumed a milder form than in most countries of "real socialism," yet to the Soviet saying "They pretend to pay us and we pretend to work" there exists a Yugoslav parallel: "No matter how little they pay me I can work even less."

Yet standing in endless lines, resorting to bribery and personal connections in order to obtain even the bare necessities, and fear of tapped telephones and secret police were definitely not hallmarks of everyday life for the vast majority of ordinary people in Yugoslavia, at least since the early 1970s.

As in many other areas, Yugoslavs tended to perceive themselves as *something in between.* In this case, they were in between Soviet or east European everyday life and that of developed Western countries.[4] At times, this sense of being neither one nor the other was a source of pride. It was possible to feel that we were unique and that our way of life combined the good sides of both systems. There is, however, another option, a thesis that lays the blame for our present predicament precisely on our being better off than our Soviet Bloc comrades. Tito's "benevolent" or "operatic" communism muddied the waters and hopelessly corrupted us.

Mud, Slush, and Red Mists

Elsewhere (Živković 1998a) I note the ubiquity of images of *mud* in Serbian self-presentation and (intimate) self-understanding. True, in a region in which paved roads still seem to be the exception rather than the rule, mud is more than common in its many varieties and grades (mire, ooze, quagmire) as a simple empirical datum. This is, after all, what, together with the stink of pigs, greets a visitor as the most familiar trait of a typical Serbian village. Mud in its many variations could be seen as belonging to a whole family of idioms in which a periphery expresses its sense of in-betweenness by resorting to images of mixedness, ambiguity, amorphousness, and miscegenation (see also Todorova 1997). Yet, I would argue that in Serbia, mud is not just a shorthand expression for in-betweenness or "our backwardness." It is not simply a synecdoche for a complex of traits associated with countryside and peasants, a way of indicating one's own primitivity or that of one's neighbor in the Balkans, but also a ubiquitous metaphor for the confused experience of living in Milošević's Serbia.

"In Serbia all politics turned into gelatin and our consciousness is slush," wrote the Belgrade journalist Nenad Stefanović in the article titled "Sviču crvene magle" (Red mists are dawning):[5] "Here we can neither fight it out nor sit down together like human beings. Corrupted and neglected for decades, we are living through a morally provisory period in which absolutely everything is possible, including the revival of disastrous utopias. They [the communists] are coming. They are coming because they never left" (Stefanović 1994: 16).

The thesis advanced in the article is that "communism is returning to Serbia riding on the corpse of tarnished (*okaljani*) nationalism" (Stefanović 1994: 14). It might appear, Stefanović argues, that nationalism could be differentiated into two sorts: authentic (supposedly operating among the people) and cynical (operating on the level of leadership). The distinction, however, has become hopelessly blurred in Serbia, where the "mimicry is an octopus which intertwines sincere with useful feelings" (15). Milošević's (cynical) nationalism, which he used as a lever in his internal party showdown in 1987, was popularly interpreted in Serbia as anti-Yugoslavism, anti-communism, and, even more surprisingly, a call for the revival of Orthodoxy. A line from a newly composed folk ode to Milošević that Stefanović quotes puts this confusion in a nutshell: "You are, Slobo, a communist, we love you like Jesus Christ" (Ti si Slobo komunista, volimo te k'o Isusa Hrista) (15).

Stefanović is trying to disentangle a nauseatingly muddled situation in which the authentic could not be distinguished from the cynical and in which supposed political opponents regularly swap ideological hats overnight. Even an octopus with its eight tentacles impossibly entwined seems like a model of clarity in this situation, and compounded mystifications and simulations blur reality in a way that defies metaphors such as "mimicry" or "facade." In fact, my unwitting mixing of metaphors[6] in the first line of this paragraph already signals the predicament of those trying to make sense of Serbia in the last 10 or so years—you cannot untangle something that is muddled.

During the last few years (roughly 1991–1996) that I focus on, talk about the legacy of socialism figured most prominently, I would suggest, in what I came to call Serbian jeremiads (see Živković 1996), a genre of "lamentations over our condition" that closely corresponds to a genre of Russian talk which Nancy Ries (1997) calls "litanies and laments." Fifty years of communism were blamed in various ways by various people (with various agendas) as corrupting their "character" and "moral constitution" and are cited as the reason, or one of the reasons, that they are still mired in the twilight semipostsocialist nightmare. Stefanović's article is an excellent example of the genre. Among other things, the article advances what I came to call the *bearable evil* thesis. The expression comes from a prominent

Serbian writer, Milovan Danojlić, who provides perhaps the clearest version of this widespread argument.[7]

Living in Bearable Evil

In the Yugoslav case, the blame for half a century of communist rule could not be shifted to the "evil Soviet Empire" to the extent that was possible in other eastern European people's democracies. If we were corrupted by communism, as many domestic critics were saying, then, in all honesty, we have only ourselves to blame. And the internal dichotomy of "us"—the (unwilling) subjects of a communist regime—versus "them"—the party, authorities, and so on—tends to dissolve under the realization that, by assenting to the "life in a lie," everybody was implicated in the system, confirmed the system, made the system, was the system, to paraphrase a classic passage from Havel's "Power of the Powerless."[8]

"The moment some notions are put beyond the reach of free debate," writes Milovan Danojlić in his *Muka s recima* (Trouble with words) (originally published in 1977), "other relationships are also disturbed, the perspectives become skewed. That which is passed over in silence throws its shadow upon that which is spoken openly; the lie swallows up the remaining truth. Thinking about public matters turns into a farce: people talk and write as if freely, wisely and responsibly, yet everyone knows what is forbidden and cannot be uttered" (Danojlić 1990: 79).

A prominent domestic writer, a one-time dissident of sorts, and a social critic, Danojlić is a good guide to the dilemmas confronting people in Serbia today at the confluence of those two large themes—the legacy of socialism and the resurrection of nationalism in the late 1980s. He is a fully qualified "native" when it comes to Yugoslav socialism; he wrestled with it both outwardly and inwardly for decades and wrote penetrating analyses and critiques of it that invite comparison with Havel, Konrad, and Michnik. Born to peasant parents (like most people in Serbia), he shuttles between Paris, Belgrade, and his native Šumadija (the "heartland" of Serbia). He feels himself both a cosmopolitan in self-exile and a deeply rooted native, both owing allegiance to his nation and called on to criticize its flaws mercilessly. Moreover, insofar as his position is structurally similar to mine, by presenting his dilemmas I can also talk about my own.

Writing in the late 1970s Yugoslavia, Danojlić addressed the problem of living in an already highly adapted system.[9] What he was up against was a much stronger popular feeling that "nothing is wrong with our way of life" than was presumably the case in Soviet-dominated people's democracies at that time.

Havel, on the other hand, sets up an absolute autototalitarian world of *living in a lie,* against which *living in truth* shines with the complementary brilliance of absolute morality. And this is the image he beams to the West: "There are times when we must sink to the bottom of our misery to understand truth" (Havel 1986: 89). ". . . do we not in fact stand (although in the external measures of civilization, we are far behind) as a kind of warning to the West, revealing to it its own latent tendencies?" (54). "It may even be said that the more room there is in the Western democracies (compared to our world) for the genuine aims of life, the better the crisis is hidden from people and the more deeply do they become immersed in it" (116).

And it is exactly this relative lack of the Soviet-type of total control in Yugoslavia, this relatively larger "room for the genuine aims of life," as Havel would put it, yet itself "shadowed" and ultimately "swallowed by the lie," that Danojlić sees as morally, mentally, and spiritually more damaging than the absolutely totalitarian system. "We lived in *bearable evil*," he writes; "it devastates the soul worse than tyranny" (*Politika,* March 11, 1995; emphasis added).

The average Yugoslav of that time, however, might not have experienced his or her life as morally, mentally, and spiritually degrading (I certainly didn't), and this difference between "ordinary" people living their day-to-day lives and the analysis of "intellectuals," I suggest, is something that researchers of socialism have to keep in mind. On the other hand, it is possible that intellectuals were just putting into sharp relief what was vaguely felt by a significant number of ordinary citizens as well.

Whether felt acutely or just vaguely, by the end of the 1980s the lie "got bloated and disintegrated," as Danojlić writes in 1995 in one of his *Letters to a Belgrade Friend* (a series that was printed every Saturday in the *Politika* daily). "Like pieces of a broken ship we emerged into—what? Not into freedom, but into emptiness. Yearning for the end of the lie, we couldn't have imagined that the flood would suck the truth into the abyss as well, and even our very life" (*Politika,* March 4, 1995).

With the disintegration of the lie, "the official calendar of non-events"[10] has "cracked," and "the lava of life"[11] has rolled out. It was not, however, the individual—some Serb greengrocer—who was supposed to simply straighten his backbone and start living in greater dignity;[12] it was the nation. "Serbia will bow down no more" and "Serbia has regained its dignity" were the slogans that made Milošević and won the elections for his "Socialist Party."

After 50 years of enforced silence, it was now possible to talk openly. But that talk was not nearly as much about civil society, market economy, or parliamentary democracy[13] as about issues left unresolved since 1945, when the Yugoslav Communist Party, "our overseers," as Danojlić puts it, "hauled a heavy lid over the abyss" (*Politika,* March 4, 1995).

These questions concerned borders, territories, and the establishment of nation-states as ethnically homogeneous as possible—a formula invented in that same western and central Europe which now condemned the belated Balkan practitioners of it as anachronistic nationalists. Europe and the Western world were cosmopolitan, internationalist, all for tolerance, removal of borders, and universal human rights. They proclaimed nationalism "a Balkan scourge and Asiatic plague" (*Politika,* May 20, 1995).

According to my experience, talk about the socialist past in Serbia during the last few years has been but part of a more dominant type of talk—that revolving around the questions of borders, war, national destiny, belonging or not belonging to Europe, being civilized or barbarous, being Eastern or Western, being modern or traditional (see Gal 1991; Verdery 1991). What seemed to exercise people most, what figured most prominently in political speeches and intellectual debates, were questions of national identity and destiny in a geopolitical environment perceived as threatening and actively hostile. The questions of consumerism, of living standards, of transition to a market economy, and of civil society and political freedoms, which seemed to occupy central stage in other postsocialist societies, tended to take secondary importance or were viewed largely in connection with national destiny and survival.

For Danojlić, then, the story of How We Were Crippled by Communism becomes enveloped within a larger dilemma of how a cosmopolitan, critical, Serbian intellectual is to deal with national homogenization, a seemingly anachronistic slide into nationalism, the war for territories and borders, and the demonization campaign unleashed in the Western media against his own people. And it is this dilemma that I, both as a native and as an ethnographer who has to represent the Serbian story to natives and to Western audiences alike, share to some extent with Danojlić.

How to Deal with Nationalism (of One's Own People)

Since the war in former Yugoslavia started, I have been exposed to the Western media, which without hesitation identified the Serbs as the only "bad guys" and thought nothing of blankly accusing them of being the present-day Nazis perpetrating a second Holocaust. It is very hard for someone who wasn't mesmerized by the media campaign surrounding the "wars of Yugoslav succession" and who didn't feel implicated in it to appreciate the multiple moral warps that twisted the minds of those who were. Thus I understand Danojlić quite well when he writes in the first of his *Letters to a Belgrade Friend:*

I found myself in a strange, unforeseen situation. Although I was against this war from the very beginning, although I never understood either the military or the political sense in shelling of civilians, . . . I was forced to declare my allegiance. If the empty-headed blabbermouths I listened to one evening after another [in Paris] are for love between nations, then I am for hate. . . . They have forced me into the pack from which I have always kept a distance, if for no other reason than because of what I do [write] and the way I live [in self-exile]. I felt repentant tenderness toward our huge misery and woeful stupidity, toward our childish immaturity and suicidal despair. (*Politika,* October 22, 1994)

What exposure to such media coverage does is to make one deeply suspect any appeal to universal human rights, tolerance, and cosmopolitanism. Danojlić writes:

The worst type of cosmopolitan is the one who demands that we fight against narrow-mindedness of our community using reasons and arguments of a foreign community no less narrow-minded. A cunning strategy, no doubt: to fight one's own nationalism in the name of a foreign, competing nationalism! Recently from all quarters they are warning us of universal human responsibilities; one could hardly find fault with that save that there are other, very selfish, interests behind those warnings. (*Politika,* June 3, 1995)

If we assume (as realist doctrine does) that we live in a world where any appeal to higher principles should be taken as rhetoric in the service of selfish national aims, then indeed, as Danojlić asked in 1988, "why should another's egotistical reasons be closer to me than my own?" (Danojlić 1989: 404). And when the cannons start thundering, he wrote in 1995, "the individual will make the least mistake if he sticks with his own kin" (*Politika,* June 3, 1995).

This, however, does not resolve my dilemma (nor does it resolve Danojlić's), for I still refuse to join my "own tribe" uncritically. As an anthropologist, moreover, a social scientist and member of a scholarly community, I want to be able not only to describe but also to evaluate and criticize the values I study.

Criticizing values of other cultures is a thorny issue for anthropology, with its legacy of cultural relativism. It is a predilection of anthropologists to delight in the particular ethos, even "genius," of "their" people, not to criticize it. If it makes sense within a particular cultural logic, even head-hunting is beyond reproach. On the other hand, anthropologists are also defamiliarizers and demystifiers. They delight in showing how what is taken for granted and assumed to be natural is actually constructed and arbitrary, and they could thus act as powerful critics of invented traditions, ethnic myths, and other paraphernalia of various nationalisms.

The anthropological enterprise, says Richard Handler (the demystifier of Quebecois nationalism), is

to reveal that human beings live according to culturally constructed values that are neither timeless nor universal nor scientifically correct. When anthropologists study the values of non-Western peoples who have been subjugated by Western power, our responsibility has been to argue that those non-Western values be respected. When, however, anthropologists study modern values, such as the values of nationalism, our responsibility is to deconstruct those values, to refuse to accept them as unquestionable truths about the world. (Handler 1993: 73)

So we are to have two standards—one for subjugated peoples and one for modern nationalisms. But what of peoples who are as powerless as those "subjugated" in respect to the West, yet have bought into the "modern values of nationalism"? After all, this Western-dominated world of ours is still a universe of nationalist values, and, as Handler himself observes, "this is the only language that power will understand" (1993: 74). Is one then to celebrate uncritically the nationalism of the powerless, or should one "speak to them critically about those values" (Handler 1993: 74)?

Keith Brown in this volume shows a dilemma facing an anthropologist working in Macedonia, a largely powerless latecomer to the world of established European nation-states. The established nation-states of Europe can afford to expose their own nation-building (and nation-crafting) historiography as "invented tradition" now that their borders and identities are secure. Isn't it then hypocritical for them to demand the same from Macedonia, where neither identity, nor language, nor borders, nor even the name of the state and the flag are securely established? Any suggestion that a particular version of the past held by the local people is open to multiple interpretations and constructed as an "imagined continuity" crafted by native historians is perceived there as dangerous and destabilizing, and not entirely without reason. What is a Western-trained social scientist to do then? Pursue demystification according to the standards of his or her discipline or abstain from it insofar as it undermines (or is seen to undermine) the legitimate claims to statehood of the people he or she is studying?

In a world of unequally powerful nation-states that still operate very much according to nation-state logic (notwithstanding the rhetoric of globalization), deconstructing the nationalism of the powerful and established societies will have different consequences from deconstructing the nationalism of the weak. And even if scholarly representation of such issues does not in fact carry real political consequences (and it rarely does, at least in the secluded world of American academia), there remains the ethical dilemma of a researcher, whether native or outsider, whose work is read by the people he or she studies (see Brettell 1993).

My response to the above dilemmas is to present the stories Serbs have been telling themselves and others in the last few years. I presented some fragments of Danojlić's story in this chapter. Like his agonizing *Letters to a Belgrade Friend,* these stories are themselves very much about the predicaments of a European periphery struggling to define its identity, its borders, and a livable society in a bewildering post–Cold War world where the logic of nation-states is entwined with the logic of globalization. They reflect a situation of a society that is both threatening (and deadly) to some of its neighbors (i.e., Bosnian Muslims and Kosovo Albanians) and threatened by them and by the powerful West (NATO). Moreover, these stories oppose and contradict each other, revealing opposing agendas of the social actors who tell them. In that sense, they often offer the most acute criticism of each other: they act as mutual deconstructors. No need to go far and wide: Enlightenment Universalism is fighting Herderian Volk Romanticism, and Liberal Capitalism is fighting (Postsocialist) Socialism right there, within Serbia itself.

Notes

An early draft of this chapter was presented in the Anthropology of Europe Workshop at the University of Chicago, and I benefited greatly from comments and suggestions I received there, especially from Matti Bunzl, James Fernandez, and Alexandra Hrycak. I also want to thank Bruce Grant and Caroline Brettell for useful comments at the end of the road. The writing of this chapter was greatly facilitated by a generous grant from the Council for Advanced Studies on Peace and International Cooperation at the University of Chicago, where I was a fellow during the 1995–1996 academic year. All translations of quotations from sources published in Serbo-Croatian are my own.

1. The position of a native or an indigenous ethnographer carries its own set of practical, epistemological, and political-ethical problems apart from those facing ethnographers in disintegrating, postsocialist societies. The problems of native ethnography have recently been widely debated (see Abu-Lughod 1991; Altorki and El-Solh 1988; Barrios 1994; Bennoune 1985; Brettell 1993; Carrier 1992; Fahim 1982; Fox 1991; Kondo 1990; Messerschmidt 1981; Narayan 1993; Ohnuki-Tierney 1984; Srnivas 1966), and I will address them only insofar as they intersect with the more specific problems of my fieldwork in Serbia.

2. The roots of what I here call geopolitical imaginings, following James W. Fernandez (1997: 726), lie in the wider European (and arguably worldwide) practice of regional or ethnic stereotyping along north–south and west–east axes as a reflection and reinforcer of unequal distribution of power. The northerners and southerners, to take one of the axes, label each other with contrasting sets of adjectives which have, from the first time North assumed political and economic supremacy in Europe, ascribed cerebral qualities of rationality, control, and mastery to northerners, and visceral ones of emotionality, unreliability, and general looseness to southerners (Herzfeld 1987; Fernandez 1986a). The South and the East themselves, moreover, tend to transfer the same odium that they receive from those positioned further "up" to regions and peoples lying further "down" the gradient. In Yugoslavia,

positioned as it was in the southeastern margins of Europe, those two symbolic axes combined to give this general schema its peculiar Balkan twist. In their influential article, Milica Bakić-Hayden and Robert Hayden explored some of the twists and turns of that rhetorical strategy as it played itself out on the eve of Yugoslavia's breakup, referring to it in their title as "Orientalist Variations on the Theme 'Balkans'" (Bakić-Hayden and Hayden 1992; see also Bakić-Hayden 1995). More recently, Maria Todorova (1997) argued for the specificity of "Balkanism" and the need to distinguish it from Said's "Orientalism." In their 1992 article, before the breakup, Bakić-Hayden and Hayden gave several examples of the "Orientalist" rhetoric coming from the northwestern parts of the country (Slovenia and Croatia), whereas the southwestern regions (mostly Serbia and Montenegro) were presented as "Balkan," "Oriental," and "Byzantine" with their largely unquestioned connotations of backwardness, authoritarianism, crookedness, and violence—thus inherently presenting them as undemocratic in contrast with the industrious, rational, and democratic northwest. Such invidious comparisons and ethnic stereotyping were, on the one hand, oriented toward the domestic scene as, among other things, a means of strengthening emerging national (as opposed to Yugoslav) identities. On the other hand, they were meant for Western consumption as a bid on the part of northwesterners to escape the sinking Yugoslav ship and join the European community by presenting themselves as more modern, rational, democratic, and so forth—in a word, more "European" than their rivals (see Živković, 1990, 1998a).

3. To present any of these "stories," or motifs, here would necessitate presenting them in the form of a brief synopsis. This would, however, defeat the very purpose of my project, which is to show how situated social actors put widely different twists or spins on a story in order to promote their own agendas. I therefore never, in fact, deal with *a* story or *the* story but with multiple versions spun by actors engaged in "dialogical narration" (see Bruner and Gorfain 1984; and Herrnstein Smith 1981).

4. This was not only the conceit of Yugoslavs who looked down upon neighboring "people's democracies." In 1979, following the trial and sentencing of Václav Havel, Milan Kundera wrote: "A communist system also exists in Yugoslavia. But to the extent that it is a communist system outside the Russian sphere, day-to-day life for a Yugoslav resembles much more that of a Frenchman than that of a Soviet citizen" (quoted in Havel 1986: 258).

5. A reference to an insidious change observable in the regime-controlled media at that moment (spring 1994) that signaled a turn from (cynical) nationalism to a sentimental, sugary, and nostalgic appeal to the "Left"—a soft revival of communism spearheaded by Milošević's wife, Mirjana Marković.

6. See Pesmen 1991 on mixed metaphors.

7. This kind of argument recently appeared, for instance, in a dialogue between a prominent Croatian historian who teaches at Yale, Ivo Banac, and a Serbian historian from Belgrade, Milan Protić, in the Radio Free Europe show "Most" (Bridge), published in *Naša Borba* (May 31, 1997). The dialogue was moderated by Omer Karabeg and titled: "After Tito, Tito." Both historians agreed that Tito's rule was characterized by "an illusion" of reform. The nature of the system did not in fact allow for any true reforms, yet the "illusion of reform was very ingeniously main-

tained over a long period" (Banac). In the countries of "real socialism," on the other hand, the impossibility of reform was crystal clear, which made it possible for these countries to embark on real reforms once the communist regime collapsed. In words of Milan Protić, "When the Eastern Bloc and its ruling ideology disintegrated, real changes occurred in these countries. That, however, did not happen to us precisely because we have for the longest time believed that reforms were an advantage of Tito's regime."

8. "Individuals need not believe all these mystifications," writes Havel in 1978, "but they must behave as though they did, or they must at least tolerate them in silence, or get along well with those who work with them. For this reason, however, they must *live within a lie*. They need not accept the lie. It is enough for them to have accepted their life with it and in it. For by this very fact, individuals confirm the system, fulfill the system, make the system, *are* the system" (Havel 1986: 45).

9. Havel admits a possibility that the regime can and does adapt: "Adaptation is the positive dimension of the regime's response. . . . Some circles may try to integrate values or people from the 'parallel world' into the official structures, . . . to become a little like them while trying to make them a little like themselves. . . . Such reforms are usually halfway measures. . . . They muddy what was originally a clear demarcation line between living within the truth and living with a lie. They cast a smoke screen over the situation, mystify society and make difficult for people to keep their bearings" (Havel 1986: 107).

10. "The more rational the construction of *the official calendar of non-events* over the years, the more irrational the effect of a sudden irruption of genuine history" (Havel 1986: 30; emphasis added).

11. "No wonder, then," Havel writes, "that when the crust *cracks* and *the lava of life rolls* out, there appear not only well-considered attempts to rectify old wrongs, not only searchings for truth and for reforms matching life's needs, but also symptoms of bilious hatred, vengeful wrath, and a kind of feverish desire for immediate compensation for all the endured degradation" (Havel 1986: 31–32; emphasis added).

12. "Living within the truth . . . not necessarily belongs to the category of dissident movements. In its most original and broadest sense . . . it covers a vast territory . . . full of modest expressions of human volition, the vast majority of which will remain anonymous. . . . Most of these expressions remain elementary revolts against manipulation: you *simply straighten your backbone and live in greater dignity as an individual*" (Havel 1986: 84–85; emphasis added).

13. In 1989, writing about Havel, Michnik, and Konrad, and their idea of central Europe, Timothy Garton Ash observed: "Why, even today, in a region largely and terribly purged of its two greatest minorities—the Jews, of course, and, yes, the Germans—nationalism still has a stronger appeal than Konrad's internationalism, even to many independent intellectuals, let alone to the general public. What is the greatest single issue (apart from declining standards of living and growing inequalities) for public and intellectual opinion in Hungary today? Is it human and civil rights? Is it democracy or 'the struggle for civil society'? No. It is the plight of the Hungarian minorities in Transylvania and Slovakia" (Ash 1989: 207–208).

References

Abu-Lughod, L. 1991. Writing against culture. In R. G. Fox, ed., *Recapturing anthropology: Working in the present,* 17–62. Santa Fe, N.M.: School of American Research Press.

Altorki, S., and C. F. El-Solh, eds. 1988. *Arab women in the field: Studying your own society.* Syracuse, N.Y.: Syracuse University Press.

Ash, T. G. 1989. Does Central Europe exist? *The uses of adversity: Essays on the fate of Central Europe,* 178–213. New York: Random House.

Bakić-Hayden, M. 1995. Nesting Orientalisms: The case of former Yugoslavia. *Slavic Review* 54 (4): 917–931.

Bakić-Hayden, M., and R. Hayden. 1992. Orientalist variations on the theme "Balkan": Symbolic geography in recent Yugoslav cultural politics. *Slavic Review* 51 (1): 1–15.

Barrios, E. M. 1994. The return of the native point of view to anthropology: From authenticity to professional authority in "native" anthropology. Unpublished M.A. thesis, University of Chicago, Chicago.

Bennoune, M. 1985. What does it mean to be a Third World anthropologist? *Dialectical Anthropology* 9: 357–364.

Brettell, C. B., ed. 1993. *When they read what we write: The politics of ethnography.* Westport, Conn.: Bergin and Garvey.

Bruner, E. M., and P. Gorfain. 1984. Dialogic narration and the paradoxes of Masada. In S. Plattner and E. Bruner, eds., *Text, play, and story: The construction and reconstruction of self and society,* 56–79. Washington, D.C.: American Ethnological Society.

Carrier, J. G. 1992. Occidentalism: The world turned upside down. *American Ethnologist* 19: 195–212.

Cerović, S. 1995. Policijska bajka. *Vreme* (June 12): 6–7.

Cohen, L. J. 1992. *Regime transition in a disintegrating Yugoslavia: The law-of-rule vs. the rule-of-law.* Pittsburgh: University of Pittsburgh Center for Russian and East European Studies.

Cohen, L. J. 1993. *Broken bonds: The disintegration of Yugoslavia.* Boulder, Colo.: Westview Press.

Danojlić, M. [1977] 1990. *Muka s recima.* 5th expanded ed. Belgrade: I. Čolović, I. Mesner, M. Danojlić.

Danojlić, M. 1989. Ko smo, sta smo, kuda idemo? In Z. Stojkovic, ed., *Serbia i komentari za 1988/89,* vol. 1: 403–421. Belgrade: Zaduzbina Milosa Crnjanskog.

Drakulić, S. 1993. *How we survived communism and even laughed.* New York and London: W. W. Norton and Company.

Fahim, H., ed. 1982. *Indigenous anthropology in non-Western countries: Proceedings of a Burg Wartenstein symposium.* Durham, N.C.: Carolina Academic Press.

Fernandez, J. W. 1986a. Andalucia on our minds: Two contrasting places in Spain as seen in a vernacular poetic duel of the late 19th century. *Cultural Anthropology* 3 (1): 21–35.

Fernandez, J. W. 1986b. *Persuasions and performances: The play of tropes in culture.* Bloomington: Indiana University Press.

Fernandez, J. W. 1997. The north–south axis in European popular cosmologies and the dynamic of the categorial. *American Anthropologist* 99 (4): 725–730.

Fox, R. G., ed. 1991. *Recapturing anthropology: Working in the present.* Santa Fe, N.M.: School of American Research Press.

Gal, S. 1991. Bartók's funeral: Representations of Europe in Hungarian political rhetoric. *American Ethnologist* 18 (3): 440–458.

Glenny, M. 1992. *The fall of Yugoslavia: The third Balkan war.* London: Penguin.

Gordy, E. D. 1996. The destruction of alternatives: Everyday life in nationalist authoritarianism. Unpublished Ph. D. dissertation, University of California, Berkeley.

Grant, B. 1993. Dirges for Soviets passed. In M. E. George, ed., *Perilous states: Conversations on culture, politics, and nation,* vol. 1. Chicago: University of Chicago Press.

Handler, R. 1993. Fieldwork in Quebec, scholarly reviews, and anthropological dialogues. In C. B. Brettell, ed., *When they read what we write: The politics of ethnography,* 67–74. Westport, Conn.: Bergin and Garvey.

Havel, V. 1986. *Living in truth.* London: Faber and Faber.

Herrnstein Smith, B. 1981. Narrative versions, narrative theories. In W. J. T. Mitchell, ed., *On narrative,* 209–293. Chicago and London: University of Chicago Press.

Herzfeld, M. 1987. *Anthropology through the looking-glass: Critical ethnography in the margins of Europe.* Cambridge: Cambridge University Press.

Kondo, D. 1990. *Crafting selves: Power, gender, and discourses of identity in a Japanese workplace.* Chicago: University of Chicago Press.

Messerschmidt, D. A., ed. 1981. *Anthropologists at home in North America: Methods and issues in the study of one's own society.* Cambridge: Cambridge University Press.

Narayan, K. 1993. How native is a "native" anthropologist? *American Anthropologist* 95 (3): 671–686.

Ohnuki-Tierney, E. 1984. Native anthropologists. *American Ethnologist* 11 (3): 584–586.

Pesmen, D. 1991. Reasonable and unreasonable worlds: Some expectations of coherence in culture implied by the prohibition of mixed metaphor. In J. W. Fernandez, ed., *Beyond metaphor: The theory of tropes in anthropology,* 213–243. Stanford, Calif.: Stanford University Press.

Ramet, S. P. 1992. *Nationalism and federalism in Yugoslavia.* 2d ed. Bloomington: Indiana University Press.

Ries, N. 1997. *Russian talk: Culture and conversation during perestroika.* Ithaca, N.Y., and London: Cornell University Press.

Srnivas, M. N. 1966. Some thoughts on the study of one's own society. In Srnivas, *Social change in modern India,* 147–163. Berkeley: University of California Press.

Stefanović, N. 1994. Sviću crvene magle. *Duga* (Belgrade) 525: 14–16.

Todorova, M. 1997. *Imagining the Balkans.* New York: Oxford University Press.

Verdery, K. 1991. *National ideology under socialism: Identity and politics in Ceausescu's Romania.* Berkeley: University of California Press.

Woodward, S. L. 1995. *Balkan tragedy: Chaos and dissolution after the Cold War.* Washington, D.C.: Brookings Institution.

Živković, M. 1990. Representing the Balkans: Symbolic geography of the southeastern margins of Europe. Unpublished manuscript, University of Chicago Department of Anthropology (available at http://anthro.spc.uchicago.edu/~mdzivkov/course).

Živković, M. 1994. The wish to be a Jew, or the struggle over appropriating the symbolic power of "being a Jew" in the Yugoslav conflict. Paper read at Ninth International Conference of Europeanists, March 31–April 2, 1994, at Chicago (available at http://anthro.spc.uchicago.edu/~mdzivkov/course).

Živković, M. 1995. The Turkish taint: Dealing with the Ottoman legacy in Serbia. Paper presented at the American Anthropological Association Annual Meeting, November 15–19, 1995, at Washington, D.C. (available at http://anthro.spc.uchicago.edu/~mdzivkov/course).

Živković, M. 1996. Too much character, too little *kultur:* Serbian jeremiads 1994–1995. Paper read at CASPIC MacArthur Scholars' Conference, October 5–6, 1996, at Chicago (available at http://anthro.spc.uchicago.edu/~mdzivkov/course).

Živković, M. 1997a. Violent highlanders and peaceful lowlanders: Uses and abuses of ethno-geography in the Balkans from Versailles to Dayton. *Replika,* Special Issue, *Ambiguous Identities in the New Europe,* 107–119.

Živković, M. 1997b. We are Gypsy people cursed by fate: Dealing with Balkan stigma in Serbia and Croatia. Paper read at the Second Conference of the Association for Balkan Anthropology (ABA), September 4–7, 1997, at Bucharest, Romania (available at http://anthro.spc.uchicago.edu/~mdzivkov/course).

Živković, M. 1998a. Serbia's place in European geopolitical imaginings. Unpublished manuscript, the University of Chicago Department of Anthropology (available at http://anthro.spc.uchicago.edu/~mdzivkov/course).

Živković, M. 1998b. Inverted perspective and Serbian peasants: The Byzantine revival in Serbia. Paper read at Negotiating Boundaries: The Past in the Present in South-Eastern Europe, September 6–8, 1998, at Lampeter, Wales (available at http://www.ac.wwu.edu/~kritika).

PART 2

FIELDWORKERS IN THE POSTSOCIALIST FIELD

Field Issues: Negotiating the Shifting Terrain(s) of Postsocialism

Relationships between insiders and outsiders, between center and periphery, and the position of the ethnographer are central to the battle to redefine and categorize history and practice. De Soto argues that ethnographic research in postsocialist eastern Germany forces the fieldworker to engage in reflective self-examinations on several levels in order to understand both the deconstruction and the construction processes of old and new, Orientalist and Occidentalist categories and hierarchies. Having considered herself a "halfie" anthropologist (born and reared in western Germany, but completing her education and now living in the United States) while undertaking fieldwork in a western German mountain village, she describes the challenges to this identity she encountered when she entered postsocialist eastern Berlin to do fieldwork among women. De Soto calls for a feminist ethical practice in which researchers move beyond immediate utilitarian aims and work toward a "politics of solidarity," especially with people for whom the transformations mean a potential move toward social exclusion, as a means for examining the fast-developing systems of cultural and material inequalities in postsocialist fields, especially those systems that tend to turn human beings into objects.

Kuehnast, the first American ethnographer to conduct fieldwork in postsocialist Kyrgystan, takes issue with constructions of new categories and clichés that developed after she had entered the field. By describing three different contexts of her fieldwork on women and poverty development, she chronicles the process of construction of new categories in regard to the American woman, the fieldworker, and the process of "othering" during the transformation. Kuehnast shows that this process is related to the Cold War legacy, postsocialist poverty development, and new Western visual imperialism. She suggests that for fieldwork during revolutionary transformations, in which people are in the middle of an "unpredictable current," the people and the fieldworker must navigate as though in the middle of an avalanche.

Reflecting in his chapter on the concepts that might be used to explain the process of doing fieldwork under conditions of extreme social change, Barsegian suggests that the term *transition* has been constructed from Western experience in Third World countries and notes that the West now uses this concept as a framework to explain postsocialism and promote a new world order. He criticizes Western social scientists for imposing the concept on the postsocialist field to define it as a space in transition toward the "advanced" West. Ethnographers, he argues, by definition work between cultures, translating the field of one culture into texts for another culture. The current emotional and cognitive preference for emphasizing the fundamental similarities of postsocialist and Western society in order to make the postsocialist societies easier to explain and predict results in ethnographic texts that unwittingly impose Western constructs on postsocialist reality. When these texts reenter the field, they reinforce the gap between perform-ances: the West originally created the image of "starving Armenians" and projected it upon Armenia; Armenians adapted the image for their own purposes; and Westerners now pick up this image and use it to explain the field. Barsegian suggests one avenue out of the impasse for insider anthro-pologists who are not always able to bridge the gap in understanding with-out feeling that they are betraying their own community. He urges social sci-entists not to ignore real differences and to describe and use more native categories.

Anderson cautions that "in the post-Soviet states, the act of writing ethnography is . . . politically charged" and notes that his identity as a for-eign scholar opened doors because the Evenkis and the Dolgans, indige-nous peoples among whom he carried out fieldwork, actively pressured him, as a foreign anthropologist, to censure their "backward" local prac-tices and affirm their idealization of the West. Anderson takes issue with Barsegian, however, arguing that Western anthropologists have an obliga-tion to broaden local perceptions and attack stereotypes of the West, rather than allow themselves to be imprinted by local categories. Anderson takes a more activist approach, urging ethnographers of postsocialism to act as "clinical ethnographers" by engaging people in discussion about their eth-nic future or to help deconstruct binary Cold War stereotypes.

4

Crossing Western Boundaries
How East Berlin Women Observed Women Researchers from the West after Socialism, 1991–1992

Hermine G. De Soto

During my fieldwork in eastern Germany, there was much that east German women wanted to tell me about their socialist and postsocialist experiences, especially their increasing sense of being objectified by Western researchers in the new postsocialist society. In order to understand their positions, I needed to reflect critically on my previous fieldwork position and identity in western Germany, to examine why and how my fieldwork identity and epistemological positions became a challenge to me as a "halfie" anthropologist in eastern Germany. My identity conflict also entailed a "concern with how the researcher constructs and reconstructs her identity and deals with her positionality vis-à-vis the researched" (D. L. Wolf 1996: xii). Its resulting disclosure opened new insights, new fieldwork dilemmas, and new friendships during my 1991–1992 research in east Berlin after the opening of the Berlin Wall and up to the present.

Shifting Positionalities

While the former German Democratic Republic collapsed at the end of 1989, I prepared to defend my doctoral dissertation, in which I explained how contemporary small-scale farming families in a village in the Upper Black Forest, in the Federal Republic of Germany, are affected by, and culturally cope with, late modern national and transnational politics and policies.[1] During this time I had considered myself to be a halfie (Narayan 1993). "Halfies . . . are people whose national or cultural identity is mixed by virtue of migration, overseas education, or parentage" (Abu-Lughod 1991: 137).[2] After the defense, in addition to my professional status of being an anthropologist, I was—from a structural point of view because of my bicultural socialization and education—also a mixture of white, middle-class, west German and North American female. By 1989 I had lived half of my life in western Germany and half of it in the United States, and I had been married for 16 years to David, a middle-class Chicano from California, whose cultural and linguistic sensitivity to eastern and western Germany have invaluably assisted me in all stages of my research.[3]

In following reflective debates in anthropology, it matters not only how anthropologists position themselves within anthropological epistemologies but also how they reorient themselves on the global map and into which discourses they reenter the construction of knowledge (Asad 1973; Herzfeld 1987; Rosaldo 1989; Stocking 1983, 1991). As reflective anthropologists have explained, such contextual positioning is related to what one chooses to study and how one bridges the gap between oneself and the people one studies. That positioning also sheds light on whether or not the new knowledge will help to reduce social inequalities, social injustices, and many other forms of human rights violations (Diamond 1974; Harding 1987, 1991; Abu-Lughod 1991; Trouillot 1991; Messer 1993; Walter 1995).

However, the intersectional position of a halfie initially only assisted me to realize that the supposedly admired "field work objectivity" or "the view from nowhere" (Harding 1991: 273) is actually, as Abu-Lughod called it, a "view from somewhere" (1991: 141). During fieldwork in western Germany, this reflective positioning as halfie had helped me understand the connection between my own position in knowledge and my perception of my position vis-à-vis the anthropological "other." In concrete terms, I had conceptually entered my field situation (Asad 1991: 318) within a critical and dialectical sociocultural framework in order to explain problems of differentiation and economic transformation, processes with which the anthropological other—the farming families—were confronted during the time of my fieldwork. For example, while many people in the village assisted me in comprehending their current economic, social, and cultural reconstitutions, what was most important is that I began to learn to understand my life from their perspective. In retrospect I understand that people in the village perceived my half-American and half-German identity with poise and wit and inventively used my mixed identity for their own purposes. For instance, whenever my behavior departed from particular known behavioral patterns, such as visiting local taverns alone for coffee, I was teasingly reminded that this must be "typically American."[4] Or, after I had studied the local dialect with my "adopted fieldwork grandmother," I was praised for still being half-German. Or, whenever I was introduced to visitors from other villagers, I was proudly introduced as "our" American who not only spoke Swabian but also "our" own Alemannic dialect.[5] During our working conversations we also began to share our different cultural knowledges. I was asked to share my experiences from the United States and had to explain for many hours how farming families in Wisconsin worked and lived and how they coped with the long, cold winters (see also Anderson, this volume).

Today I still hold both a subjective and an objective relationship with the people in Kroningen, a relationship that also consists of what Rosaldo has called the "defamiliarization" phase of fieldwork. In my case, in order to work toward an ethnographic analysis and presentation that would appear "humanly made, and not given in nature" (Rosaldo 1989: 39), this phase has included a reading and critique of the text by various people from Kroningen. Yet only during fieldwork in postsocialist eastern Germany did I discover that both of our identities—the halfie identity and the west German villager identity—were built upon the assumption that, despite our similarities and differences, we were part of the same Western system.

After my dissertation defense I began a year-long preparation for fieldwork in eastern Germany. I was motivated to switch from west to east Germany by the uncertainty of how east and west Germany would be reunified, especially in regard to the legal problem of reunifying two different abortion laws. Progressively oriented west German women hoped that reunification would open up a new space for liberalization and for replacing the restrictive west German abortion law with a law similar to the east German one. This problem, however, developed into a specific postsocialist east-west German nationalistic dilemma, one that I wanted to research ethnographically from the perspectives of the east German women who became the major contestors of this particular legal, political, and national context.

Before I left for east Berlin, I thought that there would be a kind of affinity between east German women and me, that I would have some kind of immediate understanding because I had been born German, albeit west German.[6] In retrospect, and after several years of residing in, visiting, and revisiting east Germany, I find that emotionally I had wished for some kind of affinity, yet intellectually I was doubtful or uncertain. This uncertainty, I think, was also part of my motivation to go to east Germany after the fall of the Berlin Wall.

During this time I began to face an important question: As women's bodies in the revolutionary process in eastern Germany became contested objects for German nationalistic politics, would it be possible to discover knowledge *from* women and *for* women within traditional epistemologies?

My research in eastern Berlin would focus on how eastern German women contested their personhood during shifting revolutionary times in which the two different post–World War II German nation-states—the democratic socialist and thus "eastern," and the democratic capitalist and thus "western"—became reunified, an experience that the women with whom I worked in 1991 called colonization.[7] After German reunification in 1990, east German women's previous economic, legal, social, cultural, and educational statuses were evaluated by west German standards and *dequalifiziert* (disqualified) (De Soto 1993). Women in the former GDR system were integrated into a socialist paternalist nation-state (Verdery 1996: 62–82) that in the previous 40 years had institutionalized various social rights and welfare policies, policies that were different from the policies of the capitalist west German patriarchal nation-state (De Soto 1992).

Before I left for eastern Germany, I began to reposition myself in order to strengthen my epistemological foundation. I initially entered eastern Berlin as a halfie from a women-centered perspective, that is, from a non-positivist feminist epistemology that does not assume "distance and non-involvement between the researcher and researched [nor] . . . that the researcher can objectively see, judge, and interpret the life and meanings of his/her subjects" (D. L. Wolf 1996: 4). I intended my fieldwork to be feminist research, to be "contextual, inclusive, experiential, involved, socially relevant, . . . complete but not necessarily replicable, inclusive of emotions and events as experienced" (Nielsen 1990: 6). I wanted to use my "outsider within" position as halfie (Abu-Lughod 1991) to help bring people, as Harding (1991: 282) has emphasized, "from the margin into the center of analysis" and to offer analyses from "women's perspectives on our lives." Yet, however much I agreed with these positions, I faced nearly insurmountable empirical dilemmas during fieldwork.[8]

Arrival in East Berlin

I arrived in east Berlin by taxi from west Berlin in the spring of 1991. Before I left the United States I had arranged, through previous contacts, that Anna,[9] an east Berlin woman from the women's movement, would pick me up at the train station, Bahnhof Zoo, in west Berlin. Anna, however, was not at the Bahnhof. Although I had a list of telephone numbers and addresses from people in east Berlin, the telephone connections between east and west Berlin were still out of service. Leaving my suitcases locked at the Bahnhof Zoo station, I decided to drive to the main public meeting place in former east Berlin, the Alexander Platz, and began from there to try to contact Anna by phone. After several hours I was successful, and Anna came to meet me at Alex.[10] Anna, a former teacher who had been an active participant in the women's uprising in 1989, had, like many other women, lost her job after reunification. She told me that after she realized that I might be at the train station in west Berlin instead of arriving on the east Berlin Hauptbahnhof, she knew that she was not ready, after 40 years, to make the 15-minute drive with her car to the train station in "the west." When she heard that I still had to pick up my suitcases from the west, Anna showed signs of experiencing fear and disorientation in her "own" (new) city,[11] worrying that she might not be able to drive through the faster traffic in the west, that she might get lost, that she might be unable to comprehend on short notice the different traffic signs of west Berlin. After pondering for an hour how to get there and after I told her that I also was new and unfamiliar with the streets in Berlin, we encouraged ourselves to drive to west Berlin. After several detours, we picked up my suitcases and arrived late that evening, "exhausted but safe at home in east Berlin," as Anna said. In the following days I moved into a small one-bedroom apartment in the so-called Scheunenviertel, in the east Berlin district, or *Kiez,* known as Stadt Mitte.

My initial weeks of fieldwork were absorbed in introducing myself and being introduced to various *Mitfrauen* of the east German women's movement. During the revolution, east German women had begun to change male-oriented membership terms. Women who had joined the movement were now called Mitfrauen (women participants). With this linguistic revolt women confronted the traditional, male-favoring membership term *Mitglied,* a word in which the suffix *-glied,* I was told, can also refer to the penis.

After some time and with the help of many women, I became acquainted with the movement's headquarters, in the Haus der Demokratie, and with the regional Mitfrauen and their offices, which were located in the other five new eastern German federal states.[12] During daily meetings and long conversations I learned that I was the only female anthropologist from the West who worked on problems facing women during the time of reunification and "dass andere Westfrauen kamen um uns zu erforschen" (that other women from the West had come to study us). The east German women were quite astonished that most *Westfrauen* researchers who came to study east German women during the reunification period did not live in east Berlin but instead visited east Germany from their respective residences in west Berlin. Most of these "women from the West" were political scientists, but some were from other fields such as sociology, German literature, and history. The east German women with whom I worked generally put all researchers from the West, whether from the United States, or Great Britain, or western Germany, into the category of Western researcher. However, in many cases, they added to west German researchers the status of the colonizer, the *Besser Wessi* who knows the east German situation much better than the east Germans themselves do (see also Berdahl, this volume). The

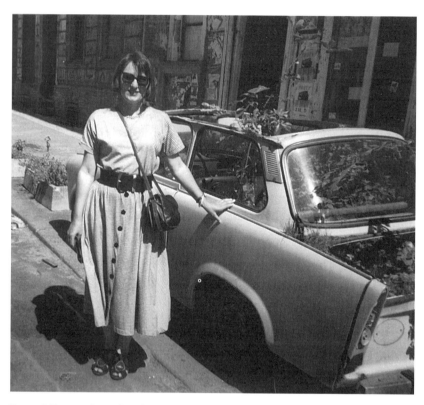

Postsocialist transformations im Scheunenviertel, the author's fieldwork neighborhood and home in 1991 and 1992. After reunification, neighbors converted their eastern German Trabi (Trabant) into an herb garden. (Photograph by Fahrünnisa Kulluk)

east German women said that these west German researchers patronized them, looked down on them, and perceived them as backward and in need of development.

From the beginning of my stay in east Berlin, women identified me as a "Westfrau aus Amerika." This surprisingly new fieldwork identification— quite different from my accustomed fieldwork identity from the village in west Germany—raised many questions for me. Why *Westfrau,* and why *American?* Why not *halfie?* Did my half-German and half-American identity not provide me with at least a small ethnographic favor or advantage as a half-indigenous fieldworker? Why were all women researchers lumped together as Westfrauen?

The east German women with whom I worked referred jokingly at times to my television German with a Swabian accent, yet, throughout my stay, I was seen as an American. While I spent weeks reflecting on my new identity, I discovered that my previous anthropological halfie position had, unknowingly, prevented me from understanding a fundamental critical dilemma in regard to social histories (see also Brown, this volume): if east German women who were part of the women's movement had accepted my halfie position, then they also would have had to accept, knowingly or unknowingly, a common German history after World War II. To hold such a historical acceptance, they would have had to deny their own east German subjectivities and individual women-histories, histories that they had collected and acquired in a different German nation from the one I was born in after World War II, the one I remembered as a halfie from the other side of the Atlantic. Recently, Verdery (1996: 62) has theoretically pointed to such differences: "Gender and nation exist in part as an aspect of subjective experience (national or gender 'identities' for instance)—as a subjectivity that orients persons in specific, distinctive ways according to the nationness and gender attributed to or adopted by them. This subjectivity is, in turn, the joint product of prevailing cultural understandings and people's social situations." While the realization brought about by the rejection of my unstable halfie identity was emotionally frustrating, it also helped me to understand that these east Berlin women had to teach me to grasp, acknowledge, and appreciate this historical difference before I could explain how they struggled and contested newly arising patriarchal inequalities. Otherwise I would contribute to the objectification of their personhood, a process that had begun at the moment of the opening of the Berlin Wall.

Ciao Bella

What the West meant to the east German women, in concrete terms, unfolded slowly during my fieldwork, although for me this process began in the first week of my stay. Not long after I had acquainted myself with various women and their organizational map of the new east German women's movement, women from the headquarters office began to invite me for coffee during working breaks, after work in the evening, and sometimes on weekends. Many of the politically active women who, in 1989, had begun the revolution against the previous socialist paternal state were physically and mentally exhausted in 1991. Although their movement had successfully fought the previous Eastern paternalist domination (De Soto 1994: 85), at the very moment of the upheaval they felt defeated by a new Western class-based, patriarchal, and subordinate position. Confusion, fear of unemployment, and mental remapping in private and public everyday life often expressed a fractured self-esteem, a situation that Dölling (1991) has described as "between hope and helplessness." Most of the women I met and worked with on life stories either had become unemployed, or were put into early retirement, or worked in short-term subsidized jobs, many of which were terminated during my fieldwork (see Kuehnast, this volume).[13] Often I heard "I can't take that anymore," or "I don't know how to continue," or "What should I do with my children, our day-care center is gone?" or "My children don't like the new west German schoolbooks," or "Now they [west German TV companies] have taken away our east German Sandmännchen, my children's favorite bedtime TV show."

During our informal conversations we further learned from each other's different experiences, but whenever we finished our informal visits I was jokingly wished good-bye, with "tschüss, bis bald, ciao bella" (so long, until soon, ciao bella), a phrase that I wittily returned with "ciao, adios amigas!" Yet, with passing time I mused, why *ciao bella?*

After exhausting days in which the other women and I unsuccessfully attempted to convince the west German press to include coverage of east German women's deteriorating employment situation, we would visit the Café im Haus der Demokratie, which then was collectively run by members from diverse east German citizen movements who had occupied the former state building after the fall of the Honecker government. Before we began our usual good-bye ritual, I jokingly referred to and asked about *ciao bella.* After some hesitating moments, Kirstin, with a smiling face, expounded:

"During the first phase of our movement, while we were feverishly organizing our opposition, a woman in a revolutionary esprit, and with a large hat, climbed up the six staircases to our headquarters office and, while cheering us on, said she was looking for our leader, whom she wanted to invite for a trip to the United States to participate in a TV show on the feminist revolution in east Germany. We all were stunned. We had no idea that this woman was a well-known American women's activist. After we told her that we had just fought against our leaders, and that our new movement had no single leader, and that we needed every woman here during these exceptional times, Ms. Bella Abzug left without a woman leader."

After a pause, Kirstin teasingly asked if I also had planned to take a woman with me to the United States.[14] Her implicit meaning was that, during the first phase of the revolution, the new east German women's movement immediately began to distance itself from the GDR's traditional leadership principles and to oppose single leadership in their movement. It can be argued, as Grant (1998, personal communication) has insightfully suggested, "that this willful eschewing of traditional leadership [became] part of a postsocialist heritage and/or response not found, for example, in west Berlin" and, I would add, not found in west Germany or the United States.

This same evening this group of women and I continued to reflect on feminist cultural misunderstandings. Although after that time they stopped the ritualistic practice of sending me off with "ciao bella," this symbolic expression pointed to a postsocialist research dilemma that continued during my fieldwork. East German women expressed that in the course of time they had become the other, or the research objects for Westfrauen.

How East Berlin Women Observed Women Researchers from the West

Women in east Berlin recalled that, from their perspective, the construction of and frustration with the Westfrau began soon after women researchers came to study east German women after the opening of the Berlin Wall on November 9, 1989. Between 1989 and 1991, eastern Germany was swept by breathtaking political changes: masses of east German people began to escape to Hungary on their way to west Germany; shortly thereafter east German citizen movements such as the women's movement, Demokratie Jetzt (Democracy Now), and Demokratischer Aufbruch (Democratic Beginning) entered the revolutionary phase; then the first trains with east German runaways left the German Democratic Republic for the Federal Republic of Germany (FRG); and soon followed Gorbachev's visit to east Berlin, where he attempted, in vain, to convince the former GDR leaders to reform socialism. In the aftermath of Gorbachev's visit, urban mass demonstrations began in the city of Leipzig, while in east Berlin the Women Lilac Offensive entered the revolutionary fervor. One week later the Honecker government collapsed, and a new socialist GDR government was founded. During this same time the east Berlin population staged the biggest demonstration in GDR history, and east German women professors and women researchers published the pamphlet *Geht die Erneuerung an uns vorbei?* (Does the renewal pass us over?). On November 7, 1989, the GDR government resigned, and two days later on November 9 the Berlin Wall was opened.

After the Wall opened, a new GDR government under Hans Modrow was formed. Some days after this, on December 3, 1989, the east German women's movement (Unabhängigen Frauenverband [Independent Women's Union], or UFV) was founded with the revolutionary aphorism "Ohne Frauen ist kein Staat zu machen" (States cannot be made without women). This was the time of the now legendary grassroots democratic "round table government," in which the east German women's movement successfully fought for women representatives in the east–west political negotiation process. During this time Chancellor Kohl and the new east German leader, Modrow, agreed to establish an east–west German contractual community (*Vertragsgemeinschaft*) and, with Gorbachev's approval, to reunify Germany. One month later the word *socialism* was removed from the GDR constitution, and for a short time Lothar de Maizière became the new prime minister. The first East/West Women's Congress was held in Berlin,

Social change im Scheuenenviertel. The translation of the writing is "Revenge: raped and beaten women should call the number 3733008 in an emergency." (Photograph by Hermine De Soto)

and on June 13, 1990, the Berlin Wall began to be torn down by GDR border troops. Nine days later the FRG and the GDR signed a unification contract in which the west German economic, financial, and social system became binding for eastern Germany. In August the GDR government signed the unification contract, and two weeks later the GDR left the Warsaw Treaty Organization. In the new state elections of October 1990, the Christian Demokratische Union (CDU) won in the GDR, and with this electoral victory the GDR population legitimized reunification with the FRG. On October 3, 1990, east and west Germany became reunified.[15]

During my fieldwork in 1991, it seemed that the former Cold War "culture of suspicion" (Sampson and Kideckel 1989: 162) no longer existed. Yet, in east Berlin, a combination of major west German press coverage and politicians' speeches aimed at the eastern German population continued to reproduce undifferentiated discourses that resounded with Cold War convictions. One example of this discourse is the remark that "from the Free World's perspective, the conflict revolves around Western freedom versus Eastern repression" (Sampson and Kideckel 1989: 162).

As I collaborated with east German women on life-story projects, we found, as McBeth (1993: 145) has described, that "intimacy result[ed] from listening to and telling stories." One such friendship developed between me

East German Mitfrauen demonstrate against the west German abortion law, paragraph 218. The poster reads: "Also we women from Thuringia [new federal state after German reunification] want to continue [after German reunification] to decide about abortion and our bodies." (Photograph by Hermine De Soto)

and Carola, a woman active in the movement and to whom I had been introduced through a Bulgarian friend in east Berlin. In 1989 Carola had participated in the women's uprising and became one of the founding Mitfrauen of the east German independent women's movement. A former east German teacher without any previous political training, Carola was elected to become one of the first feminist politicians in the parliament of the reunited Germany. Since 1991 she has represented east German women's interests—in such areas as unemployment, social welfare, pensions, and violence—in the national political arena. Together we recorded her experiences from 1992 up to the present and reflected on the revolution and the contemporary social and cultural changes of the reunified Germany.

Carola's Narrative and Hermine's Response

Carola actively participated in our tape recording of meetings, and she assisted in the editing and presentation of her life story. She also collaborated with me in reading part of her narrative in English at the 1995 American Anthropological Association conference. I have chosen Carola's narrative to illustrate the increasing disappointment, anger, and retreat of the east

German women and to detail the research distress that these women often discussed during our life-story conversations. My response (Hermine's) represents the position not of the Westfrau but of a reflective, Western-trained woman researcher, with reflexivity understood "as opening the way to a more radical consciousness of self in facing the political dimensions of fieldwork and constructing knowledge" (Callaway 1992: 33, quoted in Herzfeld 1997). This narrative and analytic response are constructed here in a way that leaves Carola's voice as unchanged as possible.

CAROLA: For us everything began in September and October of 1989. From there on until you came, we women from the movement were completely absorbed with our *Aufbruch* [uprising or awakening], and we did not have time to recognize how many Western women researchers had come to study us. At that time we did not feel that this was something to be concerned about. I personally think that many women from the West during that time had an authentic sympathy for the uprising that we had accomplished. I think west German women, in particular, found in us a way to compensate for something that they were unable to make happen: a practical change. The west German women's movement was never politically able to bring feminist politics explicitly into the German parliament, except through the Green Party, which was a special situation.

With us in east Germany things went very fast, especially how Gisela—the other east German feminist politician—and I had entered the German parliament. Women from the west German feminist movement saw in us something that they had never accomplished. At the beginning, we east German women thought that the west German women's feeling of compensation was neither exploitative nor negative. Perhaps, as I see it now, they began to make the mistake of putting too much hope into us and thought that we could solve their problems. As you know, this has something to do with German unification. West women thought that we, the so-called east German Power Women, would not let west German patriarchs take away our women-oriented institutions and rights such as public day-care centers and reproductive rights.

During this initial struggle between east and west German women, the first American women researchers came to study us. First we had a tremendous curiosity about the idea of being studied. For us that was great (*toll*) that they suddenly came to us. We saw it as an enrichment to have connections with such women. These first contacts provided us with some ideas about issues of Western feminism. We did not have much background in such issues, especially those women who were unable to engage subversively in the study of Western feminist literature. Take me, for example. I did not belong to those women who came from that section of training in which women's literature was openly read. I developed my feminist sensibilities through Professor E., but I did not belong to the tiny group (not more than ten belonged to it) who read Western feminist literature in the underground.

For most east German women the women's uprising did not define itself theoretically and exclusively as a feminist movement. We came very pragmatically into it. It was a very concrete beginning, but it also had a specific theoretical level because the beginning was carried out, most of all, by women who came from academic and political backgrounds. Most of the women had specific educational backgrounds, and some of them were familiar with Western ideas. However, the advantage for us women was that these ideas were not taken over in pure Western form.

Following our initial curiosity about Westfrauen researchers, we began to develop negative feelings toward them. Our initial perception of Westfrauen was a neutral one and was more geographically oriented. However, after our first meetings with women from the West, we began to form a cliché. For us, Westfrauen became women who were cool, successful, and spoke with us in rhetorically trained discourses about our identities, while their main focus was on career, jobs, and money. They had very different socializations, histories, and experiences. We learned that their cliché about us was that we were overworked, exhausted, naive, and veröstlichte [ossified] *Mutti* types [Easternized mommie types].

HERMINE: I hear in Carola's account that, in response to the Orientalist clichés of West women about women from the East, eastern German women constructed a new Occidentalist image of the Westfrau.[16] (Construction of Orientalist clichés during research has a long history in Western scholarship [Said 1978].) This dialectical relationship entailed essentialist representations of both Western women and eastern German women. Such a process, as Carrier (1995: 3) has explained, is a manifestation of a more general process by which a set of people seeks "to intensify its own sense of itself by dramatizing the distance and difference between what is closer to it and what is far away."[17]

CAROLA: During research interviews I felt squeezed like a sponge. They simply wanted to know everything. I think it is good if Western women ask "naive" questions, but then I realized that every time they asked me something, I had to begin my interview with what I call the origin of human beings. I mean just everything, so that I began to learn about the superficiality of the researchers.

HERMINE: Carola finds so frustrating here the need for a "myth of origin." Such a need seems to refer to the "statist ideological" positions held by the Western women researchers, for this myth of origin "denies historicity to those they [in this case, the researchers] regard as the embodiment of otherness" (Herzfeld 1987: 44, 191). Further, as Herzfeld (1987: 191) has suggested, the "search for ultimate origins" implies a researcher's aim to remove "social experience from theory." Similarly, Tiffany and Adams (1995:

6) have explained the "quest" for origin stories as an expression of a "researcher's heroic adventure of first contact with a pristine people—of experiencing a time warp to an original state of nature." Bruner and Appadurai have productively added to this demystification process, arguing that origin stories expose an "ideology of authenticity" in which the "authentic native" has to be discovered (Appadurai 1988). In such beliefs, a person's authenticity is not "constructed, sought, fought over and reinvented," but instead is perceived as "inherent in an object . . . , a thing [that] has to be discovered or unearthed" (Bruner 1993: 326).

CAROLA: I wished they [the researchers] had asked questions in a naive but professional way, for example, questions about everyday life and how this life reflected itself in my consciousness. One needs ability and sensitivity for that. Most did not show such sensitivity, and that's why they never established a dialogue with us women. It could have been a real pleasure for us to be interviewed. Instead, with most Western women researchers there was only a one-way street. Most often we did not know anything about their own positions because they didn't talk about that. They were not open with us. I think this is probably the most important point for us. If one is open with us, has a real curiosity, and is ready for new information from us, then this information, which might reflect issues and ideas different from those of Western women, could even change the interviewer's held positions. Most women researchers were unable to learn from our perspectives. We learned that we had become research objects for Western women.

HERMINE: Feminist anthropologists have begun to address this issue of objectification, to critique dichotomous notions in which asymmetrical object and subject constructions reveal a dualism that resembles the traditional research construction of objects and objectivity. Abu-Lughod (1990: 12, 15) has called such a "gendered objectivity" "a mode of power" in which the ethnographic practice is not based on relationships, equality, and attachment, but rather is built upon distance, domination, and disinterest. To work against this othering of the other, Behar (1993: 301), in agreement with Abu-Lughod, calls for a feminist ethnographic practice in which research principles foremost require a focus on a "relationship to other women." For McBeth (1993: 146), this practice concretely means forming a "collaborative approach," especially in life-story meetings in which both the woman telling her story and the ethnographer recording it are working intimately to interpret a woman's experience.

CAROLA: First we found it attractive to have connections with foreign women. Many of us were cut off in the past from such connections. However, when Western researchers came en masse and all wanted to collect interviews and grab up our papers and archives in the UFV, then we became skeptical. This was especially nerve-racking. We had to call an emergency meeting to decide what to do. We also became skeptical when we realized that many women did their research only on a few papers in our offices and nothing else. Most papers in our women's archives were rather sketchy during the transition.

HERMINE: There are exploitive practices in research encounters that are grounded in the process of turning subjects into objects and in which a researcher's first aim is to control the subjects and the research situation. Wolf (1992: 52) has suggested that feminist ethnographers "need to search for a way to do ethnographic research that not only will not exploit other women but will have positive effects on their lives." Such a practice would include subjects who "identify, and design the research projects they think are needed, who retain control over written outcome of the research. . . ."

CAROLA: I think it could have been great if there had been a reciprocal give-and-take. The optimal situation would be if both Eastern and Western women would have an equal amount of curiosity to learn to know each other. Since we Eastern women were so occupied with our own problems during the initial transition, it was very difficult for us to develop an interest for the women's movements of the West. Often we did not have energy left to ask Western women about their experiences, their biographies, and their movements. This is a critical point even now in my political faction. Most Eastern women did not constantly push for information and experiences from west German or from American women. Surely, this has something to do with our socialization in the GDR. One is somewhat limited in one's view. I do not mean narrow-minded or stupid—one simply did not grow up so *Welt offen* [open to the world], and that's why our interests and options were more limited.

And then, suddenly, everything came so fast. We had to go through so much so fast along several political paths! Eventually we had enough of whatever came from the West. Always you imagined the West was the best. And now we are constantly told that we have to evolve ourselves into this Western feminist image.

HERMINE: Western women researchers' assumption that non-Western women are victims creates problems. In her discussion on victimhood and Third World women, Mohanty (1991: 57) calls for challenging such notions and writings because "feminist theories which examine [Third World women's cultural practices or, in this case, "eastern" German women's practices] as 'feudal residues' or label us 'traditional' also portray us as politically immature women who need to be versed and schooled in the ethos of Western feminisms."

CAROLA: That's why we developed an allergy to the West and began to insist on doing our own movement. We thought it would bring us much more if we critically analyzed the New, including Western women. We could gain experience this way. But reaching this level was very difficult. Reaching an equal level between us would be a real women's revolution. For example, if

Eastern and Western women's experiences had been joined, acknowledging different socializations and history and the women's ideas of social change, we could have accomplished something. However, we have missed this moment of change.

This should be a lesson for future social change and for women. For now, we have lost the majority of women. In part this happened because the Western women came toward us and still do, with their "global" ways. They speak a different language. They already express themselves with this tremendous self-assuredness! I'm sure they must compensate a lot for what they did not accomplish, particularly when they contrast themselves with us and what we had in the past. Granted, we did not have to struggle for it. Women from the West had to fight and struggle much more than we did because the state gave it to us.

For me, we become objects when the interviewer is only a questioner and when the questions asked express no individuality. I think that there are only dumb questions, no dumb answers. If an interviewer only squeezes the interviewee like a sponge, then she makes an object out of the person because she does not bring herself as subject into the dialogue, but simplifies her work. This is especially painful when women do that to each other.

I felt particularly hurt when women came and followed me, and wherever we went they took their open notebooks with them, even into cafés. They demanded facts, facts, facts. For me this was nerve-racking. I had a few interviews with very intelligent women journalists. These interviews were enriching and a lot of fun. The women asked very smart questions while they thought along. They were also well prepared. This was an important part of a good interview because then I did not have to start with an origin story. If one is prepared and knows the basic historical background, then the interview can become an enrichment for us. We are not introductory textbooks. An interviewer should want to know how I, a woman, subjectively dealt with specific life situations in the past and in the present. It should be exciting for a woman researcher to ask which view do I, Carola the woman, have about women's constitutional rights. It is much nicer for me if I can discuss specific issues with the researcher during an interview.

During the time when I was the east German election leader in the historic election about German unification, I was often interviewed. [Carola was part of the electoral organizational team, and she was also one of the leading independent list candidates.] None of the interviews sticks in my memory except one—the most beautiful one. Ms. Lange, a remarkable journalist from a prominent west German newspaper, *Die Zeit,* conducted an excellent interview. I felt as if she had known me all of her life. She wrote even tiny small and humorous details about my mother, for example, that my mother wore the kangaroo emblem of the UFV[18] and that she left the

DFD (Demokratischer Frauenbund Deutschlands [Democratic Women's Union Germany]).[19] Ms. Lange was able to capture the significance of me (that is, my understanding of emancipation). I learned a lot from this interview. I did not feel like an object. I told her that during this awful political situation in 1990 and amongst those political actions and fights, I was unable to articulate my own political understanding. All along, I had to present a neutral position and remain in the background. She told me that she heard something similar from Mr. Modrow [the last GDR president]. This gave me a kind of comfort and new courage for the coming weeks. She told me, "Ms. Carola, you have now the same role to play as Mr. Modrow. This is now your thing, and with that you will also objectively empower the east German women's movement." That's how it was. This was a great learning experience for me. It was both research and interview together.

I do not want to say that great ideas, which help me to learn, should be part of every interview. However, if researchers do not give anything of themselves in their interviews, then there is a one-way street, which means that they construct objectifying power hierarchies in which we are made objects for their careers. Objectification of women in feminist research could be further avoided if the researcher would include the interviewee in the reading of the written text and most of all in revisiting the people. I find it most disturbing if a woman-feminist researcher uses us and then later politically criticizes us without having told us about her disagreement during the interview—I mean, of course, independent of a woman's political position.[20]

HERMINE: I hear Carola referring to the importance of respect and trust in interviews with other women. Patai (1991) has discussed such ethical concerns in regard to feminist research. Respect and trust cannot develop if we "utilize the interview as an occasion for forcing on others our ideas of a proper political awareness, however we understand that," for to do so is "to betray an implicit trust" (Patai 1991: 148).

CAROLA: It would be much better if the researcher would be honest about her position, so that we could discuss/debate differences. In such a situation I would be a subject and not an object that is being removed from context and time.

The key for both is to be curious. Of course curiosity can be positive or negative. This we found out between Eastern women and Western women. Many Eastern women have a noncompetitive approach in their interaction with people and life. We were not socialized as competitors. That's why it is important for us that Western women open up to us and tell us about themselves, and not [approach it as] "How can I use this or that from her so that I can write an article or a dissertation?" In an interview I tell things and I think about things, and if I get a new idea I feel great about it. This way I can grow with the interview. However, if I continually get the feeling that a woman over and over exploits me, then I only end up getting headaches. HERMINE: This sense of curiosity connects with a sense of play with the rhythm of time in ethnographic research. Rosaldo (1993) has recently artfully expressed that such play displays the respect of the ethnographer in her relationship with people's rhythm of time. A fieldworker's known predictable tempo often does not allow for unpredictability and thus is socially ungraceful. On the other hand, "social unpredictability has its distinctive tempo, and it permits people to develop timing, coordination, and a knack for responding to contingencies. These qualities constitute social grace" (Rosaldo 1993: 256).

CAROLA: I know this is academically difficult, but an ethical person who can connect with a human being would be able to do that. It is thus no coincidence that I developed friendships with initial researchers who were not artificial and did not enter the house with "I need an interview quickly. I need to know everything. Bye-bye, so long."

Many women in the UFV complained that numbers of women researchers did this. They came, told us that they wanted to write dissertations, and found all our doors open. They came and took everything. And so the time came when we couldn't take it anymore. It is painful if you continually see outsiders with the luxury to come, to meditate, and to reflect about all the things for which we don't have time because we have to struggle so that we don't lose everything. That's how our pain and feeling of outrage developed. It was painful to read research conclusions made by others about our feelings. Now there are inflationary and fashionable waves of researchers who study what kind of identities former east German women had. Often such research is done by women who have never had enough courage to come to us in the past. It is such developments that we can't take anymore. Outsiders can never write about our identities in the past. This has to be done by insiders. Neither west German women nor other Western women can do this for us because most of them have missed the opportunity to visit us in the past.

HERMINE: Feminist scholars have recently begun to examine critically the theoretical debates concerning epistemic privileges in feminist methodologies and issues of representations. Women of color have critiqued epistemological notions based on "hegemonically universalist subject positions available in dominant modes of theorizing," while various feminists have begun to critique standpoint theorems that privilege "marginality" (Lal 1996: 198, 199). Because "the construction of subjugation, nativity, and insiderness as privileged epistemic standpoints from which to counter the universalism of Western theory are all premised on maintaining the same borderlines between Us and Them, Self and Other, and Subject and Object that they wish to question in the first place" (Lal 1996: 198), we should approach our research agendas with "attempts to theorize from the locations of multiple and hybrid identities," remembering that, for either the insider or the outsider researcher, "there is no easy or comfortable in-between location that transcends these dualisms" (Lal 1996: 199).

Thus I respond to Carola that Western women researchers who are aware of power relations "and the unequal hierarchies or levels of control that are often maintained, perpetuated, created, and re-created during and after field research" (D. L. Wolf 1996: 2) should, *together with* women from east Germany, enrich the theoretical and research agendas and debates, since "*all* of us live in contradictory locations, and not just those of us who are perhaps involuntarily placed into those contradictions" (Lal 1996: 199; emphasis added).

Leaving East Berlin

A few weeks after I had arrived in east Berlin, I met Marion, a former east German worker and Mitfrau of the new women's movement, who had become unemployed after German reunification. We soon became friends and began to collaborate on her life story. At the beginning of our friendship, I asked her how it felt to live through the time until the Berlin Wall was opened. Marion could not talk about the emotional level of living with this much change; in the middle of recording our conversation, she broke down and could not go on. Too close to the social change of the breakdown of the former east German system and of the Wall and having had no time to reflect on the experience, Marion could not be detached emotionally. We could not continue our conversation.

Two days before I had to leave again for the United States, Marion and her two daughters came to say good-bye. Birgit, 8, and Julia, 10, had photocopied, as a good-bye present, their favorite children's book, *Die Zauberin Uhle* (The witch Uhle), a Romanian children's novel (Terschak 1994). After reunification, the state-owned east German bookstores were closed and, with privatization, west German bookstores opened in east Berlin and The Witch Uhle disappeared from the east German book market. Birgit and Julia wanted me to have "ein echtes kleines Stückchen von unserem Osten" (a real little piece of our East, before it will be forgotten).

Marion handed me an envelope and said, "Remember, you had asked me a year ago how I felt in the last two years? Please open this envelope in Madison, and don't forget to write." Marion had written the following poem, a poem that expresses how very difficult it is for east German women to talk about the painful emotional times surrounding the end of the socialist state and German reunification and that indicates there still has not yet been enough time for these women to distance themselves from the experience and to sort things out individually. In the postsocialist "fresh time" of my stay in Berlin, it was easier for Marion to express her emotions in a poem than in prose words or through conversation.

REMEMBERING THE WALL: BEFORE AND AFTER

Silence—
You encounter in your rage,
In your pain,
In your mourning,
Always again, this overwhelming wall.

Sealed tightly by invisible powers,
By many fit-together stones,
You see neither cement, wood, nor nail
To hold together this gigantic wall.
No stone can be loosened,
No path leads alongside her.
You always run up against her,
Scream at her—implore her, cry—
You beat your body sore on her,
But she always swallows your rage, your pain, your grief.

No echo returns from the wall,
Nobody taught you how to demolish her,
Until you begin to tear a stone out of her,
A stone of you in this wall.
This stone begins to come alive in your hand.
A warm rain begins to flow from your hands,
And the wall starts coming to life.
Fragile greens sprout from its stones,
And the stones begin to give you warmth.

Stones transform themselves into birds—
Birds with soft voices.
Behind the mountains of living stones
You see friends
Who conceal themselves from their own fears.
Together you begin to pick up the debris from the wall,
But always again there are ditches—
Out of fear, injury, misunderstandings between us.
These ditches cannot be filled in
With the debris from the wall—
Otherwise new walls would arise again.

Only if you talk about yourselves, laugh, cry,
And grieve with one another,
Only then will this never happen again.

                    May 1992, east Berlin (translated by Hermine G. De Soto, 1993)

I began this chapter by reflecting on how my shifting fieldwork identities became related to my conceptual repositioning before, during, and after my fieldwork engagements in western and eastern Germany. From a feminist epistemological position, Carola and Marion, east Berlin narrators, and I have pointed toward dilemmas between feminist theoretical insights and research about women's experiences of their political struggle during revolutionary times undertaken in a postsocialist setting. Especially by including Carola's narration from the margin, we have tried to show how the process of othering the other began after Westfrauen researchers crossed Western boundaries and came to east Berlin after the opening of the Berlin Wall. As indicated above, we can try to understand and learn from women in postsocialist countries only if we listen carefully to what they tell us and reformulate and further sensitize feminist ethnographic practices and ethics. In such a project "we write with insider's voices [that] bring both perspectives to bear on understanding culture" (Walter 1997: 17).

Not so long ago, Patai (1991: 150) seemed to ask, Is it possible in an unethical world to do ethical research? I concur with her implicit answer, that such problems "are political and require not only transformations in consciousness, but also, and above all, political action for their solution" (see also Silverman, this volume). While I accept that not all postsocialist research needs to be based on "action and participatory research," I strongly agree with Diane L. Wolf's (1996: 28) assessment that "research with a more participatory component challenges feminist scholars to practice what they believe: more egalitarian approaches to empowerment that are *with,* and not simply *for,* the researched population." If we miss such ethical practices, then it seems to me that we will also bypass "bringing women from the margin into the center of analysis," and thus we will build new Orientalist and Occidentalist walls, new research objects, new forms of exploitations and dominations, and new gender inequalities. Instead, what we need now in our emerging relationships with women in postsocialist societies is a "politics of solidarity" (Harding 1986: 196) combined with research about, for, and with women that women can use in their struggle against the expanding national patriarchies that are presently reconstituting themselves not only in the reunified Germany but also in various other postsocialist societies.

Notes

I wish to thank all the east German women who helped me in eastern Germany during 1991 and up to the present. I am also especially grateful to Carola B., to David J. De Soto, and to Mary Jo Heck, whose continual editorial suggestions improved this chapter. Part of this research was generously supported by the National Council for Soviet and East European Research; however, I am solely responsible for my research findings. I am also grateful for the continuous support of the Women's Studies Program and the Women's Studies Research Center at the University of Wisconsin–Madison. I am most thankful to Nancy Ries and Martha Lampland for their helpful comments on an earlier version of this chapter that was presented at the American Anthropological Association Meetings, 1995. Additional insights were forthcoming from Caroline Brettell, Bruce Grant, Rosalie M. Robertson, Nora Dudwick, Kathleen Kuehnast, Lynn Walter, Stanlie M. James, Aili Tripp, and Frances Olsen. I am most thankful for all their critical, constructive, and supportive comments.

Since 1989, many unexpected and dramatic events have occurred in many postsocialist societies. In eastern Germany, 10 years after the opening of the Berlin Wall, my friend Carola B. was elected to serve as the vice president of Parliament. She is the youngest vice president ever elected in German history.

1. In this study I utilized the analytic concept of transnationalism as it was developed by Nina Glick-Schiller, Linda Basch, and Christina Blanc-Szanton (1992). For more on my ethnographic study in western Germany, see especially "Reading the Fools' Mirror: Reconstituting Identity against National and Transnational Political Practices," in the *American Ethnologist* 25 (3): 471–488.

2. Lila Abu-Lughod writes that she adopted the term *halfie* from Kirin Narayan.

3. Although I conducted my various field engagements without my husband, his periodic visits to my fieldwork locales in western and eastern Germany and our weekly telephone and letter correspondence offered an invaluable space for reflections and conversations. His encouragement and support became especially important during my research in east Berlin in the second part of my stay. During their experience of this demanding transitional phase, several women friends suffered from mental and physical exhaustion.

4. A more uncomfortable situation arose in relation to gender inequality. As a female ethnographer I had to negotiate unspoken subtleties daily in regard to the "appropriate" norms of womanhood roles in the village. Jill Dubisch (1995) insightfully discusses such female fieldwork experiences and negotiations in "Lovers in the Field: Sex, Dominance, and the Female Anthropologist."

5. I was born in the region known as Württemberg and lived until 1969 in Stuttgart, the capital of the state of Baden-Württemberg. The dialect spoken in Stuttgart is called Schwäbisch, or Swabian. In the village in the Black Forest where I conducted my fieldwork, the dialect is Alemannic.

6. I wish to thank Caroline Brettell for helping me clarify this point.

7. Colonization for east Berlin women has meant west German structural domination and hegemonic degradation of women's experiences and life histories acquired in the last 40 years in the GDR. Recently Christa Wolf (1996: 406), one of the most prolific east German women writers, addressed east German colonization in this way: "East German territory is being colonized by West German administrators who get extra 'jungle pay' for their laudable service in an underdeveloped country." For Wolf, "colonization becomes a fact only if [east German] natives behave like colonized people, either slavishly integrating themselves with the new bosses or exhibiting childish defiance."

8. Aili Tripp, writing on the women's movement in Uganda, refers to similar research dilemmas involving problems of inequality and power relations in research, "especially in research that seeks to be more egalitarian, more collaborative and concerned with hearing and giving voice to women at the grassroots." See *Women and Politics in Uganda* (2000).

9. All the women with whom I worked prefer to be addressed in the text with fictitious names.

10. In summer 1983, I spent two months in Weimar studying east German culture and literature, and several weeks in east Berlin. During that time I learned that the Alexander Platz, particularly the area around the *Weltuhr* (world clock), is a favored meeting place for the east Berlin population. In vernacular terms, the abbreviated name "Alex" is often used for Alexander Platz.

11. I wish to thank Bruce Grant for his description of this dissonance as a sense of experiencing fear and disorientation in their own (new) city.

12. The new federal states in east Germany are Brandenburg, Sachsen, Sachsen-Anhalt, Mecklenburg-Vorpommen, and Thüringen. East and west Berlin became a united city-state after unification. In addition to the status of city-state, the reunited Berlin became in 1992 the capital city of the new Germany. For more on this process see my work, "(Re)Inventing Berlin: Dialectics of Power, Symbols and Pasts, 1990–1995" (De Soto 1997).

13. The same structural development began in rural east Germany. Christel Panzig and I analyzed this process in "From Decollectivization to Poverty and Beyond: Women in Rural East Germany Before and After Unification" (De Soto and Panzig 1995). Similarly, Kathleen Kuehnast (1993, 1996) describes how such processes affected women in the postsocialist Kyrgyz Republic.

14. It is important to understand that these women at the headquarters of the new east German women's movement had very little information about the women's movements in other countries. The name "Bella Abzug" initially meant nothing to them when they met her; they had no knowledge of her roles in American politics or American feminism. I also had to undo their notion that I had been sent by Ms. Abzug and to explain that among the many diverse aspects of the women's movement in the United States, an academically connected position such as my own was quite separate from the kinds of political arenas in which Ms. Abzug worked.

15. The east–west confrontation-debates were in part published in German in the following works: Herta Kuhrig (1995), "'Mit den Frauen—für die Frauen': Frauenpolitik and Frauenbewegung in der DDR"; Christina Schenk (1994), "Der Politikbegriff von ostdeutschen Frauen am Beispiel des Unabhängigen Frauenverbandes (UFV)"; Gisela Notz (1994), "Frauenemanzipation und Frauenrealität in Ost and West"; Birgit Bütow (1994), "Frauenforschung in Ost und West vor der Aufgabe der Neu- und Umorientierung?"; Karin Rohnstock (1994), *Stiefschwestern: Was Ost-Frauen und West-Frauen voneinander denken;* Ulrike Helwerth and Gislinde Schwarz (1995), *Von Muttis und Emanzen: Feministinnen in Ost- und Westdeutschland;* Daniela Dahn (1996), *Westwärts und nicht vergessen;* and Hildegard Maria Nickel (1995), "Frauenforschung und Muttipolitik."

Although he does not focus on studies of women during the east German transformation, John Borneman has offered insightful anthropological perspectives on contemporary east and west German relations, including identity classifications and reconfigurations. Especially relevant to the initial transformation questions are *After the Wall: East Meets West in the New Berlin* (1991) and *Belonging in the Two Berlins: Kin, State, Nation* (1992).

16. For a different form of Orientalist construction in postsocialist Yugoslavia, see Bakic-Hayden and Hayden 1992. Frances Olsen (1997: 2219) discusses "the Orientalist division of the world between the advanced West and backward East."

17. A critical examination is provided in Graf, Hansen, and Schulz 1993.

18. The kangaroo emblem was worn by several mothers during the formation of the independent women's movement. According to Carola, this time-specific symbol meant that "hopping mothers with children" were a significant part of the movement.

19. The DFD was the official women's organization of the former GDR state. The UFV, or independent women's organization, was formed in opposition to the DFD.

20. Carola referred to an article that was published in an American journal. She kept the names of both the journal and the author undisclosed.

References

Abu-Lughod, L. 1990. Can there be a feminist anthropology? *Women and Performance* 5: 7–27.

Abu-Lughod, L. 1991. Writing against culture. In R. G. Fox, ed., *Recapturing anthropology: Working in the present*, 137–162. Santa Fe, N.M.: School of American Research Press.

Appadurai, A. 1988. Putting hierarchy in its place. *Cultural Anthropology* 3: 36–49.

Asad, T. 1973. *Anthropology and the colonial encounter.* Atlantic Highlands, N.J.: Humanities Press.

Asad, T. 1991. From the history of colonial anthropology to the anthropology of Western hegemony. In G. W. Stocking, Jr., ed., *Colonial situations: Essays on the contextualization of ethnographic knowledge*, 314–324. Madison: University of Wisconsin Press.

Bakic-Hayden, M. B., and R. M. Hayden. 1992. Orientalist variations on the theme "Balkan": Symbolic geography in recent Yugoslav cultural politics. *Slavic Review* 51: 1–15.

Behar, R. 1993. *Translated woman: Crossing the border with Esperanza's story.* Boston: Beacon Press.

Borneman, J. 1991. *After the Wall: East meets West in the New Berlin.* New York: Basic Books.

Borneman, J. 1992. *Belonging in the two Berlins: Kin, state, nation.* Cambridge: Cambridge University Press.

Bruner, E. M. 1993. Epilogue: Creative persona and the problem of authenticity. In S. Lavie, K. Narayan, and R. Rosaldo, eds., *Creativity/anthropology*, 321–334. Ithaca, N.Y.: Cornell University Press.

Bütow, B. 1994. Frauenforschung in Ost und West vor der Aufgabe der Neu- und Umorientierung? In B. Bütow and H. Stecker, eds., *Eigenartige Ostfrauen*, 315–321. Bielefeld: Kliene Verlag.

Calloway, Helen. 1992. Ethnography and experience: Gender implications in fieldwork and texts. In J. Okeley and H. Calloway, eds., *Anthropology and autobiography,* 29–49. London: Routledge.

Carrier, J. G. 1995. Introduction. In J. G. Carrier, ed., *Occidentalism: Images of the West,* 1–31. Oxford: Oxford University Press.

Dahn, D. 1996. *Westwärts und nicht vergessen: Vom Unbehagen in der Einheit.* Berlin: Rowohlt.

De Soto, H. G. 1992. *Contesting female personhood: Comparison of east and west German legal cultures in the process of unification.* Washington, D.C.: National Council for Soviet and East European Studies.

De Soto, H. G. 1993. Equality/inequality: Contesting female personhood in the process of making civil society in eastern Germany. In H. G. De Soto and D. G. Anderson, eds., *The curtain rises: Rethinking culture, ideology and the state in eastern Europe,* 289–304. Atlantic Highlands, N.J.: Humanities Press.

De Soto, H. G. 1994. In the 'name of the folk': Women and nation in the new Germany. *UCLA Women's Law Journal* 5: 83–101.

De Soto, H. G. 1997. (Re)Inventing Berlin: Dialectics of power, symbols and pasts, 1990–1995. *City and Society* (Annual Review for 1996): 29–49.

De Soto, H. G. 1998. Reading the fools' mirror: Reconstituting identity against national and transnational political practices. *American Ethnologist* 25 (3): 471–488.

De Soto, H. G., and C. Panzig. 1995. From decollectivization to poverty and beyond: Women in rural east Germany before and after unification. In D. A. Kideckel, ed., *East European communities: The struggle for balance in turbulent times,* 179–195. Boulder, Colo.: Westview Press.

Diamond, S. 1974. Anthropology in question. In D. Hymes, ed., *Reinventing anthropology,* 401–429. New York: Vintage Books.

Dölling, I. 1991. Between hope and helplessness: Women in the GDR after the "turning point." *Feminist Review* 39: 3–18.

Dubisch, J. 1995. Lovers in the field: Sex, dominance, and the female anthropologist. In D. Kulick and M. Willson, eds., *Taboo: Sex, identity, and erotic subjectivity in anthropological fieldwork,* 29–50. New York: Routledge.

Glick-Schiller, N., L. Basch, and C. Blanc-Szanton. 1992. *Towards a transnational perspective on migration: Race, class, ethnicity, and nationalism reconsidered.* New York: New York Academy of Sciences.

Graf, W., W. Hansen, and B. Schulz. 1993. From THE people to ONE people: The social bases of the East German "revolution" and its preemption by the West German state. In H. G. De Soto and D. G. Anderson, eds., *The curtain rises: Rethinking culture, ideology, and the state in eastern Europe,* 207–230. Atlantic Highlands, N.J.: Humanities Press.

Harding, S. 1986. *The science question in feminism.* Ithaca, N.Y.: Cornell University Press.

Harding, S., ed. 1987. *Feminism and methodology.* Bloomington: Indiana University Press.

Harding, S. 1991. *Whose science, whose knowledge? Thinking from women's lives.* Ithaca, N.Y.: Cornell University Press.

Helwerth, U., and G. Schwarz. 1995. *Von Muttis und Emanzen: Feministinnen in Ost- und Westdeutschland.* Frankfurt am Main: Fischer Verlag.

Herzfeld, M. 1987. *Anthropology through the looking-glass: Critical ethnography in the margins of Europe.* Cambridge: Cambridge University Press.

Herzfeld, M. 1997. The taming of revolution: Intense paradoxes of the self. In D. E. Reed-Danahay, ed., *Autolethnography: Rewriting the self and the social,* 169–194. Oxford: Berg.

Kuehnast, K. 1993. Women and economic changes in Kyrgyzstan: Coping mechanisms and attitudes towards social policies. Unpublished internal document of the World Bank, Human Resources Division, Washington, D.C.

Kuehnast, K. 1996. Canaries in a coal mine? Women and nation-building in the Kyrgyz Republic. *Anthropology of East Europe Review* 14 (2): 21–33.

Kuhrig, H. 1995. "Mit den Frauen—für die Frauen": Frauenpolitik und Frauenbewegungen in der DDR. In F. Hervä, ed., *Geschichte der Deutschen Frauenbewegung,* 209–243. Köln: Papy Rossa Verlag.

Lal, J. 1996. Situating locations: The politics of self, identity, and "other" in living and writing the text. In D. L. Wolf, ed., *Feminist dilemmas in fieldwork,* 185–214. Boulder, Colo.: Westview Press.

McBeth, S. 1993. Myths of objectivity and the collaborative process in life history research. In C. B. Brettell, ed., *When they read what we write: The politics of ethnography,* 145–162. Westport, Conn.: Bergin and Garvey.

Messer, E. 1993. Anthropology and human rights. *Annual Review of Anthropology* 22: 221–249.

Mohanty, C. T. 1991. Under Western eyes: Feminist scholarship and colonial discourses. In C. T. Mohanty, A. Russo, and L. Torres, eds., *Third World women and the politics of feminism,* 51–80. Bloomington: Indiana University Press.

Narayan, K. 1993. How native is a "native" anthropologist? *American Anthropologist* 95: 671–686.

Neilson, J. M. 1990. Introduction. In J. M. Nielson, ed., *Feminist research methods: Exemplary readings in the social sciences,* 1–37. Boulder, Colo.: Westview Press.

Nickel, H. M. 1995. Frauenforschung und Muttipolitik. In *Die stille Emanzipation: Frauen in der DDR.* Frankfurt am Main: Fischer Verlag.

Notz, G. 1994. Frauenemanzipation und Frauenrealität in Ost und West. In B. Bütow and H. Stecker, eds., *Eigen Artige Ostfrauen,* 302–314. Bielefeld: Kleine Verlag.

Olsen, F. 1997. Feminism in central and eastern Europe: Risk and possibilities of American engagement. *Yale Law Journal* 106: 2215–2257.

Patai, D. 1991. U.S. academics and Third World women: Is ethical research possible? In S. Berger Gluck and D. Patai, eds., *Women's words: The feminist practice of oral history,* 137–153. New York: Routledge.

Rohnstock, K., ed. 1994. *Stiefschwestern: Was Ost-Frauen und West-Frauen voneinander denken.* Frankfurt am Main: Fischer Verlag.

Rosaldo, R. 1989. *Culture and the truth: The remaking of social analysis.* Boston: Beacon Press.

Rosaldo, R. 1993. Ilongot visiting: Social grace and the rhythm of everyday life. In S. Lavie, K. Narayan, and R. Rosaldo, eds., *Creativity/anthropology,* 253–269. Ithaca, N.Y.: Cornell University Press.

Said, E. W. 1978. *Orientalism.* Harmondsworth, England: Penguin.

Sampson, S. L., and D. Kideckel. 1989. Anthropologists going into the cold: Research in the age of mutually assured destruction. In P. R. Turner and D. Pitt, eds., *The anthropology of war and peace: Perspectives on the nuclear age,* 160–173. Westport, Conn.: Bergin and Garvey.

Schenk, C. 1994. Der Politikbegriff von ostdeutschen Frauen am Beispiel des unabhängigen Frauenverbandes (UFV). In B. Bütow and H. Stecker, eds., *Eigen artige Ostfrauen: Frauen Emanzipation in der DDR und der neuen Bundesländern,* 285–299. Bielefeld: Kleine Verlag.

Stocking, G. W., ed. 1983. *Observers observed: Essays on ethnographic fieldwork.* Madison: University of Wisconsin Press.

Stocking, G. W., ed. 1991. *Colonial situations: Essays on the contextualization of ethnographic knowledge.* Madison: University of Wisconsin Press.

Terschak, R. 1994. *Die Zauberin Uhle.* Bukarest: Ion Creanga Verlag.

Tiffany, S. W., and K. J. Adams. 1995. Feminist re-reading the Amazon: Anthropological adventures into the realm of sex and violence. Women in International Development Working Paper No. 253. Michigan State University, East Lansing.

Tripp, A. 2000. *Women and politics in Uganda.* Madison: University of Wisconsin Press.

Trouillot, M. R. 1991. Anthropology and the savage slot: The poetics and politics of otherness. In R. G. Fox, ed., *Recapturing anthropology,* 17–43. Santa Fe, N.M.: School of American Research Press.

Verdery, K. 1996. *What was socialism, and what comes next?* Princeton, N.J.: Princeton University Press.

Walter, L. 1995. Feminist anthropology? *Gender and Society* 9 (3): 272–289.

Walter, L. 1997. Teaching culture: The history of a feminist anthropology course. Unpublished manuscript, on file with author.

Wolf, C. 1996. Parting from the phantoms: The business of Germany. *PMLA* 3 (3): 395–407.

Wolf, D. L., ed. 1996. *Feminist dilemmas in fieldwork.* Boulder, Colo.: Westview Press.

Wolf, M. 1992. *A thrice-told tale: Feminism, postmodernism, and ethnographic responsibility.* Stanford, Calif.: Stanford University Press.

5

Ethnographic Encounters in Post-Soviet Kyrgyzstan
Dilemmas of Gender, Poverty, and the Cold War

Kathleen Kuehnast

The ethnographic encounter is always a complex negotiation in which the parties to the encounter acquiesce to a certain reality.
—Vincent Crapanzano, *Tuhami: Portrait of a Moroccan*

On my first fieldwork trip to Kirghizia in 1990, Soviet propaganda lined the roadway that stretched between Manas Airport and the capital city of Frunze. Statues, billboards, and monuments were vivid reminders of the Communist manifesto of Marxism-Leninism. What amazed me about the propaganda art were the numerous representations of women—in fact, twice as many as those of men. While we drove along that day, I commented to my new Kyrgyz friend, Almash, that in my own nation's capital few statues of women exist. She was surprised to learn that in the United States, the birthplace of the feminist movement, statues of women are not ubiquitous. As Almash and I exchanged stories that day about our childhood impressions of each other as Cold War enemies, neither of us had any inkling of the changes that were about to occur throughout the Soviet Union. Moreover, we were unaware that within one year's time, the small mountainous Republic of Kirghizia, with fewer than 5 million people, would become independent Kyrgyzstan, and its capital city would be renamed Bishkek. The new country would then embark on seismic political and economic reforms while it disengaged from the once-monolithic Soviet system. Along with these structural changes would come a challenge to the Soviet notion of the emancipated Central Asian woman, a theme that had dominated communist policies in Kyrgyzstan for 70 years. Likewise, other social forces would also begin to contest this former gender ideal, especially the revitalization of Islamic practices and ideologies, the reinstitution of Kyrgyz oral traditions, and the penetration of Western capitalism and international development objectives into the Kyrgyz economy. These changes would further intensify social cleavages in regard to gender, ethnicity, and class in Kyrgyz society.

One Kyrgyz described the rapid societal change in this way: "Imagine traveling along in a vehicle for seventy years. Then, suddenly the road disappears, and you don't know where to go." The economic upheaval in Kyrgyzstan between 1990 and 1996 created many unexpected challenges for the Kyrgyz people. The repercussions of the process of change on the daily lives of my informants were impossible to ignore. I had begun fieldwork in 1990 to research the impact of Sovietization upon Kyrgyz women and to understand how this remote group of Islamized, seminomadic herders had accommodated Soviet gender ideals. By 1996, I found that my research had necessarily shifted to encompass the devastating economic and social repercussions for women in their newly independent country, including issues of their decreased status, unemployment, and growing poverty, the last two affecting men as well.

The upheaval in the lives of the Kyrgyz also brought unexpected challenges to my work as an anthropologist. Reflecting the overall theme of this book, my chapter addresses three dilemmas that are particular to fieldwork in the postsocialist states. First, I begin by examining the persistence of Cold War ideologies in the post-Soviet period and the ways in which the fieldworker is consciously and unconsciously affected by this legacy. Likewise, our informants interpret us not only as individuals but also as members of the cultures from which we come. I argue that our informants' "readings" of us, and ours of them, have been indelibly shaped by this unique historical relationship and, thus, are reproduced in our representations of each other.

The complex encounter between anthropologist and informant is further complicated in post-Soviet Kyrgyzstan by the impact of the rapid infiltration of American popular culture. The global media was first introduced in 1992 on Kyrgyz television. It provided previously censored images about the rest of the world, especially the United States. These visualized scenarios of America (especially the B-rated television programs and pornographic films) seemed to convey a message to many of my informants that violence, sex, and consumerism are core American values. The Kyrgyz swiftly assimilated these new global images into their day-to-day lives, in part because they filled the ideological vacuum left by the demise of the Soviet Union. The speedy collapse of Soviet-controlled television and the extensive penetration of the global media were like trading one form of visual hegemony for another. As a result, problematic assumptions about the outsider (ethnographer) were communicated, and gender biases were transferred from one culture to another (see Kuehnast 1992).

My final point in this chapter is concerned with poverty, one of the more perplexing repercussions of a difficult economic transition from the Soviet-centralized controlled economy to free-market capitalism. For many Kyrgyz, the transition has drastically reduced their standard of living. Although fieldwork among impoverished groups is not new to anthropology, I argue that the unprecedented speed in which people found themselves impoverished and the peculiar circumstances of the postsocialist milieu make the issue of poverty among post-Soviet peoples unique. I examine how relations altered with my informants during the transition from the Soviet to the post-Soviet period.[1] To be sure, the rapidly changing social, economic, and political situation in post-Soviet Kyrgyzstan has created an unpredictable current for most Kyrgyz to navigate. Likewise, I suggest that such unexpected dilemmas hold true for the anthropologist as well.

Cold War Notions of the "Other"

Although the relationship between anthropologist and the "other" is not a new concern in anthropology (see Bourdieu 1977; Crapanzano 1980; Herzfeld 1987; Rosaldo 1989; Brettell 1993; Jenkins 1994), fieldwork in the postsocialist states yields another set of complex issues through which to explore such an association. A pertinent issue to consider in the postsocialist framework is the preexisting predicament standing between the anthropologist and informant. In the case of postsocialism, this dilemma includes the conscious and unconscious assumptions held about the "other" as the result of a half century of Cold War ideologies perpetuated by the Soviet Union and the United States. As Timothy Jenkins points out, the fieldwork encounter is not just between individuals; it is also a historical encounter between groups. He elaborates that "the anthropologist is not an individual without a history face to face with his or her 'people,' but is in a sense a multiplicity, a certain kind of person who will be 'read' in certain ways by those encountered" (1994: 447). It follows that the anthropologist doing fieldwork in a postsocialist state brings his or her own predisposition about the former Cold War enemy; likewise, the informant does the same.

It is important in the context of postsocialist fieldwork to consider the far-reaching influence of the Cold War. For as Katherine Verdery argues, the Cold War was more than simply a political face-off between the United States and the Soviet Union; it was also a form of knowledge, a virtual "cognitive organization of the world" (Verdery 1996: 4). It is precisely this deep cognitive organization of the other's world that makes the post–Cold War relationship between former ideological enemies more difficult to decipher than, say, relationships between Americans and Europeans or Asians who are not part of the postsocialist world. Not only did the Cold War affect individuals' impressions of each other, but ultimately it also encompassed a sophisticated, powerful, and convincing discourse which, over the past 60 years, permeated the social sciences, popular culture, and literature in both the Soviet Union and the United States. Similarly, the Western notions of capitalism, privatization, and civil society fervently applied in the postsocialist states, Verdery argues, are ideological remnants of the Cold War as well.

In part, the Cold War was as much about the absence of knowledge as it was about misconstruing knowledge. Certainly, methodological hurdles that existed for Sovietologists added to this gap in understanding. Prior to 1991, Western researchers were rarely allowed interaction with everyday Soviet citizens. As a result, the theoretical orientation of Soviet studies in the United States between the 1950s and the late 1980s was a top-down view of the communist system as amassed from archival material. Consequently, very little field research was generated at the grass-roots level about how people actually experienced their everyday Soviet lives. But recent ethnographic research in the postsocialist states provides new evidence about the ways that individuals dealt with multiple ideological projects during the communist period (see Funk and Mueller 1993; De Soto and Panzig 1995; Kideckel 1995; Shahrani 1995; Grant 1996). These postsocialist ethnographies critique previous polemic literature that emphasized a totalitarian view of Soviet domination without allowing individual experiences to enrich and give voice to a complex set of cultural exchanges. In this way, the postsocialist ethnographic research not only explicates Soviet experiences, but also challenges our own sophisticated, powerful, and convincing Cold War ideologies that have tended to accentuate the failure of communism and to minimize the positive features of Soviet socialism.

Indeed, I initially anticipated that my informants would tell me that they had been oppressed by the Soviet system and were now greatly relieved to be done with the old imperialistic mentality. In most cases, however, I found the opposite. Kyrgyz women expressed highly positive opinions about their Soviet experiences.[2] Even six years after its collapse, numbers of Kyrgyz women I interviewed invariably praised the Soviet system and emphasized the Soviet contribution to the emancipation of Central Asian women, especially in terms of educational and work opportunities.

When I began my fieldwork in 1990, I had not fully comprehended the degree to which my presence—a female anthropologist from the West— was indeed unusual in Kyrgyzstan. During the 70 years of the Soviet Union, only a handful of foreigners had been allowed to travel to the Central Asian republics (see, e.g., Hughes 1934; Maillart 1934; Bacon [1966]

1980), and among the Kyrgyz, few had ever ventured beyond the borders of their remote region. With so little direct experience of one another, the ideas and expectations that formed the foundation of our relationship were gleaned through persistent Cold War notions. These residual belief systems about the "other" seemed to permeate my postsocialist fieldwork experience at unexpected moments, reminding both the anthropologist and informant how resilient outmoded ideas can be, especially in the absence of knowledge.

One of the more vivid encounters of residual influences of the Cold War occurred one morning in 1994 when my friend Aigul called me on the telephone. She was very excited about seeing a photograph of me in the previous evening's newspaper along with an article which quoted my research about the changing status of Kyrgyz women in their post-Soviet society. I had just awoken. "What photograph? What article? No one has recently interviewed me, nor has anyone taken a photo of me!" Aigul explained, "The photo shows you in a long nightgown, leisurely sipping a cup of coffee." I knew that this was not a photo of me, yet the mystery image was placed next to an article about my research entitled (in translated form), How we are reflected in statistics: A woman from America about the women from Kyrgyzstan (Sorokina 1994). I was confused by this juxtaposition and, thus, surmised that I was still not correctly interpreting Aigul's excited Russian. I wanted to run down the street immediately to the local bazaar to see for myself this unbelievable photo. Yet, before I had finished my morning coffee, the phone rang three more times. Each caller described the same article and photo that he or she presumed to be of me. No one seemed to think that the photo was odd. Indeed, I was the only one who seemed confused by it.

Once I had the newspaper in hand, I discovered that the article was an unauthorized excerpt from my report for the World Bank concerning the impact of the economic transition on women in Kyrgyzstan (Kuehnast 1993). The study had been translated into Russian, making it easily transferable to any local newspaper. But what of the photograph, which was someone other than myself? Later that day, I found a plausible explanation. I arranged a meeting with the newspaper editor, for I was not only interested in her impression of the research but also wanted to learn more about why she had chosen the photo in question.

Since my study highlighted the worsening economic conditions for women, I had surmised that the photo was meant to represent an unemployed Kyrgyz woman in a state of depression because she was unable to find a job. Yet, as my Kyrgyz friends had informed me, they had each interpreted the photo to be a picture of me. I asked myself, and then the editor, How could such a serious study about the deteriorating living conditions for women be illustrated with a photo of an improbable researcher lolling about in her nightgown sipping coffee? The editor explained that her readers were interested in an American's interpretation of their country's current economic crisis, especially its impact on women. Regarding the photo, she replied that her secretary had selected it from their photographic files, believing that it best represented how women in Kyrgyzstan imagined what the "dream life" is like for an American woman. When I failed to understand what she meant by *dream life,* she curtly responded, "As Soviet women, we dreamed of being able to lounge around in our nightgowns and drink coffee. This was considered a luxury. This is how we imagine that women from the West live day to day."

Until this fieldwork encounter, even as my research delved into the contradictory gender ideologies emerging among the post-Soviet Kyrgyz, I had not fully appreciated the degree to which my own identity and the inherent cultural contradictions of the West were also being analyzed and interpreted by my informants. Indeed, the editor's interpretation of American women, and consequently of me, is reflective of Michael Herzfeld's observation that "we are participant observers only as far as we are also prepared to accept our informants' right to the same title" (1987: 90–91).

Certainly, the myths we carry about the other, such as the one that American women lounge around all day drinking coffee, are also found in Western research about former Soviet women. The relevance of this mutual problem of Cold War mythologies became clearer to me, ironically, as the result of a photo of mine that was on the cover of the same report mentioned above. The photo proved to be both perplexing and bothersome to a group of elite Kyrgyz women. My research report about the postsocialist economic burden of women had been widely distributed throughout the upper echelons of the government (see Kuehnast 1993). On the cover was a black and white photograph of an elderly Kyrgyz woman and her daughter-in-law, holding a baby, each dressed in worn clothing of seminomadic herders. I had taken the photo in a region that was experiencing a great deal of difficulty as the result of the privatization of collective farms. Since the report focused on vulnerable groups of women, I had concluded that the photo represented the pride and the tenacity of these families in the face of such hardship. Yet, as it turned out, some Kyrgyz women in governmental positions were offended by this particular visual representation. The comment I heard most often was, "Why did you choose the photograph of *these* women? The photo does not represent our country to the world in a very good light." Initially, I dismissed their concern, because I felt that the photo told an important story about the devastating effects of the rapid privatization ventures on many nomadic Kyrgyz. But eventually, with the help of several of my Kyrgyz colleagues, I began to recognize that these government

A young Kyrgyz mother with her young son and her mother-in-law, standing in front of their yurt in the Issyk Kul Oblast. For five months a year, these seminomadic herders traverse the mountainous terrain in search of good pastureland for their sheep and horses. (Photograph by Kathleen Kuehnast)

workers had "read" my photo of Kyrgyz women as a negative image that undermined their efforts to succeed in the new economy.

The response of these Kyrgyz women to my photo led to a contemplation of my own unconscious Cold War assumptions. Had I reproduced a Cold War belief that Soviet women were living in servitude to communism? To the Kyrgyz women who challenged the appropriateness of the photo, I had not represented the facts: Soviet women, as a group, were among the most well-educated work forces in the world. And Kyrgyz women, among the Muslim central Asian republics, were some of the most accomplished and held more scientific research positions than many of their Muslim counterparts elsewhere. Had my photograph of these nomadic women inadvertently romanticized or aestheticized them, as *National Geographic* photographic images tend to do (see Lutz and Collins 1993)? Such contemplations also made me reevaluate my own experience with the newspaper photo of "an American woman": Did representing me in a nightgown reveal Soviet notions about women from capitalist societies as being lazy? The manner in which both my Kyrgyz colleagues and I took offense at each other's visual representations may also reveal other cultural notions we hold about ourselves. Might the Kyrgyz' protest be more a distaste for visually portraying their country's economic hardship because it goes against well-ingrained Soviet ideologies that portrayed the female worker as strong, competent, and vital? And what of my reaction to their photo of me? Did my reaction reflect my own cultural biases that equate certain kinds of leisure with laziness, namely, an image from my childhood of American housewives watching soap operas or gossiping at coffee klatches?

Obviously, these considerations are contemplations and not conclusions, which, nevertheless, return us to the question raised earlier: To what extent do Cold War discourses still affect our postsocialist research? Although it is an intangible question, it can be made more perceptible by considering in this instance how we visually represent one another. Mead (1975), Ruby (1980), and de Lauretis (1987) have suggested that our visual representations of the "other" reveal as much about the creator as about the subject. In the examples cited above, the Kyrgyz newspaper editor's photo choice of the woman in a nightgown sipping coffee offered little information about the anthropologist in the article, but instead imparted Soviet impressions about the lackadaisical life of women from the West. Likewise, my photo of the impoverished Kyrgyz family communicated the negative repercussions of the economic transition while diminishing the successes that had also occurred in Kyrgyzstan. With these examples, I have suggested that material artifacts, such as visual representations, expose at least one way in which Cold War discourses still operate within the post-Soviet and the American imaginations. Moreover, social scientists doing fieldwork in postsocialist states need to consider how their presence in a country is interpreted through Cold War notions about the other and how their own stereotypical (and suppressed) Cold War ideas come to influence their research.

Pop Culture, an Unchallenged Interloper

The experience of being a female American anthropologist in Kyrgyzstan altered after 1992, when this small country was suddenly saturated with mass-produced products of American popular culture, especially television programs, movies, music, magazines, and the computer Internet. What was once a form of Soviet imperialism—that is, the Communist Party's strict control of the media, in which it was illegal to portray violent or blatant sexual behavior—was unilaterally transformed by the introduction of global capitalism and its wares of consumerism, cinematic violence, and pornography. Instead of acquainting the former Soviet countries with new concepts of democracy and capitalism through educational media programs, the ideological vacuum left by the demise of the Soviet Union was filled with American soap operas, MTV, B-grade and X-rated movies, and television reruns. This rapid infusion of globalism into the day-to-day lives of my informants not only created a current of excitement, especially among the younger generation, but also brought about serious reservations on the part of those Kyrgyz over 35 years old regarding the values perpetuated by the American media and its potentially negative influence on their children. Because of their new exposure to American culture, I found that my informants' interpretation of my presence in Kyrgyzstan was also drawn from imported American television programs, which typically portray Americans as wealthy.

In Kyrgyzstan, as in the former Soviet Union at-large, television-watching has long been a daily ritual for most families. Ellen Mickiewicz (1988) cites that television-viewing was a key factor influencing political change and upheaval in Soviet society during the late 1980s. Certainly, the strategic use of the visual image was not new to the Soviets. In helping to craft "socialism with a human face," Gorbachev's ambassador to Canada, Alexander Yakovlev, declared that "the television image is everything" (quoted in Mickiewicz 1988: 217). Fifty years earlier, Lenin had claimed that cinema was the most important of all the arts. Both Soviet leaders were brilliant propagandists who understood the immense power of persuasion that the controlled-media image could elicit, including the mobilization of millions of diverse Soviet people toward common ideological goals.

It is important to emphasize that the Soviet TV medium was not used for entertainment per se or as an outlet of advertising, but was employed, as Mickiewicz notes, "to supplement policy" (1988: 29). One implication of such an orientation was that this Soviet medium was perceived more as a vehicle of party information than as a font of entertaining fiction. This orientation toward television as a source of information instead of entertainment was notable in 1993 during my interviews with a group of 18-year-old Kyrgyz students about the introduction of the market economy in their country. They explained their own understanding of capitalism by referring to an episode of the 1980s American soap opera *Santa Barbara*. For them, the soap opera was not entertainment per se but a medium imparting important factual information about how capitalism operates at the household level. Indeed, their analysis pinpointed the large information gap occurring between the average post-Soviet person and the reforms underway. While foreign economists and investors were attempting to intervene in the former socialist states and create a market economy, the general population was viewing the globalization process through the lens of American popular culture. The keen interest in information about the West, in general, was so intense that an article from the Kyrgyz newspaper *Izvestia* (September 1992) reported that the management of a collective farm outside Bishkek had to cut off electricity in order to tear workers away from daytime television. Apparently, too many employees were skipping work to watch episodes of the 249-part Mexican soap opera *Bogatie tozhe plachiut* (The rich also cry). What were only entertainment programs for the Western viewer were considered the equivalent of "educational" television for the nascent Kyrgyz viewer who was seeking further information about his or her new postsocialist world.

Although I had noted the impact of imported television programs on my Kyrgyz informants, I had not considered the new TV medium's impact on my own research. I got a glimpse of the indirect effect on my fieldwork when one evening in October 1993, after watching the nightly news *Vremia,* my colleagues Daniyar and Medet asked me whether I had noticed any differences in the way Kyrgyz men treated me now as compared with several years prior. The question puzzled me, since I was rarely queried about my own experiences in Kyrgyzstan. Daniyar went on to explain that in early 1992 the first showings of violence and pornography occurred on Kyrgyz television. My colleagues, both trained social scientists, were curious whether the programming had affected the way in which Kyrgyz men responded to me, since so many of the women in the new programs were "Western" and blond. Daniyar seemed somewhat nervous about posing the question, but I knew that his query stemmed from a protective, even brotherly, feeling that he held toward me. Up to that point, I had not noticed a change in my relations with Kyrgyz men, but then I primarily interacted with women in my research. I asked them to answer their own question. Both men stated that there had been an attitudinal shift among Kyrgyz men toward women from the West since the imported television programs first began to appear. According to them, women from the West were generally thought to be less modest and perhaps more open and receptive to male advances and pornographic fantasies. Daniyar noted my incredulity and reiterated, "Don't worry, Ketlin. You see, in this cultural vacuum other people's fantasies are filling our own emptiness, since we have no other ideology anymore." It was this interaction that brought to my attention the possible effect that the imported TV medium was having upon the Kyrgyz and their perceptions of me.

Not only were such television programs from the West affecting how the Kyrgyz interpreted who I was, but also many of the low-quality programs were beginning to cast a shadow for some Kyrgyz on the desirability of a "democracy," and increasingly there were demands for stronger government controls on television. One afternoon while I had tea with my Kyrgyz friend Altinay at a Bishkek *chai khana,* she explained to me some of the negative effects of the imported programs. Altinay lamented in Russian about her situation: "Even though I really never liked going to Pioneer Camp (communist youth programs), at least I knew what was important, what it meant to be a good citizen. Now, what can I offer my children? There are no children's camps. Few of us can afford the good schools. Movies cost too much. No one attends the theater anymore. All that seems left is television. It is free and easy while our lives are expensive and difficult."

Altinay then began to discuss the quality of the new television programming. She told me about how early one evening several weeks prior, she and her children and their grandmother were watching an American movie about a filmmaker. "At first it looked like an entertaining story, but then it suddenly became pornographic and violent—the filmmaker strangled a naked woman. I was so shocked that I didn't think to turn the television off. I didn't know how to explain this to my son and daughter. You know, we never saw such things during the Soviet period. But I have to admit that when I see things like this on television, I am not sure if it is such a good idea that our country becomes like the West." Altinay compared the ways women were visually portrayed during the Soviet period. "I was always concerned about Soviet realism, especially how women were made to look like King Kong monsters. Just look at the statues on Chui Prospect! But now I ask myself, What is worse?" She then referred to a popular Russian television advertisement where a man attempts to explain something to a woman who does not appear to be understanding his point. He turns to the camera and says, "She may be beautiful, but she's stupid. For those who *can* understand this message, call this phone number." Altinay continued, "I think maybe things are worse for women now. The idea that a woman can be owned has been put into men's minds by this new television. It seems that men behave toward women in the same way they now see things on television."

The analysis of how visual images affect the relationship between ethnographer and informant is pertinent to the discussion of fieldwork dilemmas facing anthropologists in the postsocialist states. Prior to 1990, very little information existed in the Soviet Union about the individual lives of American women, and vice versa. This dramatically changed during the initial years of postsocialism (1991–1996), when the vacuum was filled by images of American popular culture. Although visual representations are not in and of themselves facts but rather interpretations of someone's reality, Richard Rorty reminds us of the power that visual representations hold over our conceptions of others when he writes, "Our desire to represent is really a desire for constraint, to find foundations to cling to, and frameworks so one will not stray" (1979: 315). Indeed, Rorty points out the dilemma challenging ethnographers in postsocialist states, that is, how exported American myths and stories have unwittingly become a narrow framework in which to define Americans, for better or for worse.

Deconstructing Socialism: Experiencing Poverty

The ideological and material shift away from socialism toward capitalism in the former Soviet Union has been more difficult than any economist could have predicted (see Bauer, Green, and Kuehnast 1997). Since 1991, when Kyrgyzstan became an independent country, the majority of the population has experienced a marked decline in their standard of living. The United Nations 1998 economic figures on Kyrgyzstan report that nearly 59 percent of all households there are living below the poverty line, and a fifth of the population lives under extreme poverty.[3] Such dramatic economic changes have affected nearly every aspect of Kyrgyz daily life. As an anthropologist studying Kyrgyz women and the postsocialist period, it was disturbing to observe the increasingly burdensome predicaments for many of my Kyrgyz informants (Kuehnast 1995b).

Most notably, the economic decline of the household has undermined women's self-confidence and their ability to plan for the future. When comparing my field interviews between 1990 and 1996, I noticed that the once easily articulated, culturally cohesive Soviet ideology about work and family life had all but fallen away. Before the breakup of the Soviet Union, my female informants were much more assured about their future. In spite of the daily uncertainties, for instance, whether bread would be available or not, daily life in the late Soviet era was relatively predictable (see Kuehnast 1995c). During the years 1990 and 1991, women communicated a much clearer sense about their identities as both mothers and workers. They had planned for the number of children they wanted and how long they would be on maternity leave (typically three years); they depended upon the government benefits they would receive for each child; and, last but not least, they were able to fulfill their immediate and extended family obligations. In contrast, in the post-Soviet economy, many women were having difficulty knowing how to plan for their future. Uncertain and fragmented plans seemed to mark their days. They were often unable to meet extended family obligations, such as life-cycle celebrations, because they lacked the time and money to do so.

Many Kyrgyz women expressed a deep sense of loss about the end of Soviet socialism, since they had been key recipients of its major benefits, including free education, guaranteed employment, state child-care centers, and food subsidies. As one of my informants said, "Socialism is better for women. Capitalism is better for men." The situation in the early 1990s was one in which the majority of jobs held by women during the Soviet period had been government-subsidized work in preschools, health clinics, youth camps, cultural centers, and collective farms. Thus, with the international impetus toward privatization of all state-run programs, women bore the

The author (*center*) conducting an ethnographic interview with two generations of Kyrgyz women (Photograph by Leonid Azapovich Akmadeev)

brunt of this change. In addition, the rising cost of living also forced women to leave their professions, in order to make "fast" money working in *spekiuliatsiia*—the resale of products and goods for a higher price at local bazaars. This type of work was becoming more common for teachers, physicians, university professors, and government bureaucrats, whose low monthly salaries ($30) could hardly keep pace with inflation.

It is important to keep in mind when examining the postsocialist situation in Kyrgyzstan that the material benefits of the Soviet system were notable, especially for women. These Sovietized women had been raised and educated to place a high value on being contributing members of society. Having internalized the ideological expectations and norms of the communist system, many considered it a personal failure in the postsocialist period not to be contributing to the overall productivity of the country. For Kyrgyz women, being unemployed was demoralizing. They were embarrassed to discuss their unemployed status, feeling it was perhaps indicative of their lack of ability. Unemployment represented more than simply being without an income. Losing one's job had many other social ramifications as well (see De Soto, this volume). Kyrgyz women explained that unemployment also meant being disconnected from many important socioeconomic networks. They likened a job to a one-stop service center that provided everything from family benefits and a child-care center to housing and in-kind contributions of food and fuel. Survival in their former command economy encouraged a high degree of interdependency in which many informal transactions took place through an intricate system of cohorts "helping one another out." For the rural regions, postsocialism meant that daily living conditions for women were even worse, since many collective farms had been downsized in the privatization process. Few employment options and rising costs of transportation added to rural women's sense of isolation, as well as their fear of leaving their homes in the evening, since gangs of drunk young men often hung out in the deserted streets.

Because of the changing economy and deteriorating living standards for many of my informants, the conditions in which I began my fieldwork in 1990 changed dramatically in just a few years' time. Of significance to the research process was the reduction of the available time my informants' could spend with me, since many of them had taken a second job. Although I accompanied some of my informants to their new job (typically at the local bazaar), it was evident at times that my presence was an additional burden to their already stressful living circumstances associated with the uncertainty of the economic transition. These factors, along with my informants' sense of bewilderment regarding the rapid decline in their economic security, reduced access to fieldwork opportunities that were once more commonplace. For example, by 1994, my informants were less able to afford the expense of making obligatory trips to relatives' homes of which I had once been a regular guest. During these previous visits, I had gained a greater understanding of the Kyrgyz kinship system, as well as a better appreciation for Kyrgyz life-cycle celebrations. Many Kyrgyz had stopped visiting their relatives because of social reciprocity norms, which required them to return the favor whenever their relatives accommodated them. In an increasingly precarious economic situation, many Kyrgyz simply could not reciprocate. In a culture where accommodating a guest is nearly an art form, the curtailment of hospitality to their relatives and friends was seen as a great personal shame among many of my informants. Even in less familiar circumstances—for example, when I was completing a survey of 600 women throughout Kyrgyzstan in 1993—many could not offer the obligatory tea and bread (a nomadic custom of offering nourishment to the guest). I found the women were deeply embarrassed by this inability to extend such hospitality to their guests.

The economic uncertainty and increased societal problems, including violent crime, loss of social benefits, and high unemployment, introduced a feeling of scarcity different from the once Soviet fear of "not enough." The post-Soviet experience of scarcity for the Kyrgyz was also found in their ambivalence about letting go of the past. At the same time, they expressed little faith in the new government's experiment with capitalism. By 1996, the collective euphoria created by state independence in 1991 had transmuted for many into individual disillusionment. I found that my Kyrgyz inform-ants, especially those over 35 years of age, seemed to be psychologically and socially disoriented. They euphemistically recalled the past, and even the problems and limitations of former Soviet times seemed preferable to the vague, uncertain realities of the present. This paradoxical comfort of the fa-miliar pains of the previous system and the uncertainty of the present were expressed by one Kyrgyz journalist: "We are very trapped. We're on a bro-ken bridge between two different societies. We can't take pleasure in the new and we can't leave the old" (quoted in Nantes 1994: 4).

In the Avalanche of Postsocialism

When Roy D'Andrade wrote, "Fieldwork in the twentieth century is like at-tempting to study the physics of moving bodies while living in the middle of an avalanche," he aptly forecast the condition of conducting ethnographic research in postsocialism (D'Andrade 1984:111). Consider the different ways in which my presence in Kyrgyzstan between 1990 and 1996 was ex-plained to me. According to some of my Kyrgyz associates, my first visit in 1990 was seen as a manifestation of *glasnost,* an openness which allowed me to travel with few restrictions and even to stay as a guest in the home of my new Soviet friends. A year later, after the collapse of the Soviet Union and the emergence of an independent Kyrgyzstan, such ethnographic visits be-came viewed as hopeful signs that the Cold War was truly over. I became viewed as the *de facto* representative of the West on any given topic and was periodically interviewed by newspapers, television, and radio. In 1992, I was still one of the few foreigners working in Kyrgyzstan, but by 1993, I re-turned to a country suddenly bristling with foreign embassies and the head-quarters of a number of international aid and business organizations.

A dual economy was emerging. The local economy had acquired its cur-rency, the *som,* ending a century of shared monetary allegiance with the Russian ruble. The other economy, based on the American dollar, was de-veloping at a rapid pace as the result of the growing number of foreign busi-nesses and foreign visitors with cash. By the time I returned for my sixth field experience in 1994, I was amazed to find Chinese and Turkish restau-rants, Kodak one-hour film processing services, Coca-Cola billboards, and 60 brand new Mercedes automobiles parked outside the Kyrgyz House of Government. These less-than-subtle changes coming from the outside were commensurate with greater personal expectations of me on the part of my informants and acquaintances alike. Many assumed that I could "open doors" to the presumed riches of the West, while others considered me as a hoped-for vehicle to opportunities abroad (see also Silverman, this volume). I found that my fieldwork experiences were being shaped by the macroeconomic, social, and political changes underway in Kyrgyzstan, just as the Kyrgyz understanding of the outsider was being transformed by such external influences as the global media.

During my eight months of fieldwork in 1994, I found myself, like many of my informants, longing for the former Soviet era. I recalled my earlier fieldwork experiences (1991–1992) at local bazaars in which I was routinely asked if I were Estonian, since Soviet citizens from the Baltic republics often made their way to the mountain resorts of Kyrgyzstan. Such an assumption about my origins occurred not only because of my light-brown hair, I was told, but also because of the relative isolation of Kyrgyzstan, which meant that few foreigners ever traveled the distance. But by 1996 thousands of foreigners lived in Bishkek. I was seldom asked anymore if I was "Estonka," since my identity as an outsider in Kyrgyzstan became more associated with that of a foreigner. The new assumption about me was that if I was not a local, then I must be from the West. With this shift, I found myself longing for my former anonymity, that is, for the Kyrgyz assumption that I were a Soviet woman. It was not that I wanted to deny my origin or to minimize my work as an American anthropologist, but previously my role had been less encumbered by expectations about what people from the West could offer and by the growing assumption that I must be wealthy like Maria of the soap opera *Prosto Maria,* for how else did I get to Kyrgyzstan?

Conducting fieldwork in the postsocialist era is an ethnographic opportunity for negotiating identities between anthropologist and informant. Whether these identities are remnants of the Cold War or fragments of the global marketization of popular culture, a reflexive approach is necessary to reexamine our assumptions about the other. Nietzsche called reflexivity "the burden that we can neither carry nor throw off" (quoted in Lawson 1985: 53). It is a positive force that rejuvenates the worn and outmoded ideas that permeate our thinking. Indeed, this is a critical challenge of fieldwork among any group, but even more so, I argue, in fieldwork between American anthropologists and our postsocialist informants, in which 70 years of anti-American and anti-communist rhetoric has inevitably shaped our views of each other.

D'Andrade (1984) describes the dilemma of studying culture in a rapidly changing world where the observer and the observed are constantly redefining one another. Certainly, the ethnographer from the West encounters the transformation of cultural boundaries in postsocialist fieldwork, where old ideologies are readily substituted, nationalities are reinvented, and global media permeate every household. The abrupt end of one way of life and the bewilderment that has followed present an interpretive challenge for the anthropologist working in post-Soviet Kyrgyzstan. New approaches to fieldwork and interpretations are needed in order to understand the many influences and ideologies affecting the Kyrgyz today.

As I witnessed first-hand the changes in my informants' lives, my ethnographic position also altered. Once an exotic Cold War outsider, my role as an anthropologist acquired dramatic images associated with the West, especially those from imported soap operas. Such dramas present a reality that starkly contrasts the increasing levels of poverty in Kyrgyzstan. When I interpret my ethnographic encounters in these contexts, it is easier to understand how a local Kyrgyz newspaper would represent a Western social scientist in a news report by using a photograph of a woman in her nightgown, leisurely sipping a cup of coffee.

Notes

An earlier draft of this chapter was presented at the invited session Human Dilemmas of Doing Fieldwork in Disintegrating Post-Socialist States, during the annual conference of the American Anthropological Association, December 2, 1994, in Atlanta, Georgia. Sections of this chapter also appear in my dissertation: "Let the Stone Lie Where It Has Fallen: Dilemmas of Gender and Generation in Post-Soviet Kyrgyzstan," University of Minnesota, 1997.

I gratefully acknowledge the following institutions for support in my fieldwork research and dissertation write-up: the Social Science Research Council Dissertation Fellowship, 1995–1996; the University of Minnesota doctoral dissertation fellowship, 1994–1995; IREX long-term research grant, 1993–1994; the Wenner-Gren Anthropological Foundation, 1993–1994; and the University of Minnesota block grants, 1991, 1992, 1993. I would also like to express my sincere appreciation to Gloria Goodwin Raheja for her substantive remarks and to acknowledge Caroline Banks, Caroline Brettell, Cate Cowan, Hermine De Soto, Nora Dudwick, Bruce Grant, Kenneth Rasmussen, and Rosalie Robertson for their editorial comments on various drafts of this chapter.

1. Kyrgyzstan has experienced an economic depression since the breakup of the Soviet Union in 1991, when it became an independent country. The Asian Development Bank findings from a 1996 study show that the economic crisis is continuing. Although both men and women suffer from issues of impoverishment, including unemployment and a reduction in life quality, women disproportionately carry the domestic burden, which includes the care for the young, the elderly, the disabled, and all household responsibilities, all of which are made more difficult by impoverished conditions.

2. According to anthropologists Caroline Humphrey (1983) and Bruce Grant (1996), the influence of Soviet socialism among the peripheral, non-Russian populations of the Soviet Union was so effective that even in the reconstitution of their post-Soviet ethnic identities, Soviet ideals persist.

3. During the Soviet period, it was estimated that 5 percent of the population lived below the poverty line. It should be emphasized here that it is not only difficult to compare Soviet and post-Soviet demographics regarding poverty but also misleading, since they are based on different economic indicators.

References

Bacon, E. [1966] 1980. *Central Asians under Russian rule.* Ithaca, N.Y.: Cornell University Press.

Bauer, A., D. Green, and K. Kuehnast. 1997. *Women and gender relations: The Kyrgyz Republic in transition.* Manila: Asian Development Bank (ADB).

Bourdieu, P. 1977. *Outline of a theory of practice.* Cambridge: Cambridge University Press.

Brettell, C. B. 1993. Introduction: Fieldwork, text, and audience. In C. B. Brettell, ed., *When they read what we write: The politics of ethnography,* 1–24. Westport, Conn.: Bergin and Garvey.

Crapanzano, V. 1980. *Tuhami: Portrait of a Moroccan.* Chicago: University of Chicago Press.

D'Andrade, R. 1984. Cultural meaning systems. In R. Shweder and R. LeVine, eds., *Culture theory,* 88–119. Cambridge: Cambridge University Press.

de Lauretis, T. 1987. *Alice doesn't: Feminism, semiotics, cinema.* Bloomington: Indiana University Press.

De Soto, H. G., and C. Panzig. 1995. From decollectivization to poverty and beyond: Women in rural east Germany before and after unification. In D. A. Kideckel, ed., *East European communities: The struggle for balance in turbulent times,* 179–195. Boulder, Colo.: Westview Press.

Funk, N., and M. Mueller. 1993. *Gender politics and post-communism: Reflections from eastern Europe and the former Soviet Union.* New York: Routledge.

Grant, B. 1996. *In the Soviet house of culture.* Princeton, N.J.: Princeton University Press.

Herzfeld, M. 1987. *Anthropology through the looking-glass: Critical ethnography in the margins of Europe.* Cambridge: Cambridge University Press.

Hughes, L. 1934. *A Negro looks at Soviet Central Asia.* Moscow-Leningrad: Cooperative Publishing Society of Foreign Workers in the USSR.

Humphrey, C. 1983. *Karl Marx collective.* Cambridge: Cambridge University Press.

Jenkins, T. 1994. Fieldwork and the perception of everyday life. *Man* 29 (2): 433–455.

Kideckel, D. 1995. *East European communities: The struggle for balance in turbulent times.* Boulder, Colo.: Westview Press.

Kuehnast, K. 1992. Visual imperialism and the export of prejudice: An exploration of ethnographic film. In I. Crawford and D. Turtons, eds., *Film as ethnography,* 183–195. Manchester: Manchester University Press.

Kuehnast, K. 1993. Women and economic changes in Kyrgyzstan: Coping mechanisms and attitudes toward social policies. Unpublished internal document of the World Bank, Human Resources Division, Washington, D.C.

Kuehnast, K. 1995a. Cultural factors influencing the employment potential of women in Kyrgyzstan. In M. Kaiser and Z. Khakimov, eds., *Labor market and social protection in the Kyrgyz Republic,* 112–121. Bishkek: Literaturny Kyrgyzstan.

Kuehnast, K. 1995b. Women and economic changes in Kyrgyzstan: Coping mechanisms and attitudes toward social policies. *Labyrinth: Central Asian Quarterly* (London: School of Oriental and African Studies) 1 (4): 39–41.

Kuehnast, K. 1995c. Women and cultural transition in Kyrgyzstan. *Surviving Together* 13 (2): 28–31.

Kuehnast, K. 1996. Canaries in a coal mine? Women and nation-building in the Kyrgyz Republic. *Anthropology of East Europe Review* 14 (2): 21–33.

Lawson, H. 1989. *Reflexivity.* La Salle, Ill.: Open Court.

Lutz, C., and J. Collins. 1993. *Reading "National Geographic."* Chicago: University of Chicago Press.

Maillart, E. 1934. *Turkestan solo.* Paris: Editions Bernard Grasset.

Mead, M. 1975. Visual anthropology in a discipline of words. In P. Hockings, ed., *Principles of visual anthropology,* 3–12. Paris: Mouton.

Mickiewicz, E. 1988. *Split signals: Television and politics in the Soviet Union.* Oxford: Oxford University Press.

Nantes, Y. C. 1994. *The status of women in central Asia.* Women in Development Monograph, Series 2. New York: United Nations.

Rorty, R. 1979. *Philosophy and the mirror of nature.* Princeton, N.J.: Princeton University Press.

Rosaldo, R. 1989. *Culture and truth: The remaking of social analysis.* Boston: Beacon Press.

Ruby, J. 1980. Exposing yourself: Reflexivity, anthropology and film. *Semiotica* 3: 153–179.

Said, E. W. 1979. *Orientalism.* New York: Vintage Books.

Shahrani, M. N. 1995. Islam and the political culture of "scientific atheism" in post–Soviet Central Asia: Future predicaments. In M. Bourdeaux, ed., *The politics of religion in Russia and the new states of Eurasia,* 273–292. Armonk, N.Y.: M. E. Sharpe.

Sorokina, E. 1994. My—v zerkale statistiki: Zhenshchina iz Ameriki—o zhenshchinakh iz Kirgizii (How we are reflected in statistics: A woman from America about the women from Kyrgyzstan). *Vechernii Bishkek,* March 15, 1994, p. 5.

Tambiah, S. 1989. Ethnic conflict in the world today. *American Ethnologist* 16 (2): 335–349.

Van Maanen, J. 1988. *Tales of the field: On writing ethnography.* Chicago: University of Chicago Press.

Verdery, K. 1996. *What was socialism? And what comes next?* Princeton, N.J.: Princeton University Press.

6

When Text Becomes Field
Fieldwork in "Transitional" Societies

Igor Barsegian

Since 1991, the principal meeting point for the realities of the West and of the postsocialist countries has become what is now referred to as the *transition,* a cultural construct which Westerners use to explain what happened and what is happening to socialist countries. As a cultural construct, transition includes within itself a multitude of derivative notions, such as development, privatization, market economy, political participation, civil society, and others. In this chapter, I use my own fieldwork in Armenia to discuss transition as a concept which, I believe, often overlooks and dilutes the specific features of postsocialist societies. This oversight and dilution result from the assumptions that transition is characterized by development toward a market society and that many important, even structural, features of postsocialist societies will only be temporary.

To some extent, the explanation for the transition construct consists in fieldwork within Third World countries by anthropologists who explored the integration of rural communities into the global economy. This fieldwork approach was based on a perceived dichotomy between Western and non-Western societies, a dichotomy sometimes described in terms of North–South contrasts. The model of transition is now applied to postsocialist societies and their expected integration with the West; this time the dichotomy to be overcome is that of the "advanced" West versus the "underdeveloped" East. It is both interesting and important to analyze the ethnographic fieldwork of these "transitional" postsocialist countries, because ethnography and ethnographic fieldwork are themselves located on a transitional continuum between different cultures. As Clifford notes, ethnography "is situated between powerful systems of meaning . . . [and] poses its questions at the boundaries of civilizations, cultures, classes, races, and genders" (1986: 2). In this chapter, I explore the experience of doing fieldwork in this transitional continuum as a local ethnographer in Armenia, and I reflect upon how being a local versus a "guest anthropologist" shapes one's interpretation of the field. I use my experiences in Armenia to suggest how the construction of transition works in the field.

My fieldwork itself has also been transitional in many senses—on the continua between socialist and postsocialist Armenia and between insider and outsider. In 1981–1983, I participated in a research project on continuities in Armenian rural traditions, and in 1988–1991, I conducted interviews with members of different ethnic minorities, mainly Jews and Russians living in Armenia, concerning the revival and reinvention of ethnic and religious identities. These two periods are divided by the collapse of the Soviet Union, in December 1991, and the emergence and development, or perhaps revival, of interethnic conflict between Armenians and Azerbaijanis. If one can describe the field of the first period (1981–1983) as quiet or stagnant, one must certainly characterize the second period (1988–1991) as a time of troubles. Yet despite the collapse of the Soviet Union and the contrast between these two periods, one can trace many continuities between them. It is these continuities, in my view, which make today's field specifically postsocialist rather than a transitory or transitional stage on the road toward a free market society.

After the Cold War: Changing Fields

During the Cold War, the socialist field was, in some respects, akin to a closed box which is only now beginning to open up. The field was particularly opaque for those Western scholars, particularly political scientists, who relied primarily on secondary sources. While certain countries of eastern Europe—notably, Poland, Romania, and Yugoslavia—allowed foreigners to conduct field research, the Soviet Union was relatively inhospitable to anthropologists and other fieldworkers. The resulting scholarly characterizations of the Soviet Union portrayed it primarily in terms of its contrast to the West: it was totalitarian, while the West was democratic; it had a centrally planned economy, while the West had a free market economy. These stereotypes, of course, ignored nuances in the complex social relationships which shaped Soviet politics, as well as the elaborate "gray" or "shadow" economy, whose operation, in fact, often kept the state-planned economy functioning. Since the collapse of the Iron Curtain and the Soviet Union, Western social scientists have gained much easier access to the field. No longer forced to rely on secondary sources, their attitudes and analyses have changed considerably. However, the possibility of carrying out fieldwork in these countries has introduced a new methodological problem: what kinds of narratives are best for describing and analyzing face-to-face interactions in these societies or, to be more precise, interactions with the people who live in them?

The Cold War logic which used to underlie descriptions of this part of the world was, as I noted above, often based on dichotomies. Part of this dichotomizing had to do with the people's predominant values. Thus, if Westerners believed in and valued democracy, human rights, and civil society, their Soviet counterparts rejected them or denied their value. When the socialist regimes collapsed, however, it became obvious that they had not, in fact, been supported by their citizens. A devastating earthquake in 1988 triggered an influx of Western aid workers, officials, social scientists, and nonscientists, who, to judge from those I met, prematurely concluded that "these people" were not so different after all. These Westerners concluded that the inhabitants of the socialist regimes actually held the same values as those held by people in the West, but they had just been unlucky and lived in repressive states. This assumption led logically to the next assumption— that the inhabitants of the socialist regimes were completely different from their states; in other words: "They are like us; it's just that they lack our technology and experience." To return to my initial comparison, one can say that social scientists and the other informed and interested observers with whom I discussed these matters after 1991 began to view the postsocialist field in the general framework of developing countries.

A few Western social scientists have opposed this post–Cold War tendency to search for similarities and instead prefer to think in terms of difference. For example, David Kideckel (1998) characterizes east-central Europe as a particular social type. In his view, this particularity casts doubt on the legitimacy of the concept of transition. He argues that theories of transition are based on the assumption that the qualities that defined the former socialist states are ephemeral and, therefore, likely to give way quickly to those of market societies.

As a "native" of the field, as a well as a professional observer, I, too, consider the postsocialist field a particular social type. Part of the reason for this particularity derives from the many features of socialist societies which persist in postsocialist societies, including an ideologized social life and lifecycle; pervasive state intervention in all spheres of social and private life; extremely ideologized perceptions of "us" and "others"; and a society extremely dependent on the state.

I would characterize the activity of those observers and scholars of post-socialism as similarity-hunting, an exercise I compare to cleansing or purification, in this case, the cleansing of socialist differences from postsocialist societies. Similarity-hunting aims to find, in the constructed and imagined social space of transition, at least enough similarity that these transitional societies can be compared with the "developing countries" more familiar to Western experience. In other words, through this process of similarity-hunting or cleansing, fieldworkers, among others, try to gain a handle on the new reality, adapt it to the mythology of transition, and, in this way, eliminate the differences that make it so mysterious or "other."

Important dimensions of this process of similarity-hunting consist of the ethical and cognitive preferences of the fieldworker (or interviewer), for these preferences result in a narration which includes both description and evaluation of the field. When an ethnographer runs into a situation where cognitive and ethical preferences seem to conflict, he or she sometimes simply tries to separate them, thus either pursuing data collection or passing a moral judgment on the society (Hastrup, as cited in Elizabeth Koepping 1994). This separation is not an easy task, even when studying stable societies. The more a society is involved in a transition or radical social change, the less one can find representative aspects or dimensions. Perhaps for this reason, some narrators/fieldworkers have found it helpful to analogize their experiences or problems in so-called transitional countries to the familiar discourse on Third World countries. This analogy, however, influences both the ethical and the cognitive attitudes during the course of fieldwork in postsocialist countries.

Narrating the field, then, cannot be a value-free exercise that takes place in a moral vacuum, as Elizabeth Koepping (1994) and Klaus-Peter Koepping (1994) have pointed out. When ethnographers select a limited number of aspects or dimensions of the field to represent this field as a whole, they are, in effect, passing a moral judgment on the field. As Tambiah (1985: 349) writes, "The close connection between the epistemological dimension and the moral requirements for achieving the epistemological aim of understanding and explaining difference becomes apparent as the virtually inseparable unity of the anthropological attitude."

Native and "Guest" Ethnographers

The meaning of *transition* for local ethnographers will become clearer if we consider the continuities between the socialist and postsocialist fields. As noted earlier, the important continuities include the extensive penetration and intervention of the state into all aspects of life as well as society's dependence on the state. These features strongly influenced the field and fieldwork in Armenia. In 1981–1983, when I was conducting research on rural communities and rural cultural traditions in Siunik, Ayrarat, and Shirak, historically defined regions in Armenia, I was "empowered" by the state to conduct interviews on any aspect of the private or social lives of the local people. My sense of being empowered came from my informants, who identified me with the state authorities, whether local or central, and saw me as someone with access to all the luxuries of urban life, from which they were so often deprived in this society of chronic shortages. This perceptual gap, between how they saw me and how I saw myself, formed a social and cultural setting reminiscent of the images of colonial anthropology, with its "white man's" detachment and objectivity.

At the same time, I was a participant in their private and social lives because they also perceived me as one of them, that is, as a fellow Armenian (see Živković, this volume, and De Soto, this volume, on the issue of being "insider" and "halfie" anthropologists). These two images set up a framework of constant oscillation between observation and participation during the fieldwork I carried out in Armenia in the early 1980s, and not only for me but for other ethnographers as well. We saw one reality in villages and rural communities—chronic shortages, lack of basic infrastructure such as roads, and steady depopulation—but we also knew what the state expected us to write about "actually existing socialism."

To a certain extent, our problem as Armenian ethnographers resembled the problem of the Western anthropologist who now arrives in the postsocialist and impoverished field, surrounded by an aura of power because he or she is seen to have access to the commodities and luxuries inaccessible to local people. This difference also creates a perceptual gap, but one which is even stronger than the one I felt in the field, because the Western anthropologist is not one of "us." In other words, while the native ethnographer can move between observation and participation, the Western anthropologist must settle for observation, his or her only accessible level of fieldwork.

My second period of fieldwork, in 1988–1991, coincided with the rapid weakening of the socialist state. For a local ethnographer to remain a detached observer empowered by the collapsing state in this polarized political setting, with ethnic tensions sharpening between Armenia and Azerbaijan, would have been practically impossible. Native ethnographers had to take sides, to participate and cease to oscillate or hesitate between observation and participation. In Armenia, the need to choose sides in turn polarized cognitive and ethical attitudes between participatory local ethnography and observant Western anthropology in an already highly polarized and ideologized postsocialist setting.

Dunja Rihtman-Auguštin (1998), a Croatian ethnographer, has observed that foreign anthropologists have a freedom and latitude, as well as a distance (in both a positive and negative sense), that are not possible for native ethnographers close to the field and its realities. For the Western anthropologist, observations and theories about postsocialism, whether it resembles "feudalism" (Verdery 1996) or "neo-capitalism" (Kideckel 1998), are both intellectually and ethically possible. For the native ethnographer, however, options are often reduced to just one—to join his or her people. The pressure to take sides is one of the important lessons the native ethnographer learns from doing fieldwork in a transitional continuum where no boundaries exist and where one chooses one's side or becomes an outsider. This is especially the case during times of trouble or war, when, as Rihtman-Auguštin (1998) observes, the field comes to the ethnographer.

In the postsocialist countries, local ethnographers have been trapped in the field: in the darkness of their apartments and departments, without electricity and without heat. In many cases, they stopped being observers and instead became part of the field itself. In Armenia, at the end of the 1980s and beginning of the 1990s, two choices opened up to local ethnographers. They could either let themselves be absorbed into the field and become political activists (thereby transforming a moral judgment into a political slogan) or try to become participant-observers (with an emphasis on the second term) by collecting data as insiders. Both positions had their professional and moral costs. This decision was no longer a matter of methodology, but rather one of professional and personal survival. Rihtman-Auguštin characterizes this notion of participation as "the moral question (and sometimes the courage) to be critically present" (1998: 141). In my view, such critical presence implies the requirement that one strive to demythologize new emerging myths, including the myths of transition. This kind of critical presence may face two challenges: one from local colleagues who have become absorbed into the myths of nationalism; the other from "authoritative" Western anthropologists who consider critical presence an unnecessary ethical spillover into a field which requires only a professional approach.

Interpreting the Field: Imagined Communities

Both native ethnographers who resist absorption into the field as activists and "guest anthropologists" encounter many pitfalls as they seek to interpret the field. When they try to balance participation and observation, fieldworkers sometimes resort, even unconsciously, to dominant images or paradigms that strongly shape their interpretation of the alien postsocialist field. For Armenia, one of the dominant explanatory patterns is based on traditional images of "starving Armenians." This image formed in the West during the second decade of this century, after the 1915 massacres of Armenians in eastern Turkey sent hundreds of thousands of Armenian refugees fleeing to Armenia and other countries of the Middle East. The stereotype was created and spread by Westerners, mainly missionaries and members of aid agencies such as Near East Relief, who described in their private letters and articles the sufferings of Christian Armenians. Later, this stereotype penetrated the academic discourse. For example, Arnold Toynbee (1915) described Armenians as a helpless people who needed protection and aid because of the persecutions to which they had been subject in the Ottoman Empire.

This image was incorporated into contemporary narratives on Armenian history, written by Western historians, mostly of Armenian origin, such as Richard Hovhannisian (1987) and others who described the suffering of Armenians caught between the hostile Byzantine, Persian, Ottoman, and Russian empires. Equally important, however, has been the impact of the fiction written about these historical events, in particular, the massacres of the first decades of this century. Both writers of Armenian origin, such as William Saroyan (1961) and Michael Arlen (1975), and non-Armenian writers, such as John Dos Passos (1966) and Arthur Koestler (1954), responded to memories of genocide by depicting the impoverished lives of Armenian refugees and their attempts to reconstruct their identity after genocide. The typical image of the Armenian people became that of a suffering people living in a small, landlocked homeland, a kind of Christian fortress surrounded by hostile "others."

The Sovietization of Armenia put an end to the stereotype of the starving Armenians, at least in Soviet Armenia; we cannot find similar descriptions in Soviet Armenian social science or in self-descriptions of Soviet Armenians. In the official discourse of the Soviet Armenian Academy of Sciences, Soviet Armenia appeared as one of the most prosperous republics of the Soviet Union and the one with the most highly educated population. Any deviation from the official line would have been defined as anti-Soviet activity.

The collapse of the Soviet Union put an end to this state-enforced interpretation. After the mass nationalist demonstrations of 1988 (described in Dudwick, this volume), the pogroms against Armenians in Azerbaijan, and especially after the earthquake of December 1988, the image of starving Armenians beset by ancient persecutions was suddenly revived. It became a mode of self-description in post-Soviet Armenia, particularly during the early years of "transition" (see Sargsyan 1990; Shnirelman 1993). Public discourse was filled with images of starving and freezing Armenians. A new addressee, the West (instead of the Kremlin), called forth a new interpretation of the field that posed images of current starvation versus future normalcy (which the West would bring) and replaced the Soviet-era images of current shortcomings versus the future normalcy of communism. In fact, this transitional mode of interpreting starving Armenians came to resemble that which developed in the West during the Cold War.

When projected into the field, this pattern overlaps with "actually existing" postsocialist reality. Certain social phenomena are selected from the field and help to create an imagined community of starving Armenians. This ideologized mode of explanation is comparable to the Soviet ethnographic explanatory pattern, which was based on an ideology asserting that people living in a socialist state could not be starving and which dismissed the actual problems of the people. Since this transitional mode of interpretation originated in the West, is rooted in Western stereotypes and perceptions about Armenians, and is addressed mainly to the West, it generates a vicious circle of representations, all of which originated in the West. Very often the real problems of local people remain outside this circle, as they often did in the ideologized fieldwork of Soviet ethnographers.

In Armenia, the image of starving Armenians became part of selective public performances for sometimes local, sometimes foreign audiences. After returning from a research trip in Armenia, for example, Nora Dudwick described to me the differences between group self-representations in a public forum and individual self-representations that emerged after the public meeting. She had attended a meeting at a school at which teachers, feeling they were particularly badly paid, discussed whether to go on strike. During the meeting, they described their everyday difficulties: ridiculously low salaries that left them unable to afford heat in winter, buy decent clothes, or even maintain adequate nutrition for themselves and their families. They spoke movingly of standing in front of their pupils to teach while almost fainting from hunger. After the meeting, when Dudwick chatted informally with the teachers, they took pains to assure her that in fact, they were well able to provide their households with food, and they stressed their ability to cope and survive. They had adjusted their collective public performance, with its political goal, to the image of starving Armenians, while privately and in interaction with a foreigner they readjusted individual images to show themselves as resourceful and fully capable of hospitality.

This account reminded me of my own interviewing experiences in 1981–1983, when people described their daily lives in terms of steady improvement, because they knew the rules of the game. At the same time, privately they complained about shortages, problems with corruption, and tensions with Azerbaijanis. The kinds of oppositions remained the same but played out in the reverse order: Under socialism, in public there were no significant problems, but in private, problems were discussed in jokes and gossip. In postsocialist Armenia, people complain in public, but privately confess that they have a whole array of strategies, ranging from remittances from relatives working abroad to unreported income from the informal economy, which help them cope and survive.

In my view, it is very important to evaluate this gap between public performance and private behavior as a continuation, not just a relic, of the socialist past, a continuation which leads many Armenians now to stress their suffering in public life as the public discourse in Soviet Armenia stressed prosperity. This gap is a very important dimension of the postsocialist field and one which creates a problem of cognitive and ethical dissonance.

This gap between public and private makes it more important for Western social scientists to think about new interpretive strategies and methodologies which will help them see behind the public "curtain." Without such strategies, Western social scientists will remain on the surface of public performances, looking for an explanation in the pattern of the "starving Armenians."

Local or native anthropologists may be able to bridge this gap between public and private by making their private life more visible in the public discourse. But this is not just a methodological problem. Sometimes it is dangerous to be accused of "washing one's clothes (or other people's) in public." This is primarily a problem of moral choice for native social scientists: How does one move from private participation to public observation and detachment? How can one put in writing what one knows privately, making it available for academic—but not only academic—communities without endangering people whom one has interviewed?

Observation and detachment are luxuries for local ethnographers living through a troubled transitional period that is filled with ethnic conflict. With the beginning of "transition" and "normalization," local fieldworkers may end up sacrificing professional observation for the sake of participation, and detached observation becomes a professional stance mainly available to foreign scholars. Sometimes, however, even foreign scholars may be pressured to join sides in ways which may challenge their professional and personal integrity (an issue Dudwick discusses in this volume).

In a different context, Mary Douglas (1991: 2) wrote about the anthropologist and "dirt" of the field: "There is no such thing as absolute dirt: it exists in the eye of the beholder. . . . Eliminating it is not a negative movement, but a positive effort to organize the environment." I agree with her first statement, that there is no such thing as absolute dirt or absolute purity in the field, that these exist in the eye of the beholder—in this case the Western scholar who has come to a "messy" postsocialist country in transition.

In the context of the postsocialist field, however, I cannot agree that eliminating dirt is a positive effort to organize the environment. Eliminating dirt can also be seen as a form of cleansing, an activity in which Soviet ethnographers once engaged and in which fieldworkers, both native and foreign, still engage when they try to rid the field conceptually of all those phenomena which do not fit either Marxist ideology about "actually existing socialism" or theories of development and transition to market societies. By eliminating those features of a field which an ethnographer considers ephemeral or "dirty" and unworthy, and therefore cognitively unimportant and irrelevant, he or she passes a moral or ideological judgment, all the more insidious because it is unconscious.

Note

This chapter was written while I was a research associate at the Institute for Russian, European and Eurasian Studies; I am very grateful for their support. I am also grateful to Bruce Parrot and Ilya Prizel, who helped me clarify some important points. I would like to thank Nora Dudwick, Hermine De Soto, Bruce Grant, Caroline Brettell, and an anonymous reviewer for their extensive and provocative comments on innumerable drafts of my chapter. I also wish to thank Mary Jo Heck, whose unusual insight helped me to develop ideas further in the chapter. Finally, I must thank Ariel Dudwick, who inspired me to complete the final draft.

References

Arlen, M. 1975. *Passage to Ararat.* New York: Ballantine.
Clifford, J. 1986. Introduction: Partial truths. In J. Clifford and G. E. Marcus, eds., *Writing culture: The poetics and politics of ethnography,* 1–26. Berkeley: University of California Press.
Dos Passos, J. 1966. *The best times.* New York: New American Library.
Douglas, M. 1991. *Purity and danger: An analysis of the concepts of pollution and taboo.* London: Routledge.
Hovhannisian, R. 1987. Foreword. In R. Hovhannisian, ed., *The Armenian genocide in perspective,* 1–3. New Brunswick, N.J.: Transaction Books.
Kideckel, David. 1998. Left behind: Labor, poverty, and subalternity in contemporary Romania. Paper presented at American Anthropological Association annual meetings.
Koepping, Elizabeth. 1994. Trust and its abuse in long-term fieldwork. *Anthropological Journal on European Cultures* 3 (2): 99–116.
Koepping, Klaus-Peter. 1994. Ethics in ethnographic practice: Contextual pluralism and solidarity of research partners. *Anthropological Journal on European Cultures* 3 (2): 21–38.
Koestler, A. 1954. *The invisible writing: An autobiography.* New York: Macmillan.
Rihtman-Auguštin, Dunja. 1998. An ethno-anthropologist in the native field: To observe or to witness? In Christian Giordano, Ina-Maria Greverus, and Regina Romhild, eds., *Reflecting cultural practice: The challenge of fieldwork,* part 1. *Anthropological Journal on European Cultures,* Special Issue 6 (2): 129–144.

Sargsyan, G. K. 1990. Nakhahaireniki Zhoghovrdi Kazmavorman yev Urartvi Masin (About the formation of the people of the proto-fatherland and Urartu). *Patma-Banasirakan Handes* 1 (128): 23–40.

Saroyan, W. 1961. *Here comes, there goes, you know who.* New York: Simon and Schuster.

Shnirelman, V. 1993. Struggle for past: Ethnogenetic studies and politics in the USSR. Abstracts. 13th International Congress of Anthropological and Ethnological Sciences.

Tambiah, S. 1985. *Culture, thought and social action.* Cambridge, Mass.: Harvard University Press.

Toynbee, A. J. 1915. *Armenian atrocities.* London and New York: Hodder and Stoughton.

Verdery, K. 1996. *What was socialism, and what comes next?* Princeton, N.J.: Princeton University Press.

7

Fieldwork and the "Doctoring" of National Identities in Arctic Siberia

David G. Anderson

Fieldwork in the Taimyr Autonomous District, 1992–1993

This chapter examines the ethical dilemmas of conducting anthropological field research in a small Siberian community of hunters, fishermen, and reindeer herders shortly after the collapse of the USSR. The field project lasted for 16 months and was situated in a variety of locations across the Russian Federation, including St. Petersburg, Moscow, Krasnoiarsk, Noril'sk, Dudinka, and the rural settlement of Khantaiskoe Ozero. This long list of locales is a product of the difficulties inherent in the study of this region. One of the necessary skills of becoming a Siberian ethnographer is the ability to negotiate one's way through a variety of settings, from the haughty academic salons of the central cities to the warm but modest welcome of a herdsman's hearth. In each of these encounters it is literally one's identity as a foreign scholar which serves as a passport to the next desk, kitchen table, or campfire. It is not difficult to imagine that being distinguished as a foreigner in a place far removed from the usual circuit of intellectuals and travelers has both its advantages and disadvantages. One's identity opens doors and people's hearts as much as it engenders suspicion or envy. All these reactions were encountered along the path to the settlement Khantaiskoe Ozero, located several hundred kilometers north of the Arctic Circle near the mouth of the Yenisei River. Rather than focus upon the dilemmas posed for the fieldworker by a puzzlement over what an anthropologist does, this

The author with harness reindeer near the river Gorbiachin (Photo by Mikhail Yelogir)

chapter will examine the dilemmas arising when people have a very clear idea of what an ethnographer is and the possible benefits that his or her learned opinion brings to local political struggles. During the harsh winter of 1992–1993, the Evenki, Dolgan, and Russian residents of Khantaiskoe Ozero gave this ethnographer a warm welcome, an honor that I accepted with reticence. Although in any fieldwork setting the professional outsider is often courted, cajoled, or ignored, in postsocialist settings the judgment of a European or American ethnographer is valued to an unusually high degree, primarily because of the ideological nature of Cold War rivalry. This leads to a special ethical dilemma. Although both common sense and the anthropologist's code of ethics dictate a strong and unconditional alliance between the fieldworker and the community, this chapter argues that, in the post-Soviet states, the act of writing ethnography is so politically charged that the student must apply his or her curiosity about culture with thoughtful caution. This is a theme shared with the contributions by Nora Dudwick, Marko Živković, and Keith Brown in this volume.

Of the year and a half invested in learning about Evenkis and Dolgans, this chapter focuses upon a small but intense portion of the project: an eight-month apprenticeship as a reindeer herder in the Number One Reindeer Brigade in the state farm Khantaiskii in 1992–1993. The time and the place are highly significant for this argument. This community is located in

one of the most northerly political-administrative districts in the Russian
Federation: the Taimyr Autonomous District. The district is paradoxically
located well away from the main centers of power and population, yet it
figures prominently in the political events which shaped the former Soviet
Union since the 1930s. The Taimyr is the homeland of five officially recognized aboriginal peoples: Nenetses, Dolgans, Enetses, Nias, and Evenkis.[1]
It is also the location of one of the largest nickel and cobalt mines and
smelters in the world, within the urban enclave of Noril'sk, populated with
300,000 immigrant workers (Bond 1984, 1985). For reasons of its proximity
to the Arctic coastline (which forms the northern border of the Russian
state) and for the strategic significance of the Noril'sk mining city, the district was closed to all foreigners until 1991. Although delegations of foreign
diplomats and engineers visited the city of Noril'sk throughout the Soviet
period, my arrival in Khantaiskoe Ozero by bush-plane in December 1992
was one of the first by a foreigner in this rural community during this century. It was also one of the few visits to be made by an ethnographer of any
nationality.[2] If the circumstances of my visit were not unique, the year of my
visit was a special one. The winter of 1992–1993 was unusual for its gale-
force winds and a snowfall that was four times the yearly average. The state-
owned aircraft which left me on the ice strip in front of the village airport
was the last to land on the lake until the same airplane (now privately
owned) landed in April of the following year. In addition to the chaos in the
transportation system, this blustery year marked the end of the regular
supply of subsidized allotments of gasoline, heating fuel, and even salaries
for the employees of the state farm, forcing them to turn inward to their own
resources. Thus the theme of what it meant to be a local person or an outsider was foremost on people's minds during the course of my fieldwork. I
have since returned to the region in years of more moderate weather (1995
and 1996) to discover that the institutionalized provision of social assistance, transport, and medical care has stabilized at a reduced level, as the
impoverished expectations of residents have. The anxiety over establishing
one's identity authoritatively before this outsider has also waned, but this
may be because my friends in the area are more familiar with my cautious
stance toward national identity and accept me more as a person than as a
visiting dignitary. Thus it is important to emphasize that my argument here
concerning the cautious use of the ethnographic gaze holds most strongly
during a particular period at the start of the much lauded "transition" and
more significantly during a particular period in my history with this particular community.

   What circumstances led me to choose this community for a doctoral thesis? My intention was to find a place and a people in the Russian subarctic
that bore a close resemblance to the geography and economy of the Cana-

dian subarctic. This design had much do with my biography. Before start-ing graduate work and before studying anthropology, I spent two sum-mers and a full year working for an Indian band government in the com-munity of Fort McPherson, Northwest Territories, between 1983 and 1986 (Ryan and Robinson 1990). My formal work consisted of assisting young Gwich'in activists in affixing boundaries and land descriptions on topo-graphical maps so that they might secure title to portions of their tradi-tional territory before it became criss-crossed with roads, pipelines, and well sites. However, the people of Fort McPherson also gave me the taste for living in an Arctic landscape, which let itself become known to people through stories, dreams, and the paths of animals. My doctoral project was designed to combine my new interest in learning more about the land with a political project of studying how economic development might be ac-complished less stressfully. Analytically, the study of an equivalent Siberian community—a community which was not struggling with the demands of privately owned mineral consortia—seemed a practical way to demonstrate that an Arctic landscape could be "developed" in a different manner. It is an irony of the anthropological enterprise that by the time my doctoral funding was arranged and my research visa approved, I found myself en route into an institutional environment governed by mineral consortia newly obsessed with privatization and foreign exports, much like in the Canadian Arctic. Although much of the critical symmetry had been erased from my research proposal by the time that I arrived in Taimyr, my knowl-edge of the Canadian North formed a very important silent part of my re-search. Much of my enthusiasm for spending long terms on the land in of-ten cold and cramped conditions came from an earlier introduction to this climate. My familiarity with cross-country skiing, splitting wood, and fetching water from under the ice kept me from being a useless, although not unclumsy, companion around the camps. Finally, my stories and pho-tographs gave a point of common contact with my Evenki hosts, for it turned out that they as well as I felt a common identity between the Cana-dian Arctic and the Russian Arctic and had a keen curiosity as to how life might be different across the polar sea.

It remains for me to introduce the people who hosted my studies. Khan-taiskoe Ozero has until recently been known as a predominantly Evenki settlement. Evenkis are members of one of the most widely dispersed na-tionalities in eastern Asia. They can be found in a wide arc starting at the northern edge of Kamchatka, descending along the Pacific interior into Manchuria and eastern Mongolia, and then ascending northwards along the Yenisei River valley into Taimyr. In the 1989 census their population within the Russian Federation was 29,901 (with 311 living in Taimyr). The Taimyr represents the northwesternmost point of their settlement. They are

Nikolai Savalevich Utokogir rounding up harness reindeer on the Number One Reindeer Brigade (Photograph by David Anderson)

perhaps best known to the English-language reader for their *hamanil* (shamans), who had privileged knowledge of the spirits of animals, people, and places (Shirokogoroff 1935). In 1969 a large influx of Yakut-speaking Evenkis and Dolgans forcibly swelled the population of Khantaiskoe Ozero from just under 300 to over 600 individuals, such that the community is now more often associated with the newcomers than with its original inhabi- tants. These new neighbors arrived by military transport carriers on one cold autumn day when district planners in Dudinka decided to "liquidate" another sparsely populated village called Kamen', located 400 kilometers northeast of Khantaiskoe Ozero. The goal of the planners was to consoli- date native peoples into larger villages to facilitate the provision of educa- tion, sanitation, and redistribution. The 1960s were a time of great resettle- ments all over Siberia (Chichlo 1981; Grant 1995; Slezkine 1994). What was significant about this resettlement was that the planners felt that the Yakut- speaking newcomers embodied a higher level of civilization and efficiency, which was bound to impact upon the local Evenkis with a "weaker culture." To paraphrase an archived manuscript of the early state ethnographer A. A. Popov, Dolgans were considered to be an "avant-garde people" (*peredovoi narod*). The enforced resettlement of Dolgans into a small Evenki commu- nity quite predictably precipitated many conflicts over accommodation and access to goods. The everyday struggle for position between native Evenkis and Dolgan newcomers often manifests itself in nationalist slurs or the occasional tragic brawl not unlike the situation described by Nora Dudwick before the explosion of armed nationalist struggle in Armenia.

The directed tidying of a diffuse ethnic landscape was only one late manifestation of applied ethnographic action in the Soviet state (cf. Anderson 1995). A hallmark of Soviet state ethnography has been a concern with inscribing those boundaries between people which later became real administrative borders. As other anthropologists have taught us, the most intense expression of ethnic distinctiveness is often at the boundaries between ethnic groups and not in their heartlands (Barth 1969; Plaice 1990). Thus in Taimyr, a meeting place of five different aboriginal "nations," the practice of ethnography is far from a naive endeavor. Unlike in similar settings in the Canadian Arctic where anthropology is distrusted for its role in first establishing and then questioning ethnic boundaries, in the former Soviet Union ethnography is read deeply for signs which reflect a nation's soul. With this introduction the stage is set to discuss the drama of conducting fieldwork in a place obsessed with generating ethnography.

Fieldwork in the Shadow of the State Ethnographers

Soviet state socialism was slow to reach the Evenkis living near the shores of the volcanic lake known as Khantaiskoe Ozero. It is tempting to accredit this fact to their physical isolation in the rocky fjords of the Putoran Mountain range or to the harsh blizzards that buffet this mainland peninsula, which extends beyond 74° north latitude into the Arctic Ocean. In fact the aboriginal peoples of what came to be known as the Taimyr Autonomous District were reticent to submit to the state the regulation of their autonomously managed trading network, which linked together three major river systems of eastern Asia. In 1923 the Soviet government claimed jurisdiction over Taimyr after an extended battle with counterrevolutionary forces in the Zabaikal region and in Yakut *guberniia.* In 1932 they quelled a civil uprising led by native leaders of three nationalities in the Taimyr settlement of Volochanka. Only in 1938, judging from trade accounts and subsidy ledgers, did the Soviet state come to regulate this peninsula legitimately. One of the first Soviet envoys to reach Taimyr in 1930, after the state veterinarian (who covertly counted wealth in animals) but before the armed troops of the state political police (who crushed the Volochanka uprising of 1932), was a state ethnographer. A careful reading of his published and unpublished work shows that the people who were reticent to surrender their freedom of movement were as cautious about representing their identity.

Andrei Aleksandrovich Popov was a pathbreaker for Soviet state ethnography. His nuanced writings on the ritual and philosophy of Nia shamans have inspired students and embarrassed partocrats (Popov 1966, 1984). Many of his finer studies remain unpublished and jealously guarded in the vaults of the Museum of Anthropology and Ethnography in St. Petersburg. His first ethnographic mission as a graduate student was to study the "Dolgano-Yakuts" of Turukhansk Territory or, more specifically, "to link the Dolgan to [one of] the Turkish, Tungus-Manchurian, or Paleoasiatic [language] groups."[3] A. A. Popov (1954) was eventually to publish his opinion that Dolgans were a "special population" distinct from Evenkis and Yakuts, although this authorized verdict as to their bounded national identity was extracted only after much political negotiation (Anderson 1995). Popov's early published and unpublished work reveals a fascination with multivalent clan appellations and complex identities, which implied that individuals had more than one nationality, or could at least change their nationality several times during their life (Popov 1934, 1946). Most interesting is the fact that his writings seem deliberately to avoid constructing pedigrees for the five neighboring nationalities of Taimyr, as if to suggest that Evenkis, Dolgans, and Sakhas blend together in a complex spectrum. Perhaps his most beautiful description of Taimyr was as a "wondrous mosaic" composed of "colorful and dappled nationalities" which "divide themselves into many different groups" belying the traditional appellations of ethnographic maps.[4] Popov's early disdain for ethnographic maps notwithstanding, the engineers of Soviet state craft declared the Taimyr to be a Dolgan territory in 1932 and signified this by placing the word in the formal name of the new district (the "Taimyr Dolgano-Nenets District"). In the same year the histories and pedigrees of Evenki-speaking people were encapsulated within the Evenki Autonomous District, located directly to the south of Taimyr. Similarly, the long tradition of a Sakha (Yakut) presence on the Taimyr Peninsula was shifted to the east within the new boundaries of the Yakut Autonomous Republic. The exact reasons for this ethnographic rationalization cannot be determined. The archival record is scarce. However, documents scattered among five cities suggest that state-makers in Moscow feared border conflicts and expansion from an aggressive Yakut republic and thus were predisposed to molding ethnographic opinion to turn a Yakut-speaking people into a "special population." In 1960 this special population became more concrete with the official renaming of many Taimyr Evenkis (as well as Enetses and Sakhas) as Dolgans (Dolgikh 1963). Physically, the shattering of the mosaic was concluded with the great resettlements of 1969, a process of ethnic tidying which owes its origin to the applied action of state ethnographers.

The politically inspired "doctoring" of Popov's subtle field diaries is a characteristic feature of Soviet state ethnography. The ethnographic tradition in Soviet Russia differed from its Euro-American cousin not so much in its method as in its practice. Russian ethnographers were carrying out stationary fieldwork with a theoretical interest before Boas or Malinowski. After the revolution, the fieldwork experience of professional ethnographers became drawn out into an entire career of multiple one-month visits, which, as Bruce Grant suggests, makes Soviet ethnography something closer to ethnosociology.[5] Although fieldwork was not foreign to Russian ethnography, the writings of ethnographers (and after the revolution, their salaries) were always tightly interwoven with the prerogatives of good bureaucratic administration. Whenever lines were carved into landscapes, ethnographers held the scalpel. The deliberate redistributive calculus of subsidies and expropriation was factored according to the lifestyles of officially recognized national groups (Anderson 1996a). State ethnographers, until recently, wrote the nationality policies for state ministries and the governing party. In the post-Soviet period, the director of the Institute of Anthropology and Ethnography, Valerii Tishkov, continues to contribute to the public agenda on nationality policy (cf. Tishkov 1998). The hierarchical staircase that professional ethnographers climbed tended to merge at its higher levels with the hierarchy of state power. According to the authors of this volume, this was not an uncommon phenomenon over the formerly socialist space (see especially Silverman on the Bulgarian Roma or the Pomaks, who "do not exist"). This genre of ethnography also should not be completely foreign to Euro-Americans. The examples of anthropologists working by the side of the colonial officers of the British Empire or contemporary anthropologists who work for departments of Indian affairs provide parallels closer to home. What is surprising for an anthropologist trained in the Euro-American tradition is the strength and casualness of people's assumptions that ethnographers are charged with a political task (Gellner 1975). I argue that this attitude, which is a distinct legacy of the mechanism of the Soviet state, forces the fieldworker to make difficult choices.

In conducting fieldwork with a brigade of Evenki hunters and reindeer ranchers in this area in 1993, I had difficulty in explaining many things about my student life in Cambridge, England, or my rural upbringing in western Canada. The least of my problems was explaining who an ethnographer was. An ethnographer "finds out who we are," "explains about our culture," "wants to hear about the old things," "comes to collect the names of things." The younger generation had read some ethnography in boarding school. The older women remembered the faces of those state ethnographers who had visited briefly during their month-long summer expeditions. Soviet state ethnographers had always been warmly accepted here, for un-

like the state economists or the state veterinarians, their job was to understand the ways in which the activities and ideas of the people were different.
The other specialists had always come to measure the degree to which the
people had lagged behind the homogeneity of the "plan." Although the
history of contact with a socialist state in the Taimyr had been short, albeit dramatic, most people shrewdly understood the potential value of an
ethnographer for the well-being of their nation.

The Invitation to Criticize

If Soviet state ethnographers were eagerly welcomed, a Canadian ethnographer was welcomed with great enthusiasm. With a pleasant but unexpected display of Cold War binary logic, it was felt that a representative of
a state which was not bothered with building socialism was automatically
eager to receive ideas of building something different and somehow better.
Over and over I was asked to recount the story of how Canadian Indians
lived on "their own lands" and "controlled their own lives" through their
reservations. Stories circulated the village, which were falsely attributed to
me, of how Canadian "Eskimo" reindeer herders used their own private hel-
icopters to drive immense herds of reindeer or of how hunters used sophisticated night-vision glasses to stalk wild reindeer at night. (Needless to say
the true authors of these stories were several American serial films which
had been shown on state television.) Anecdotes such as these must be universal to any fieldworker in Russia or, for that matter, in many other parts
of the world (see especially Barsegian; Zanca; and Kuehnast, all in this volume).

What interests me is not the negation of the perceived shortcomings of
one's own society for an emancipatory ideal of "Amerika" but instead the
eagerness of young Evenkis to win the censure of the foreign anthropologist in regard to the backwardness of many local practices (see also Zanca,
this volume). One is asked to concur with such statements: "This snowmobile is junk but it is all we have"; "I suppose in the Canadian North you
never have to wait for a helicopter-taxi so long—that is how we live"; "Have
a drink with us—these spirits are bad, but this isn't Canada you know." I
should immediately add that the requested authoritative criticism applied
only to practices and tools in the public sphere; all people were proud of
their families, hospitality, and knowledge of the land. Answering such statements proves difficult. The expected reply that "yes, indeed, this snowmobile is a pile of junk" seems to stick in one's throat, but to praise the machine
or, indeed, the idea of a helicopter-taxi is to invite a somewhat sharp and
distant smirk. To confirm such statements is to do more than to validate the
hierarchical position of the West or to surmount one's own vanity by ad-

mitting that Westerners are too weak to tolerate such conditions. It draws one into a political field wherein the anthropologist has a passive role. The topic under debate here is not the technical design of the left snowmobile piston but what is expressed with the statement, "You agree that the system has treated us badly." The implicit solution is not the importation of Bombardier snow machines (since such an act of consumer choice was then unthinkable for a state farm member) but an attack on the order of things, be it the director of the farm, the agricultural administration, or the Russianness of the faces that arrive to barter and haggle. In contrast to Barsegian's conclusions (this volume), it is my conviction that in conversations of this type the anthropologist has a duty to question directly the local value framework rather than automatically to endorse the cynicism that erodes public institutions, even though they indeed might be corrupt. This, however, does not mean that traditions of trade or economic organization need be displaced, silenced, or smirked at. With reference to the example introduced here, one might produce the curious replies: "Yes, the piston is weak, but it only costs fifty cents to replace, and not fourteen dollars"; or "The Canadian trapper must sell over one hundred marten skins to pay for a Skidoo" (as opposed to being given one free of charge). The effect of such a dialogue widens the range of political options rather than surrendering to "the market," "the state," or (worse) "the transition" the quality of being a necessary historical process. This dialogue need not be condescending, especially in a context where people themselves acknowledge the appropriateness of consulting the history of particular settings (in this case, indigenous communities in the Canadian Arctic rather than "Amerika") and, perhaps more pragmatically, in a context where one lone voice can easily be ignored.

Here I do not want to make the relativistic argument that familiar forms of power are preferable when one appreciates their context. However, this is understandably a common interpretation of such statements. It is a difficult task to communicate alternatives to the consuming and violent competition of corrupt fragments of the former state economy. Making analogies to the Soviet past is one attempt to demonstrate that things could be different, although often it is misunderstood as conservatism. My nationalist Evenki tent mate would sometimes sneer at the "rose-colored words" he presumed I kept in my voluminous notebooks. In this time of great institutional change, I feel one must resist the invitation to transplant the image of the Canadian Arctic as a shiny but bald alternative without at least attempting to build a healthy bricolage of ideas that allow people to think about *different* institutions. To continue with my example of the snowmobile parts, the comparison of the Canadian trapper's situation with that of the state farm hunter negates the implied model of state redistributive power, wherein the access to things is a reflection of one's social status, and it posits a more complex situation regarding the comparative advantage of different political and economic systems for the actor.

The dilemma of being asked to share the criticisms of others can also be found in the main core of ethnographic action. The foreignness of one's identity only accentuates the political potential of a discipline that is already assumed by one's hosts to possess the influence associated with Soviet state ethnography. In the course of fieldwork there are plenty of opportunities to get involved in local vendettas and power struggles. Again, this is a challenge in any field site, as both Nora Dudwick and Daphne Berdahl eloquently discuss in this volume. However, in this disintegrating postsocialist state, the ethnographer is presumed to possess a prescient insight into the boundaries that divide people. As outlined above, the village of Khantaiskoe Ozero is fractured into Dolgan, Evenki, and Yakut-speaking Evenki groups following the strategically planned resettlement of one entire village from the North. The Dolgan newcomers came with the frontier conviction that they had been brought to raise the cultural level of the "Tungusy" (to use their vernacular and somewhat insulting name for the local Evenkis). It must be remembered that in Russia, both popularly and in scientific articles, the word *kul'tura* (culture) is used synonymously with the word for "civilization." Having been ascribed as a cultural technician, I was proudly shown many examples of this cultural stratification in action.

The Tungusy are lazy, are they not? They are shy about wearing their national clothes, and they have forgotten their language. They are so poor. Why do you study them? There is no culture there.

The Dolgans just hoard things to themselves. They are like that. They don't even feed their relatives. When they came here, they just took over and walked around like special people. They talk about us in their own language, yet we try to speak Russian to them. Yet they are pretty backward. They always walk around in skins and beads. You can smell them in the village store.

It does not take an experienced fieldworker to know that one nod or grunt automatically shifts the scales of evolution one way or the other in this postsocialist setting, as in any other. Diplomatic distance can also be perceived as being arrogant or permissive. If the number of my house visits favored one community or the other, I could expect to be confronted on the street and questioned why I refused hospitality. An equitable investment of time is also delicate, since it once led to the rumor that "this Canadian is nothing special; he drinks with anyone at all." I never came up with a solution to this tender situation other than in the end exclusively allying myself clearly with the local, Khantaiskoe Evenkis.

However, the exclusive Evenki invitation to apply my ethnographic calipers to document the antiquity of their "forgotten history" is to this day an uncomfortable one. During my fieldwork it was often flattering to have elders create carvings on mammoth ivory to establish the originality of their designs or to have the design of a beaded pattern punctuated with explanations as to the origins of semiprecious tsarist-era beads. However, the enthusiasm with which younger herders labeled my topographical maps with Evenki appellations often had a bitter edge, as if they wished to negate the presence of their neighbors. An ethnographer's attempt to deal sensitively with this dilemma will be insufficient if he or she either romanticizes local knowledge or negotiates a clever position as an "in-betweener" (as Dudwick and Barsegian both discuss in this volume). Although in either case the ethnographer may free himself from the narrative of his home discipline, he surrenders himself to the web of power within which the discipline is understood locally. Though it may be fine to suggest, as Igor Barsegian does in this volume, that "the field" should imprint itself on the visiting anthropologist, one must remember that "the field" often craves the attention, opinion, and authoritative imprint of the anthropologist. The legacy of state ethnography in Taimyr, and in the postsocialist space generally, is such that the fluid boundaries between identity groups, be they Evenki/Dolgan, Armenian/Azerbaijan, or Vlach/Macedonian, have been made solid and impermeable partly through official ethnographic action. More tragically, it would seem that the concerted practice of state ethnographers and administrators has doctored the intersecting and multidimensional quality of identity in favor of the single word that is printed in personal identity documents or on maps. It is for this reason, I believe, that the opinion of the foreign anthropologist is eagerly sought, to inject new meaning into what in my view are very narrow and confining national categories. The ethical point here is, once again, that the foreign anthropologist should find the courage to engage in tacitly accepted constructions with the hope that "naive" (and not so naive) questioning may help local activists to look upon longstanding feuds in a different light (see De Soto, this volume). I accepted the Evenki invitation to learn about national identity, but I refused to answer the burning issue of which group was more "cultured." Instead, I often discussed similarities in the design of appliqué and in hunting practice with Evenkis and Dolgans. In my doctoral dissertation I applied myself to uncovering how the understanding of practice and culture was constructed by state managers and local hunters in concert (thus implying that it might have been constructed differently in a context where a socialist state was not so keenly interested in defining national identity).

The Invitation to Diagnose

So far I have introduced many small but apt illustrations of the management of everyday life in order to portray the peculiar tasks presented to an
anthropologist in a disintegrating postsocialist state. As my final example,
I wish to introduce not tacit but explicit demands for the professional help
of the foreigner as anthropologist.

As a result of the prescriptions of policy scientists, the organizational
characteristics of Evenki and Dolgan society have been shifted from an extensive and flexible relationship among people, between people and animals, and between people and the land to an encapsulated and, in many
ways, isolated form of social life. Elementary genealogies demonstrate that
Evenkis have become forced to imagine themselves as distinct from Dolgans, who might have been cross-cousins (or for that matter Evenkis) in another time and place. The introduction of a national pedigree when added
to generally hazardous living conditions has led individuals, usually older
women, to ask, "Will we survive as a people?" This is seen as a fundamentally anthropological question.

The question of national survival has controversial implications. Older
sisters complain that their younger siblings have no one to marry: "Who is
there for her to marry? That one drinks; she is related to that one; that one
is violent." Indeed, it is immediately obvious that the practice which is seen
by local Russians as a sign of moral decay, the practice of "finding children
from outside," is a common strategy among young women. Fathers can be
sought among a modest but sizable population of transitory professionals,
from engineers, to geologists, to humble anthropologists. There are a number of reasons to see this as a creative strategy and not as "moral decay." In
a small and isolated society, it may be difficult to follow the rules of exogamy, and this is made doubly difficult if there is a large number of deaths
in the cohort of unmarried men. Furthermore, in a highly colonized community, professionals or transient outsiders may be seen as "more cultured"
or "more attractive." But from another point of view, one should not put
such a passive interpretation on the actions of women. Although men who
stay to be resident fathers are no doubt valued, the new citizens who are labeled by the social welfare people as "single-parent children" are regardless
seen as a joy, even though they create a crying need for social security payments and for meat from the land. As one grandmother remarked: "I don't
know where she found that child, but you see now he's grown and walks
around. Isn't that good?"

Despite the joy that mothers and grandmothers have in their children,
there is a nagging thought that things have got out of control. In different
contexts the same women might complain: "There are so few real Evenkis
around"; or "The Evenkis are becoming fewer and fewer each year." Al-

Children playing between the houses in the village of Khantaiskoe Ozero (Photograph by David Anderson)

though younger women consciously respect rules of exogamy, there seems to be a new received ideology that ideally "we must marry our own." This ideology seems to overlap with and be reinforced by the moral censure of the local Russians, who see a strategy of national endogamy as a sign of pride in one's nation. This also seems to be the subtle subtext to state ethnographic texts which carefully measure and evaluate the ratio of interethnic marriages in order to qualify ethnic groups as proper nations (for example, Bromlei 1969). This mismatch of ideology and practice was thrown to me once as a professional challenge: "You have been sitting here for months writing things, working with the household registries. Well, what future is there for us? You're an ethnographer. You must know these things. Why are you silent? In twenty years, will there be Evenkis or not?" At the time I was shocked by the question and by the uncharacteristic force behind the words. I found that my answers, which expressed my upbringing of anthropological relativism, did not produce the desired effect. Theoretically, I argued, it is the mothers who bring up children as Evenkis or not Evenkis. "Everything is in their hands," I urged. Drawing examples from the Canadian North, I spoke of communities where individuals who were descended from First Nation and French or Scottish marriages either integrated themselves into status Indian communities or, more radically, proudly spoke of themselves as a métis nation. Again, I received those distant and cold eyes as a reply. My words were taken as an evasion of the question—and perhaps they were.

Reflecting now on these experiences, I wonder if I should have accepted this invitation to be a "cultural doctor" giving a diagnosis of the health or sickness of this constructed community. This is a role very similar to that of the shamans of the past or of the psychic *ekstrasensy* who from time to time give paid performances in these northern communities. Righteously, I can defend my sympathetic silence by noting that the engineered national boundaries and overcrowded houses have as much to do with me as do the acid rains and heavy metals that are spewed out over the land from the mining city of Noril'sk. I did not make them, and I do not have to answer for them. Perhaps it was too easy to emphasize that I was a foreign anthropologist and that therefore I had no opinion on a nationality program that was as strange to me as it was stifling to them. I think now that this was an equally convenient display of the same Cold War binary logic that I criticized above.

To accept the invitation to diagnose the careers of nations leads one to difficult conclusions. The answer to the old woman's question is certainly no. No: under the conditions of predatory commercial exploitation and the abdication of the Russian redistributory state, the Evenkis as a tightly defined nation cannot persist. No: by living within a narrowly defined national group, the Evenkis will not be, and perhaps should not be, a "great nation" like the Russians. To answer this question is to feel for the impossible position of the community, but I will argue it does not lead to despair. An honest answer does not begrudge the people the respect that they ask for in displaying their courage in managing a hard, encapsulated world. There is, after all, a certain pride fostered by having the strength and resourcefulness to live in difficult conditions. This is the same pride that the snowmobile operator shows in working with a weak machine or that the Dolgan settler shows in trying to "civilize" a difficult people. Perhaps it is the duty of the anthropologist to respect this courage by taking seriously their desire to understand the future. Thus while one might argue that the ethnographic tradition here has been heavily imprinted by past works of social surgery, it may be possible to subvert this role of one who "doctors nations" by instead encouraging people to imagine a life beyond the symptoms of national rivalry.

Beyond State Ethnography

Instead of following the path of the state ethnographers, this chapter encourages those who work in post-Soviet spaces to test out a different ethical position. To engage with people in the field of clinical ethnography is a somewhat different path from what is often taught in the profession; in postsocialist settings it is one that is a problem because of the residue of the Cold War. Anthropologists are trained to react to their informants with sympathy and/or with advocacy. In discussing this chapter with other students in Cambridge, I was offered a range of suggestions along this spectrum. American students suggested debating the dilemma of national identity in the public media. An Asian Indian student suggested a warm but taciturn empathy: "For what point is there in stirring up trouble if you are not there?" A Russian student suggested a different form of advocacy by alerting the state authorities to a flaw in their national categories. In all three cases the perceived needs of the culture "out there" under study are passively given primacy over the exchange of opinions about the broader question, How should people live? It is precisely this very subjective and moral question that is at issue in every interaction within the postsocialist states. By giving an honest diagnosis of how a narrowly defined national category might disappear, one accepts the invitation to think, alongside one's field hosts, about how the future can be lived without the burden of building a nation. This is perhaps a situation not unsimilar to that described by Keith Brown where a Vlach husband (C——) and a Macedonian wife (A——) prefer *not* to discuss national discreteness "here and now," but instead celebrate national solidarity. A blunt diagnosis in these contexts indicates that the anthropologist affirms that the lives of those who do not hold national identities of world-historical significance are interesting and worthy to learn about in their own right. This stance is a challenge not so much to the students of ethnic boundaries, such as Frederick Barth, as to the appropriateness of their methods. In post-Soviet places, controversial boundaries are not so much curious objects of study as *symptoms* of a complex interaction between people and state ethnographers. In a context where the relationship between state and citizen is being shaken, it may be equally interesting for the anthropologist to initiate a dialogue about these symptoms rather than assume that ethnic boundaries are intrinsic to human self-worth and health.

In this chapter I have given an impression of the types of unique dilemmas that the foreign anthropologist faces when working in that domain colonized by the state ethnographers. I argue that the anthropologist should not be drawn blindly into sympathizing with people over practices that they find unseemly or unworthy. Such a strategy of appeasement does not bring the structure of power into the dialogue. However, the anthropologist, in order to show respect for peoples living in difficult situations, should endeavor to try to initiate a dialogue by actively circulating his or her queries about the problems at hand. In this time of change, this means trying to engage with the difficult questions of how people live and what the future may hold for them. It is only through such a dialogue that the binary stereotypes of the Cold War can be gradually deconstructed.

Notes

1. English-language reference works on the peoples of Siberia are Levin and Potapov 1964; and Forsyth 1992. A recent summary of the ethnography and politics of Taimyr is Anderson 1996b. Classic Russian-language ethnographies on each people include Khomich 1976 (Nentsy); Dolgikh 1963 (Dolgany); Vasil'ev 1963 (Entsy); Gracheva 1983b (Nganasany); and Rychkov 1917, 1922, 1923 (Evenki). In this chapter I use the singular form of the name that people call themselves as a root. The terms enclosed in parentheses in the previous sentence are the Russian-language ethnographic standards.

2. For reports of other field expeditions to Khantaiskoe Ozero, see Tugolukov 1963, 1985; and Gracheva 1983a. Notes on the region surrounding Khantaiskoe Ozero can be found in Lebedeva 1960; and Vasilevich 1951, 1972; and passim in Stepanov 1835; Middendorf 1860; Kastren 1860; and Tret'iakov 1869. Ziker (1996) reports on a recent trip to the area.

3. This quotation from Popov, as well as the one on page 134, is from an unpublished report preserved in the Krasnoiarsk Center for the Preservation and Study of Contemporary Documentation (the Party Archive), F.28 op.1 d.24 1.1; my translations.

4. Manuscript Archive, Museum of Anthropology and Ethnography, St. Petersburg, F.14 op.1 d.149 1.6.

5. For engaging histories of Russian ethnography, see Grant 1995; Plotkin and Howe 1985; and Stocking 1991. For examples of early ethnography see Shternberg 1998; Bogoras 1909; and Jochelson 1926.

References

Anderson, D. G. 1995. *National identity and belonging in Arctic Siberia: An ethnography of Evenkis and Dolgans at Khantaiskoe Ozero, Taimyr Autonomous District.* Doctoral thesis, University of Cambridge. Published by University Microfilms International 9708311.

Anderson, D. G. 1996a. Bringing civil society to an uncivilised place: Citizenship regimes in Russia's Arctic frontier. In C. M. Hann, and E. Dunn, eds., *Civil society: Approaches from anthropology,* 99–120. London: Routledge.

Anderson, D. G. 1996b. The aboriginal peoples of the Lower Yenisei Valley: An ethnographic overview of recent political developments in North Central Siberia. *Polar Geography and Geology* 19 (3): 184–218.

Barth, F. 1969. *Ethnic groups and boundaries: The social organization of cultural difference.* Boston: Little, Brown.

Bogoras, W. G. 1909. *The Chukchee.* Jesup North Pacific Expedition, 7. Leiden: E. J. Brill.

Bond, A. R. 1984. Economic development at Noril'sk. *Soviet Geography* 25: 354–368.

Bond, A. R. 1985. Northern settlement family style: Labor planning and population policy in Norilsk. *Soviet Geography* 26 (1): 26–47.

Bromlei, Y. V. 1969. Etnos i endogamiia. *Sovetskaia etnografiia* 6: 84–91.

Chichlo, B. 1981. Les nevuqaghmiit ou la fin d'une ethane. *Inuit Studies* 5 (2): 29–47.

Dolgikh, B. O. 1963. Proiskhozhdenie dolgan. In B. O. Dolgikh, ed., *Sibirskii etnograficheskii sbornik.* 5, Trudy instituta etnografii AN SSSR (novaia seriia), 84, pp. 93–141. Moscow: Nauka.

Forsyth, J. 1992. *A history of the peoples of Siberia: Russia's north Asian colony 1581–1990.* New York: Cambridge University Press.

Gellner, E. 1975. The Soviet and the savage. *Current Anthropology* 16 (4): 595–617.

Gracheva, G. N. 1983a. Poezdka k zapadnym dolganam. *Polevye issledovaniia instituta etnografii 1979,* 59–68. Moscow: Nauka.

Gracheva, G. N. 1983b. *Traditsionnoe mirovozzrenie okhotnikov Taimyra.* Leningrad: Nauka.

Grant, B. 1995. *In the Soviet house of culture: A century of perestroikas.* Princeton, N.J.: Princeton University Press.

Jochelson, W. 1926. *The Yukaghir and the Yukaghirized Tungus.* American Museum of Natural History Memoir, 9. Leiden: E. J. Brill.

Kastren, M. A. 1860. *Puteshestvie v Sibir' 1845–1849.* In Magazin zemlevedeniia i puteschestvii, tom 6, chast'2, pp. 199–482. St. Petersburg: Folovoi.

Khomich, L. B. 1976. *Problemy etnogeneza i etnicheskoi istorii nentsov.* Leningrad: Nauka.

Lebedeva, E. P. 1960. K kharakteristike severnogo narechiia evenkiiskogo iazyka (po materialam govorov B. Poroga i Agaty). *Uchenye zapiski Leningradskogo Gosudarstvennogo Pedagogicheskego Instituta* 167: 137–170.

Levin, M. G., and L. P. Potapov. 1964. *The peoples of Siberia.* Chicago: University of Chicago Press.

Middendorf, A. 1860. *Puteshestvie na sever i vostok Sibiri.* St. Petersburg: Tip. Imperatorskoi Akademii Nauk.

Plaice, E. 1990. *The native game.* St. John's, England: Institute of Social and Economic Research.

Plotkin, V., and J. E. Howe. 1985. The unknown tradition—continuity and innovation in Soviet ethnography. *Dialectical anthropology* 9 (1–4): 257–312.

Popov, A. A. 1934. Materialy po rodovomu stroiu dolgan. *Sovetskaia etnografiia* 6: 116–139.

Popov, A. A. 1946. Semeinaia zhizn'u dolgan. *Sovetskaia etnografiia* 4: 50–74.

Popov, A. A. 1954. Dolgany. In M. G. Levin, and L. P. Potapov, eds., *Narody Sibiri,* 742–759. Moscow: Nauka.

Popov, A. A. 1966. *The Nganasan: The material culture of the Tavgi Samoyeds.* The Hague: Mouton and Co.

Popov, A. A. 1984. *Nganasany: Sotsial'noe ustroistvo i verovaniia.* Leningrad: Nauka.

Ryan, J., and M. Robinson. 1990. Implementing participatory action research in the

Canadian North: A case study of the Gwich'in Language and Cultural Project. *Culture* 10 (2): 57–71.

Rychkov, K. M. 1917, 1922, 1923. Eniseiskie Tungusy. *Zemlevedenie* 24 (1–2): 1–67; 25 (1–2): 69–106; 25 (3–4): 107–149.

Shirokogoroff, S. M. 1935. *Psychomental complex of the Tungus.* London: Kegan Paul, Trench, Trubner.

Shternberg, L. 1998. *The social organization of the Gilyak.* Edited by B. Grant. New York: American Museum of Natural History.

Slezkine, Y. 1994. *Arctic mirrors: Russia and the small peoples of the North.* Ithaca, N.Y.: Cornell University Press.

Stepanov, A. P. 1835. *Ocherki istorii Eniseiskaia guberniia.* St. Petersburg: Tip. Konrada Vingebera.

Stocking, G. 1991. Maclay, Kubary, Malinowski: Archetypes from the dreamtime of anthropology. In G. W. Stocking, ed., *Colonial situations: Essays in the contextualization of ethnographic knowledge,* History of Anthropology, vol. 7: 9–74. Madison: University of Wisconsin Press.

Tishkov, Valery. 1998. U.S. and Russian Anthropology: Unequal Dialogue in a Time of Transition. *Current Anthropology* 39 (1): 1–18.

Tret'iakov, P. I. 1869. Turukhanskii krai. *Zapiski Imperatorskogo Russkogo Geograficheskogo Obshchestva po obshchei geografii* 2: 215–531.

Tugolukov, V. A. 1963. Khantaiskie Evenki. In B. O. Dolgikh, ed., *Sibirskii etnograficheskii sbornik,* vypusk 5, Trudy instituta etnografii AN SSSR (novaia seriia), tom 84, pp. 5–32. Moscow: Nauka.

Tugolukov, V. A. 1985. *Tungusy (Evenki i Eveny) srednei i zapadnoi Sibiri.* Moscow: Nauka.

Vasil'ev, V. I. 1963. Lesnye entsy (ocherk istorii, khoziaistva i kul'tury). In B. O. Dolgikh, ed., *Sibirskii etnograficheskii sbornik,* vypusk 5. Trudy instituta etnografii AN SSSR (novaia seriia), tom 84, pp. 33–70. Moscow: Nauka.

Vasilevich, G. M. 1951. Esseisko-chirindinskie evenki (po kollektsiia V. N. Vasil'eva, MAE No. 1004). *Sbornik Muzeia antropologiia i etnografiia* 13: 154–186.

Vasilievich, G. M. 1972. Nekotorye voporosy plemeni i roda u evenkov. In A. M. Resehetov, ed., *Okhotniki, sobirateli, rybolovy,* 160–172. Moscow: Nauka.

Ziker, John. 1996. Problems of the North. *Michigan Discussions in Anthropology* 12: 59–75.

PART 3

NEGOTIATING PERSONAL RELATIONSHIPS IN THE POSTSOCIALIST FIELD

Interpersonal Spaces: Postsocialist Fieldworkers Reposition Themselves

The people with whom we work in the field distinguish between insider and outsider fieldworkers, tending to associate these different positions with different systems of power, fears, and hopes. What we learn from the experiences of insider, outsider, and halfie fieldworkers extends our sense of both these people's and the fieldworkers' humanity and subjectivity. While studying economic change in a post-Soviet Uzbek village, Zanca found himself in a fieldwork situation of "tumult or hurly-burly," similar to what Kuehnast called an "avalanche," and Barsegian, a "field without boundaries." During a time in which people must cope with incredible economic uncertainty, Zanca was seen as the "rich American" who might be able to help with almost everything, most important, with contacts in "wealthy America." Like Kuehnast, then, Zanca found himself caught up in Cold War values and belief systems. Emotionally and mentally overwhelmed by the villagers' demands and unable to provide them with everyday material needs, Zanca began the painful process of reflectively deconstructing his own values. He comes to see himself not as the "detached observer" but rather as an intruding fieldworker. Yet within this process Zanca creates for himself new interpersonal spaces that allow him to negotiate his fieldwork among people who had a "manic attraction . . . to the flashy capitalist societies."

Berdahl studied social change and religion in an eastern German border village after the collapse of the Berlin Wall. Chronicling how she began to negotiate interpersonal spaces as an American "halfie" fieldworker, Berdahl demonstrates how in this process of negotiation our own emotional and intellectual involvements inevitably intersect with how we position ourselves as anthropologists—how we do fieldwork—and how our personal identities connect with and are constantly changed by the changing relationships that develop between our field friends and ourselves. For Berdahl, as for Zanca, this process revealed that her values on issues of health, illness, and fear of death were embedded in a Western belief system, yet were no less humanly made than the values of health, illness, and fear of death held by her friend and key informant. This realization offered Berdahl an unexpected awareness and understanding of the dilemmas of attachment and displacement during fieldwork.

Silverman, in a chapter based on her extensive research experiences before and after socialism among the Balkan Roma in Bulgaria and among the Roma in postsocialist Macedonia and in New York City, describes the process by which she ethically transcended her fieldwork dilemmas. She shows how she widened her interpersonal spaces, bridged the insider, outsider, and halfie positions as well as the roles of analyst, documenter, advo-

cate, and friend, and came to develop a "reciprocal ethnography." Reflecting on both socialist and postsocialist dilemmas, Silverman finds that the
former fieldwork relationships focused more on informant and fieldworker
in regard to the state, whereas in the postsocialist fields citizens must refashion their lives and negotiate new choices with the ethnographer as an
accomplice. Similarly to De Soto, Silverman suggests that during periods of
transformation and people's searches for new ways and sociocultural models "advocacy and cultural analysis . . . become two sides" of the fieldworker's project.

8

Intruder in Uzbekistan
Walking the Line between Community Needs and Anthropological Desiderata

Russell Zanca

The encounter between villager and anthropologist reproduces on a small scale the relations of power in which both are enmeshed. The questions of honor and shame are thus not merely issues in village morality; they also concern the protection and penetration of an intimate view of communal and even national identity. These identities face in two directions at once; they represent a continual tension between self-presentation and self-knowledge. Self-presentation adopts the rhetoric of a cultural perfection already achieved; self-knowledge surveys the range of departures from that perfection in daily social experience.
　　　　—Michael Herzfeld, *Anthropology through the Looking-glass*

This chapter mainly focuses on my presence and role in a post-Soviet Uzbek village. I try to reconstruct my relationship to the collective farm villagers of Boburkent,[1] in the Ferghana Valley of Uzbekistan, through readings of various situations that reveal my predicament as an American anthropologist working within a part of the archetypical postsocialist world, the erstwhile USSR. For this reason I quoted Herzfeld, above, even though he was speaking of negotiations between himself and modern Greeks as a "Mediterranean" nation. I find his description of modern Greeks apt for Uzbeks, since both of these peoples among whom we worked experienced their own unique "falls from grace." With regard to the modern Uzbeks, the fall is one from socialism to an ill-defined and malformed independence.

My secondary concern in this chapter is an oblique address of the rhetoric surrounding socialism at the community level. Here socialism hardly exists, but its legacy continues to assert itself in most spheres of daily life. Socialism, as readers will soon read, plays an all-important role in village self-representations to both the intrusive, ever-wider world (Grekova 1996: 68–74) and this anthropologist; to this I attribute my title choice.

Informants and interlocutors often took pains to tell me that I had entered their lives and society at the wrong time, because "it used to be so much better." They were speaking of the time before the collapse of socialism; they wanted me to know I was not seeing them at their best, that a certain degree of self-pride and local dignity had been won and lost with the transformation-in-process from socialism to hesitant independence. My hope here is to convey a sense of the tumult or hurly-burly that significantly characterizes the "ethnographic present" of my fieldwork period, 1993–1994. I designed the following discussion with an eye toward capturing my own involvement in certain upheavals tucked into this corner of the postsocialist world, as well as toward presenting issues that account for local insecurities and hardships during this de-Sovietizing moment.[2]

American Scholars and Postsocialist Officialdom: An Uzbek Case

The experience for almost all of us who have completed fieldwork in the postsocialist states is much like the experience of working in the socialist states:[3] we need to be given scholarly status and then be placed within an appropriate institute or academy with which we have disciplinary affiliation. In order to get that far, there are a host of personalities and written forms to deal with and complete. This process can be unnerving because of all the running around we must do, the seemingly insane[4] bureaucratic practices we must endure, and the very interrogative way in which our encounters with foreign colleagues or academic hosts play themselves out. We are often subjected to unsolicited lectures about the superiority of how local scholars do their research and how their educational system (with state ideology as the lodestar) has enabled them to achieve stupendous results as opposed to bourgeois approaches. Furthermore, local anthropologists often find it puzzling that we want to spend more than a couple of weeks at most in the field; living in a village for a year strikes them as insufferable (see Hann 1987: 142). Of course, I'm not saying that tangled bureaucracies and cantankerous officials and colleagues are unique to the postsocialist states. My point, however, is that the combinations of attitudes and interactions encountered in states of the former USSR can be set apart from others because a highly competitive (antagonistic to boot!) outlook toward the capitalist order distinguished Soviet social psychology.

One of the most frustrating, though at times comical, elements of the field experience is our being seen as suspect in the eyes of the local authorities and, sometimes, our local colleagues. Even though the Cold War is dead, we continue to be treated as spies whose motivation for conducting research in a given village is to write up and sell reports to the CIA. Our hosts will joke about this *ad nauseam,* so even if it seems cute or harmless the first dozen times, it almost seems conducive to hostile intent by the 50th time some prankster brings up the topic at an evening social. And for those of us who still possess a dram of Marxism in the blood, the half-joking becomes disheartening (see Sampson and Kideckel 1989). Since some degree of scholar-espionage activities within the superpower states occurred, reasons for local suspicions about spying may not be entirely unfounded.[5] Perhaps the greatest challenge we face, aside from the ordinary demands of fieldwork, is learning how to work effectively with and gain respect from our host colleagues. Within academic institutions, one forever runs across what I call the processual paradox, which contains its own dialectical component: the unremitting hubris invoked by scholars who were scientifically inspired by socialism to commanding heights of pride and the depressing postsocialist recognition that in many ways their societies have a far lower standard of living and quality of life (especially for scholars) than is true in the case of their colleagues from the West. Actually, they probably always knew this, but they are now confronted by it directly, simply by looking across their desks and taking in the fine clothes, perfect teeth, fragrant aftershaves and perfumes, and good-quality pens, paper, and laptop computers that are the average effects of fresh-faced American graduate students who are half the age of their foreign hosts.

In the case of the former Soviet Union, the scenario sketched above stands out in glaring relief. This is the only case I know from experience, and it is an extreme case because of the former Soviet Union's superpower status. Bombastic superpower rhetoric convinced masses of people that their country was at least equal, if not superior, to all other developed nations, the first and foremost being the United States. Thus now, after the collapse of one superpower, one cannot ignore the psychological letdown frequently encountered among former Soviet citizens. Here I offer one example from a Russian woman from Kazakhstan, whom I met on a train traveling between Urgench and Tashkent:

> "Our country was a good place until that bastard Gorbachev emerged. We didn't think about any of the republican boundaries the way we have to now. It's true you had to be careful what you said, but at least we could live well on our salaries and pensions. And all you foreigners are coming in here now like you own the place (well, I don't mean you exactly), but it wasn't like that before. Back then our money was worth something, and everybody respected our country. We helped everybody out, too. . . . Now just look at this mess. I'm just thankful my children moved to Russia. . . . They keep us afloat."

Over the course of my stay in Central Asia, I found this opinion nearly proverbial, and the nationalities of the people making such a statement generally mattered little.[6] Furthermore, I am convinced that it was my very status as an American that provoked these kinds of reactions or responses to my inquiries.

If the USSR may be taken as the emblem of the socialist world, it is also credible to posit the United States as the standard of the capitalist world.

This contrast helps tell us why the competitive angle becomes all the more intense for American anthropologists. There is unquestionably so much from our ethnographic experiences that we will never feel we understand with confidence, that we are forever in the dark about, yet, as Americans, we are also "insiders," in essence, when it comes to confessional outbursts of people of the former Soviet Union: America played an undeniable role in the destruction of the USSR.

If this dialectical situation about the clash between post-Soviet and American academics is more actual than humorously imaginary, where does the synthesis fit in? The synthesis develops through sensitive exchange relationships that grow not only among colleagues but also among anthropologists and the people in the communities where we work. In this new era, participants from the opposite poles of the superpower spectrum enter a situation that is far more lopsided in favor of the Americans than was true 10 years ago. To compensate for the loss of pride *qua* power that is the result of the Soviet collapse, both host colleagues and ethnographic subjects attempt to profit from the anthropologist's visit, just as he or she derives gain from the experiences of traveling to and securing knowledge from the community in which he or she lives and works. I am not trying to allude to some sort of symmetrical exchange here; I am saying that many villages of the former Soviet Union are reeling from the deprivations that have arisen in the wake of socialism. Villagers themselves, in admitting their plight to foreign scholars, have sought compensation while trying to tap into the resources these outsiders possess. The outsiders, in turn, exact prices for sharing. In this kind of relationship, such intangibles as official permission, access to materials and physical places, and knowledge itself (the anthropologist's trophy) are converted into precious commodities.[7] Coinciding with the partial opening of Uzbekistan to the world and its shifting politicoeconomic alignment, new patterns of networking and well-connectedness have been created that are comparable to the old socialist patterns (Swain 1985: 25–50; Kideckel 1993: 66–69).

Rude Awakenings in the Field

I now relate the kinds of events and thoughts that were both formative and indicative of the ways in which my professional desires and plans frequently outstripped the possibilities to act upon them. I was obligated to subordinate scholarly curiosity to the practical needs and, occasionally, whimsical hopes of those around me. These situations will help the reader to understand the nature of exchange reciprocity in my dealings with villagers.

My wife and I planned to spend about a year living in a village not far from a Kyrgyz border town. I decided to study how Uzbeks and Kyrgyz negotiate interethnic disagreements with each other, especially because of historical disputes in many areas of the Ferghana Valley where farming Uzbeks and pastoralist Kyrgyz have lived side by side and traded with one another. In 1990 violent clashes developed in the southern Kyrgyz province of Osh, and I wanted to understand how Uzbeks viewed their neighbors, to see if interethnic disputes were deeply ingrained or superficial.

From the time I began discussing my "scientific plan" with local academic officials, I knew my dissertation goals were in for a rough ride. The notions were controversial and did little to convince the officials that my intentions were properly "ethnographic." Thanks to the old Soviet thinking in regard to foreigners who have a keen interest in the local culture, my wife and I remained in Tashkent a good three weeks longer than we had planned. Having arrived in October of 1993, I thought we would be able to head off for the field site within two weeks. We mistakenly reasoned that our status as locally certified foreign scholars would enable us to secure rapid access to the Ferghana Valley.

After we had been in the field for a while, I convinced myself that I should veer from the interethnic course and concentrate on something I presumed would be less controversial. Villagers did not seem comfortable with my initial inquiries into discord and violence between Uzbeks and Kyrgyz. I became increasingly interested in the nature of collective farming and the household economic strategies used to grapple with what I consider to be increasing peasantization of village farming, and this is what I settled on as my dissertation topic.

Uzbekistan struck me for what I perceived were its split-personality tendencies: scholar-visitors feel at once warmly received and tacitly accused by local scholars, administrators, law enforcement specialists, and villagers. Although being kept, held, or detained by people from all walks of Uzbekistani life could be extremely trying, I reminded myself that many people tried to hinder our movement more out of incredulity for who we were than out of some wish to frighten us or wring secrets from us. Thus, I softened my frustration, lack of autonomy, and the creeping sense of *Weltschmerz* experienced whenever I was deprived of my right to exercise some part of my will.

Once I was able to accept my presence as intrusive (disruptive in many circumstances), I began to understand why trying to engage people privately and publicly on my anthropological terms was often a doomed task among a people whose cultural approach to strangeness was to deflect or corral it easily and then, ironically, to convert my inquisitiveness into their own entertainment. This conversion revealed itself whenever people showed me around, showed me off, and got me to tell more about my own country than I was usually able to solicit in return. I vividly recall walking home from community events, months into my field research, feeling agitated by the strife of role reversal, asking myself such questions as, "Who's the anthropologist here anyhow? Don't they know I arrange to come to these events so they can tell me about themselves and what it is I'm witnessing?" It was then that I started to realize there could be no successfully passive approach to the project.

One of the virtues I have taken from my field experiences is "patient deference." This *modus operandi* covers interviewing practices and household etiquette as well as social intercourse with people in positions of power over the foreigner, positions which invariably signify all state service workers upon whom one depends for transportation and communication. For me, this attitude made Uzbekistan vastly different from the many other Soviet cultural settings in which I've found myself, most notably those in Russia. Displays of testiness or outpourings of insults simply do not advance one's cause in times of securing a coveted rail ticket or receiving a clear connection to an intercity phone line from local service workers. Politeness and deference in official/bureaucratic situations, instead of acting as rudely as I sometimes had been treated, always helped me to obtain my goal. I had ranted and raved initially to assert myself, and did so now and then when exhaustion and frustration got the better of me (like the time I found myself locked in a wrestling clench with a herculean farm boy who had driven me mad by cutting a line for bus tickets!). I like the Uzbek saying, "When you become angry, you lose your senses." Figuring out how to modify one's behavior in one or another sociocultural setting entails a process of doing it one's own way until one realizes the terrible futility of it and is ready to start anew.

Looking back at the way I acted whenever I rode the rails, I am amazed at how I reckoned it would be possible to shut myself off from the humanity around me, to step back into my American existence through books and magazines. All my feeble attempts at sequestration, often extending far beyond the cramped spaces of the "general car" class, finally caught up with me. This was actually fortunate, for the result was a kind of cognitive epiphany; that is, I scolded myself back to my senses: "Am I so stupid as to cut myself off from some of the deepest anthropological insights I've received during these past discomfiting months?"

The shameful answer was yes. I remember harboring terribly unfriendly thoughts toward the people around me because of their actions, habits of (un)cleanliness, nosiness, and so on, only to regret such thoughts just as soon as somebody was generous enough to offer me snacks they had cooked at home or smiled in wide-eyed astonishment upon learning of my national origin. Sometimes people were interested merely to know what English writing looked like; one man asked me to read a passage aloud "just to hear

Women making music with tambourines during their *gap* (Photograph by Russell Zanca)

English." There I was, thinking of myself as an anthropologist, yet all the while trying to remain self-centered and individualistic among a nation of people who were as culturally communal as any I had ever met. In this setting, the peculiarity of the Western scholarly ontology, with its arguably liberating advantages (*pace* Gellner 1985), with its tendency toward atomization as the linchpin of scholarly contemplation and investigation (data collection, reception of knowledge), clashes with the values of given societies wherein such scholarly behavior is antipodal to the locally constructed course of action and manners; to qualify my point, I am referring to societies where the fieldworker feels the individualist-communalist divide.

Personal Tales of Post-Soviet Withdrawal

People in Uzbekistan never hesitated to tell me how their quality of life had plummeted. One Sunday morning Ahmadjon and I were walking along a stretch of highway between Boburkent and the Nurerli district's center, Adolatobod. Each Sunday, village residents journeyed to Adolatobod, using any and all means of transportation; the lucky ones rode crammed in cars, and the unlucky rode there on bicycles, scooters, donkeys, or horses, but most people had to squeeze onto ramshackle buses bursting with Sunday shoppers. Ahmadjon haplessly tried to flag down a car because we had just missed a bus and a drizzle had begun. Before a car finally stopped for us, we walked silently, until Ahmadjon piped up:

> "This is different, too."
> "What do you mean *this*?" I asked.
> "Well, until a few years ago, we never had to put up with overcrowded and infrequent buses like this. And there were a lot more cars on the road, too. But now, . . . well, you know, gas is expensive, and if that's not the problem, spare parts are hard to come by; and then some people just can't afford to drive anymore no matter what the problem is."

At the bazaar, Erkinboi, a *kolkhoz* tractor-driver, walked from one sugar vendor to the next, hoping to negotiate a price for five kilos of sugar; in the end he settled on three. In 1994 sugar was available in state stores for a much cheaper price, but it was rationed to approximately two kilos per month per household. The sugar that formerly came from Cuba or Ukraine now comes primarily from Turkey. Marketeers sell it at inflated prices, thinking people will spend more if they can buy it conveniently, in relatively unlimited quantities, but few villagers have a sufficient amount of money in pocket to do so.

Medicines and pharmaceuticals are a key indicator of postsocialist misfortune, too. Clinics and hospitals lack the necessary equipment and medicines to perform routine surgery or to maintain outpatient care that used to be possible at the village level, including the treatment of appendicitis, postpartum complications, rashes, and so forth. People are now sent to the regional-center facilities. When someone does receive doctors' prescriptions, especially for summertime's omnipresent intestinal parasites, it is often a separate trial simply to have them filled. Many a village *apteka/dorikhona* (pharmacy) no longer functions; if it does, the prices for drugs are often so expensive that people must borrow money from relatives or friends in order to buy them. The other possibility is to bring a prescription directly to the kolkhoz bazaar, where many medicines are sold illegally, or at any rate extralegally, and often by people who have no knowledge of administering the products or maintaining their quality.

When the American television program *Rescue 911* was shown, people watched in rapt attention and marveled at the lightning response of ambulatory teams during emergencies. They would ask us, "Is it really like that in America? Does the emergency medical service come so fast with all the equipment and medicines?" Then they would claim that it used to be sort of like that in Boburkent when the USSR cohered, but now the "*skoraia/tez*" (emergency) ambulance could be greatly delayed depending on the condition of the vehicle, availability of gas, or even the availability of the vehicle itself, since some of the drivers earned extra cash by driving around the district as a livery service.

One woman, Pakhtagul, told me about a liver operation she underwent in Andijon (35 kilometers to the southeast) the year before I came. I asked her how it went:

> "Well, there were no complications, and the doctors did a good job. Just look at me now! But at the time when I needed it, I was really sick. We couldn't call the ambulance because they wouldn't have come; that's how it is now. Nuralis' father [an Uzbek woman often refers to her husband as the father of one of her children] had to drive me to Andijon. Before we left, we had to bring medicines, bedding, sheets, money, and food; otherwise, they wouldn't have performed the operation at all. Our hospitals used to be great, and they provided everything, but today we're just lucky that some of the good doctors have stayed, even though they don't get much money either."

I collected accounts involving acquaintances and friends who had had to bribe doctors for treatment on an unprecedented scale, even by Soviet standards. One friend had a very sick infant nephew who needed a blood transfusion. A week passed since she had first told us about it; then we met up again in Tashkent and took the train back to Namangan together. During the ride she told us her infant nephew had died; we expressed our condolences and rode on in silence for a while. I thought we would change the subject, but in time Nilofar opened up, telling us how her brother and his wife had spent nearly all their money in an effort to buy gifts for the doctor (local currency was so worthless for a time—November 1993 to June 1994— that people preferred tangible items instead) in order to ensure that their infant would receive the best possible treatment. However, it was all for naught. Nilofar, normally stoic in these situations, broke down and sobbed. Later she told us that so many things caused her tears, most of all that the baby should have died in so much pain without understanding anything, but also that the society which she had known from childhood, even with all its faults, still seemed so much more humane and compassionate than post-Soviet independence.

These tales represent a sample from real-life situations that betray a vast, deep ocean of postsocialist discontent because they concern the loss of one of the welfare state's most crucial institutions—namely, public health. The pernicious effects of the decline of public health spread in so many directions throughout society that people often engaged me in conversation about all manner of minor and major illnesses, to say nothing of their complaints about the care given in local facilities.

But my contacts extended beyond those who received care. The care-givers (i.e., doctors, nurses, etc.) also expressed dismay over the setbacks that faced all the participants involved in this vital institution. For care-givers, this dismay dealt with bread-and-butter issues: they could no longer support their families, a situation that forced many to seek other kinds of nonprofessional employment. In years past the health-care system show-cased the socialist way of life. Today the teetering system epitomizes mori-bund socialism, and those who praised and benefited most from it—com-mon citizens—have been reduced to asking for aspirin from a sojourning anthropologist.

Anthropologist as Anything But

Such benefits as new sources of information and alternative economic and political developments may prove the destruction of socialism worthwhile to the masses. However, the postsocialist mentality makes people think that they need only cultivate foreign contacts to establish international trade and business opportunities. In reality, rural people have little idea about which local products could be considered marketable internationally. To gain an appreciation for this, I offer apposite illustration.

 During my first walking tour of our village, an unemployed truck driver accompanied me on the rounds. We passed by the kolkhoz offices, the small canning factory, the teahouse, the everyday-life building, the hospital, and, finally, the agricultural and domestic products store. It was in this final spot where I committed the first of many gaffes. I met the store's two proprietors, exchanged greetings, and then walked around the store trying to feign in-terest in the pathetic-looking bins of consumer goods. After I had looked probingly at as many plastic toilet seats (in a village where there are only outhouses) and mutilated flatware as I thought humanly possible, and after exchanging too many minutes of excruciating smiles with the proprietors, I started—tactfully, I thought—for the exit.

 "Hey, hold on a minute," one of the guys said. "Don't you want to talk about trade for a minute?"

 "Trade [*Savdomi*]?" I repeated politely, wondering if I had understood him properly.

 "Sure," he began with a grin, "maybe you can help us trade with America. What do you think?"

 I was sure these guys were joking, and I let out a chuckle that was a bit too ro-bust. They were no longer grinning but waiting for some sort of reasoned answer. My tour host cut the tension by saying, "They have all this stuff in America already."

 Later I started thinking about so many encounters that either involved requests for business contacts or placed a premium on me as someone who

The "weighing-in." Sacks of picked cotton are weighed, and each picker is paid the equivalent of about $0.02/kg. (Photograph by Monica Eng)

could help engineer commercial development. Naturally, I tended to think of the villagers who made these requests as bumpkins who really were naive and unaware of how commodities markets and trade policies function. But that was a large, in some cases foolhardy, assumption to make, and it furthermore undercuts the wider complexity or dynamic of the whole problem.[8] It is certainly true that the people who approached me are a product of a system that tightly curtailed their access to the nonsocialist world and clearly misinformed them about many phenomena of the capitalist world. Given the Soviet state's policy of denying individual entrepreneurial activity, especially in relation to the capitalist world, an obvious consequence of Uzbekistan's turn toward new financial opportunities with the West, and given the discovery on the part of many that the West leads with regard to high-quality consumer goods and high personal income ceilings for those who do well professionally, it seems almost natural that those who are farthest from the inchoate access to the world beyond the borders would aggressively pursue new fiscal interests with the one foreigner who dropped into their midst (and one who just happened to represent the greatest consumer society on earth).

One afternoon a neighbor who worked at the local *hokimiiat* (town hall or regional political center), and who had been active in establishing district property auctions, hinted about my doing a favor for him. This was not a man given to impractical urges, so I knew he wouldn't be asking for ice cream makers, televisions, or ovens, as others already had. He first wanted to know what America could use from Uzbekistan. I told him I could not think offhand, but that there had to be a number of things, and I suggested gold, oil, and natural gas. He aimed at something more local and within his grasp, suggesting honey and onions instead, to which I replied, "You've got to be kidding." He then assented, saying, "Yeah, I'm sure you've got enough of that, but we face a terrible shortage of bovine medicines, and I was wondering if you didn't know of a way to acquire them."

In such a situations I never thought it possible to reject the ideas outright, though I always tried to stress that trade arrangements and business dealings were not personal talents. I dissimulated partly because I understood how earnest people were about their proposals; partly because I wanted to appear as more than a nuisance who spoke bad Uzbek, followed people around, and tried to get people to talk about subjects that made them uncomfortable; and also partly because I felt that I really was the only person who could possibly represent these people to the kinds of foreigners whom they would never ordinarily meet.

One young man asked me repeatedly for business cards of Americans in Tashkent. I showed him a few and asked him what he would do if he were to contact these people. He replied, "I want to get into some kind of international business, and you are the only guy I know who knows people who might be able to help." These encounters always made me feel useless, though I know there loomed an illusion of entelechy about me, as if I could regenerate their understanding of my "successes" for them through contact with Americans—a bridge to wealthy people and a wealthy world (see also Kuehnast, this volume).

Indeed, one difference between the postsocialist societies and almost all others is the kind of manic attraction many people feel to the flashy capitalist societies from which they have been shut out. I think certain people in Boburkent, Namangan, Tashkent, and elsewhere throughout Uzbekistan considered me to be their primary link to wealth from which they are prevented by the well-entrenched Soviet-style bureaucracy and the generally conservative organs of local power. To be able to avoid the state by dealing directly with an outsider offers a rare and curious experience to many people, but few interested people were willing to accept the fact that I was not a businessman doubling as an anthropologist, that I had next to no knowledge about how properly to establish international business, that I had little interest in business period.

For this reason I ask would-be fieldworkers to consider the difficulties involved in remaining to one side of the sorrows and resentments character-

Children at play in their courtyard (Photograph by Russell Zanca)

istic of much of the postsocialist world. Assuming the mantle of pure scholarship takes on a solipsistic, even exploitative, air because this attitude presents to the human objects of study the position that they are only a part of
your cerebral entertainment. The more we make ourselves available to the
needs of these communities, the further we can go in learning from and
about them (Hann 1993: 16).

Deciding What Proper Fieldwork Is: Toward an Unorthodox Methodology

To return to a discussion of fieldwork, since the interregnum between returning to America and sitting down to write—the period I term ponder-
ous drift—I can think only of how odd I have appeared to myself. There
were so many times when I tried to stress to people in Uzbekistan that I am
an anthropologist. I told them this not because they did not already know
it, but because I wanted them to consider my role in their village as meaningful (on its own terms). Everybody wanted me to perform "diverse" functions, too. I spent a lot of time trying to flee from imposed responsibilities:
requests for my help as a mediator; requests from groups of schoolchildren
who wanted me to teach English (or at least to hang around me under the
pretext of learning English); and requests from people who wanted me to
accompany them to visit friends and relatives in distant villages or towns,
so that I might be displayed as one of life's bigger oddities.

If it can be said that fieldwork is the anthropologist's crucible, then surely figuring out one's place in the field site is the crucible of fieldwork itself. Unfortunately, I was least prepared for this part of fieldwork (I doubt I am alone here) and, worse still, least flexible. I kept thinking that anthropological "moments" were something I would never attain or undergo until I became the "master" of my situation. Eventually, and somewhat happily, I learned that much fieldwork is simply about mastering oneself, since it seemed that I was going to remain controlled and manipulated to some extent by those whom I had decided to study. As an aside, I would say that this is just one of the many problems about the overall usefulness of fieldwork, about "being there," and so on. For a number of us, being there is a time spent in full-blown, hot-blooded conflict with ourselves, and for some time we feel that all the efforts made to come to this point (the site) in space and time as professionals are leading to our undoing.

However, for me to pursue better the theme of the preternatural character of fieldwork, more exposition is needed. In what are commonly termed Third World or developing countries, we usually expect to find rural peoples living in poverty, a situation which connotes a series of factors including malnutrition, rampant infectious diseases, lack of indoor plumbing, and very few technological conveniences that we in the West have taken for granted for at least two generations. In speaking about most of the countries of Africa, Asia, and Latin America, we are inclined to think of poverty as multigenerational, whether these countries became independent recently or centuries ago. When we look specifically at the former Soviet Union, however, we see many elements of the Third World (by our own standards) combined with the crucial differences that industrialized socialism brought about—namely, the general absence of poverty even in the agricultural areas from the Baltic Sea to the Chinese borders in Central Asia and southeastern Siberia. All the qualifications regarding overall quality of life notwithstanding, this was a remarkable achievement, and we find the remnants of its success in the contemporary sociocultural settings of rural Uzbekistan today.

One of the ways in which the "success" of Soviet life was forever brought home to me is the shame so many people felt for what they now lack and for how I, as a foreign guest, was sometimes impertinently treated. When my wife and I first arrived in the middle of a desolate, cold, rainy, muddy fall, our immediate hosts and neighbors would say: "You've come at such a bad time: first of all it's winter, and second, [since the Soviet Union ended] our economy has become worse and worse. We can't treat you the way we should, and you can't understand how well we used to live."

This discourse of the recent past, of the "Union" and of socialism in general, strikes me as an enormously rich source for an anthropology of so-

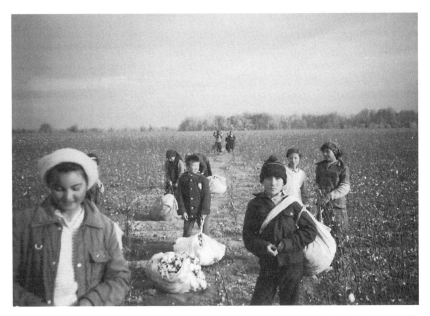

Children picking the remnants of the cotton harvest in fall 1994. Their role is close to negligible, but decreasing mechanization makes all hands necessary. (Photograph by Russell Zanca)

cialism that we can conduct through the interview process and the writing of oral histories. A part of me thinks a few more years of distance from the collapse are needed, as are a few more years of distance from the turbulence and upheaval of the present. But the danger here is to expect a sort of stability or a completion of the establishment of a new economic and sociopolitical system in the near future that will sweep aside the remnants of socialism; this is unlikely to happen quickly. As foreign scholars working within the former Soviet Union, we have a wonderful opportunity to better our understanding of modern historical processes—our understanding of the fear, the animosity, and the competitive natures that guided our thinking about one another during the past century—from the viewpoints, at least in my case, of the non-European peasant populations. The essential method for answering questions about how people experienced socialism, how it affected their social organization, cultural institutions, gender divisions, and livelihoods, is prolonged fieldwork where most people live, and that is in the countryside.

My presence among Uzbek villagers during a strained time brought about by Soviet disintegration left me feeling more an intruder than a detached observer. People of the community were determined to have me function in practical ways, to take part in the life of the village, and to serve as a primary link between their community and the outside world. At first this arrangement frustrated me, but in time I realized how important it was both to kolkhoz villagers and to my ethnographic work. Eventually, the notion that I had to give something back to the people who were helping me with my own intellectual curiosity and career development became less an obligation than a commitment.[9]

In the vignettes above, I illustrated what the declines of the de-Sovietizing period have meant for ordinary rural people by analyzing their situations, especially regarding health care, which I read as an overarching indicator of popular dissatisfaction with the fall of the empire. In sketching my position as a young scholar within the local academy and as a foreigner in various subordinate positions with regard to the bureaucracy and public life, I have discussed how best to negotiate what can be very trying circumstances. The extent to which my work was successful is bound up with the extent to which I was able to serve people through extrascholarly activity: meeting individual and community needs provided commitment to local interests and helped break down mutual suspicions.

Notes

1. I have intentionally falsified the names of local places in the Ferghana Valley, where I worked, as well as those of informants and friends. The only reason for choosing this tack is to lend a degree of anonymity to people who may not always want to see attributed to them the remarks they made or my paraphrasings of those remarks.

2. Much like Creed (1995) and Hann (1994), I am also uncomfortable with referring to this "moment" as "the transition." Creed (1995: 848) refers to the current time as one of "de-communization," whereas the one factor I'm sure I can confidently speak of is "de-Sovietization," notwithstanding its sluggish pace in rural Uzbekistan.

3. The Soviet Union was not only the colossus of the socialist world but also the largest country on earth. To mention communism or socialism is to call images of the Kremlin or Red Square instantly to mind. The USSR was the quintessence of the socialist state.

Once this extraordinary Marxist-Leninist empire fell to pieces in 1991, most of its republics declared themselves to be independent nation-states (excepting the three Baltic countries and Georgia, which had declared independence at various times before August 1991). It is ironic that Central Asia's most chest-beating nationalist leaders, from Uzbekistan and Turkmenistan, very much hoped that the USSR would survive even as it was being written out of existence; in fact, the leadership of all the Central Asian nations wanted to preserve the union. For a clear encapsulation of the political wrangling in Central Asia at the time, see Olcott 1996. Now that the dust has settled, we are left with 14 independent countries and Russia.

4. Obviously I use the word *insane* relative to my own sense of how the world should be ordered. One might be tempted to stop me and say, "What about your Uzbek colleagues? Don't they face the same barriers and hurdles?" A well-made point, but slightly off the mark. First of all, they have had an entire lifetime of learning the ins and outs of the bureaucracy, including how to fudge and forge sections of official documents that we, foreign scholars, would need years to master. They know precisely whom to approach and how to approach—the intricacies of an unofficial protocol far beyond our sojourning ken. Second, and I'll stop here, by dint of the fact that they are not foreigners, they are not nearly as threatening to officials and leaders; they are not suspected of being spies or people who may defame Uzbekistan and the Uzbeks to outsiders because of what they may publish abroad. Because the nature and methods of their doing fieldwork significantly differ from our long-term approach, they are usually granted permission to travel and work with far more speed than we.

5. Personally, I have had to fend off recruitment drives by dedicated members of both the CIA and the KGB in connection with my Central Asian studies. Furthermore, I don't think it will shock most readers to recall that throughout the Cold War period certain American anthropologists gathered intelligence in the service of the CIA. For the bright though poor this has been, *horribile dictu,* a lucrative lure from time to time. It is, therefore, almost only natural that Soviet bureaucrats and officials (I include academics) should suspect us, since they have long been on the alert for shrouded spies. Very understandable and very annoying.

6. Although such well-known eastern European intellectuals as Bauman (1976) and Sinyavsky (1990) wrote on the utter failure of the USSR as a socialist state and on its inhumane sociopolitical and economic system, field experiences of the Soviet "overthrow" prove that many citizens share a very different remembrance of its past, not one predicated solely on being ground down.

7. Rather than pleading or begging from wealthier foreigners, most people who wanted things from me had the idea that it should be based on some notion of exchange, even if they set the conditions as delayed; that is, "I know someone who could probably secure your access to those records, but it would go smoother if you agree to begin teaching English at the local government office right away."

8. All the attempts by villagers to see me as a conduit for business prospects follow from their own experiences of operating within the "second," "alternative," or "gray" economy of the socialist period. Living better usually meant having to circumvent official/state channels in order to secure a higher income. In the current, crisis-laden period, villagers have necessarily become more aggressive in quest of extra-kolkhoz income, and I served as a potential extension of that system for those who knew of me. Detailed and theoretical treatment of the "private sector" under socialism may be found in Lane 1985; Nove 1988; Kornai 1992; and Verdery 1995.

9. I must say that I am being wholly personal here; this position hardly qualifies as a prescription for others. As trite as I may read here, no two fieldwork situations and personalities involved will necessarily be alike. The amount one thinks she may

be able to give back depends greatly on one's relationships to informants and perhaps to a community at large.

Maybe because I was seen as educated and wealthy and because people knew I
had connections to fairly prominent and powerful people and institutions in
Tashkent, some thought I might be able to influence responsible leaders to improve
village conditions. On more than one occasion, people implied that I should represent the village and tell somebody how conditions and infrastructure had worsened
since the late 1980s.

Surely it was an odd feeling: a complete nobody from America all of a sudden becoming a "hope," if you will, to a community. I wanted to believe I could effect
change; however, in the end, I worked very hard to convince people that whatever I
said or wrote would probably achieve next to nothing, but that I would try in my own
minor way.

To come down from the clouds for a moment, however, I do think I was able to
give something back by lending my services as a teacher, helping children to develop
some rudimentary English. If nothing else, I provided some learning service that
children and parents enjoyed, that facilitated some cross-cultural understanding
and appreciation. Volunteer work may not be as valuable as a box of shoes, a ton of
coal, or a pot of gold, but it proved a simple measure by which I tried to show people
that I valued all the help they had given me. Selflessness in this sense rarely raises the
kind of ire or resentment that the giving away of things—as a supposed gesture of
generosity—often does.

References

Bauman, Z. 1976. *Socialism: The active utopia.* New York: Holmes and Meir Publishers.

Creed, G. W. 1995. The politics of agriculture in Bulgaria. *Slavic Review* 4:
843–868.

Gellner, E. 1985. *Relativism and the social sciences.* New York: Cambridge University Press.

Grekova, M. 1996. Restructuring of "the life-world of socialism." *International Sociology* 1: 61–78.

Hann, C. M. 1987. The politics of anthropology in socialist eastern Europe. In
A. Jackson, ed., *Anthropology at home,* 139–153. ASA Monographs 25. London
and New York: Tavistock Publications.

Hann, C. M. 1993. Introduction: Social anthropology and socialism. In C. M.
Hann, ed., *Socialism: Ideals, ideologies and local practice,* 1–26. ASA Monographs 31. London and New York: Routledge.

Hann, C. M. 1994. After communism: Reflections on east European anthropology
and the "transition." *Social Anthropology* 3: 229–249.

Herzfeld, M. 1987. *Anthropology through the looking-glass: Critical ethnography in
the margins of Europe.* Cambridge: Cambridge University Press.

Kideckel, D. A. 1993. *The solitude of collectivism: Romanian villagers to the revolution and beyond.* Ithaca, N.Y., and London: Cornell University Press.

Kornai, J. 1992. *The socialist system: The political economy of communism.* Princeton, N.J.: Princeton University Press.

Lane, D. 1985. *Soviet economy and society.* New York: New York University Press.

Nove, A. 1988. *The Soviet economic system.* 3d ed. Boston: Unwin Hyman.

Olcott, M. B. 1996. *Central Asia's new states: Independence, foreign policy, and regional security.* Washington, D.C.: United States Institute of Peace Press.

Sampson, S. L., and D. A. Kideckel. 1989. Anthropologists going into the cold: Research in the age of mutually assured destruction. In P. R. Turner and D. Pitt, eds., *The anthropology of war and peace: Perspectives on the nuclear age,* 160–173. Westport, Conn.: Bergin and Garvey Publishers.

Sinyavsky, Andrei. 1990. *Soviet civilization: A cultural history.* New York: Arcade Publishing.

Swain, N. 1985. *Collective farms which work?* Cambridge: Cambridge University Press.

Verdery, K. 1995. What was socialism and why did it fall? In N. Keddie, ed., *Debating revolutions,* 221–243. New York: New York University Press.

9

Mixed Devotions
Religion, Friendship, and Fieldwork in Postsocialist Eastern Germany

Daphne Berdahl

Most ethnographic fieldwork is punctuated by distancing moments, instances when the ethnographer's dual and paradoxical insider-outsider status becomes highlighted in particularly bold relief. Often these moments seem to confirm what we, as ethnographers, already know and feel: that we are the (uninvited) guests of those we study, our work made possible by the tolerance, patience, and cooperation of our hosts. At other times these moments may come as a complete shock, suddenly jolting us out of our feelings of satisfaction at having been approved by those around us and challenging our sense of competence in the culture (see Dubisch 1996: 115; Kondo 1990). When these incidents are shocking, they are also revelatory. We may come away with a sense of self-revelation, having gained insights into our personal and ethnographic selves (Bruner 1990), and we may experience a "revelatory incident" in the ethnographic sense (Fernandez 1986), emerging with a better understanding of our relationship to and with the people we study, with an improved sense of the relation between the processes and products of our research, and above all, with a richer perspective on the subject of our study itself.

This chapter tells three stories. It is a chronicle of a friendship, describing my struggle to come to terms with the terminal illness of a close friend whom I met in the field and with her decisions about treatment. It is an account of the dilemmas of doing research as a Westerner in a postsocialist setting, particularly in relation to the "halfie" or "hybrid" status of anthropologists working in European societies (Dubisch 1996; see also De Soto, this volume). And it is an exploration of transformations in religion, popular faith, and the Catholic church after the collapse of socialist rule in eastern Germany. All these stories converged around a single distancing moment during fieldwork, to which I shall later return. I begin, however, by describing the events and relationships that provided the context for the incident.

Of Friends and Fieldwork

Anthropologists have rarely written about "friends," for to do so would blur and thereby threaten the discipline's classically coveted boundary between observer and observed, between self and other.[1] In the authoritative voice of traditional ethnography (Clifford 1983), friendships formed and cultivated during the course of research were transformed in the course of writing through distancing concepts like informants or interlocutors.[2] Yet it is inevitable that meaningful friendships develop after living intensively with people over an extended period of time, as ethnographic fieldwork requires us to do. Thus I may be guilty of certain professional transgressions when I call Johanna my friend, but to describe her in any other terms would not only be dishonest, it would also "do violence" (Bruner 1990) to our shared experience.

I first met Johanna, a petite woman in her late 20s, on a dark December afternoon while she was working late as a secretary in the village mayor's office. I was hurriedly searching for a new field site after the one I had arranged the previous summer had fallen through, and she immediately sensed my feelings of urgency and desperation as I entered the office to inquire about possible housing in the village. Because my research focused on issues of borders, boundaries, and identities in relation to the rapid transformations in everyday life after the fall of the Berlin Wall, it was important to me to live and work in a village along the former inner-German border. After careful thought and effort, she was able to convince a local family with a vacant apartment to take me and my husband in. Johanna, then, was essentially responsible for my presence in the former East German border village of Kella between 1990 and 1992.

Because her position at the mayor's office gave her access and insights into material on everyday life before and after socialism, Johanna was also what anthropologists have often called a key informant. She patiently guided me through the confusion of the disorganized village archives, kept me abreast of the employment status of nearly all the village's 600 residents, and attentively informed me of community building projects, local factory

The author (*left*) and her friend Johanna (Photograph by Anne Baldwin)

closings, and administrative restructurings. Together we spent long hours taping conversations, often while sunning ourselves on her balcony, about the pressures and pleasures of being a working mother in the German Democratic Republic (GDR), about her perceptions of western German notions of femininity and womanhood, about the church and state during socialist rule, about her recollections of the border fortifications during the 1970s. We periodically took long walks at dusk, after she was finished with her office job and domestic chores but while it was still light, to survey the most recent renovations of local homes, new construction projects, and changes in village public space. Often our discussions lasted into the early hours of the morning, long after her husband and two children were in bed and she could speak uninterrupted by the demands of being a wife and a mother.

Throughout our interactions in which I sought insights and information (i.e., "data") for my study, I came to value, indeed at times cherish, her companionship, sense of humor, and humanity. And I believe she sought in me not only a friend and confidante, but also a certain validation of her life experience that my interest in her as a friend and inquiring anthropologist naturally provided. After our difficult good-byes when I left the field, she later told me, she would drink every morning out of a travel mug I had brought her from the United States, as if to keep my memory and presence alive. Back at home, I placed a gift from her, a glitter-encrusted cat sculpture that reflected her tastes more than mine, on my windowsill and looked at it long-ingly as I grappled with the dilemma of the returning anthropologist at-tempting to turn the particulars of fieldwork into a more general and co-herent ethnographic account (see Dubisch 1996).

Devout Struggles

Many of my conversations with Johanna during fieldwork focused on the topic of religion, a mutual interest that was the result of my research as well as Johanna's own spiritual concerns. Born and raised in a village that re-mained devoutly Catholic despite the socialist state's attempts to root out religion in the GDR,[3] Johanna became increasingly involved in the church during early adulthood after the arrival in 1982 of a new priest in the village, Father Münster, a small yet domineering man in his mid-40s who was a member and avid promoter of the charismatic Focolare ecclesiastical move-ment. Based on an ideal of world unity and universal love preached by its founder and leader, Chiara Lubich, around whom the movement's person-ality cult is centered, Focolare is one of the more powerful of the newer ec-clesiastical movements within the Catholic church.[4] Its notion of piety is also strongly connected to a glorification of suffering, reflected in and in-culcated through censured testimonial narratives told and retold at fre-quent Focolare gatherings. For Johanna, however, the movement's empha-sis on tolerance and Christian love was the logical extension in practice of religious teachings that had been central to her upbringing. She was willing to devote the substantial time and energy the movement required of its ad-herents and quickly became part of the priest's inner circle composed of the handful of villagers involved in Focolare activities. Together with Father Münster and these followers, Johanna attended local and regional Focolare meetings in the GDR; after the Wall fell, she traveled to western Germany, Italy, and Poland on behalf of the movement.

Father Münster's passionate involvement in the Focolare movement was greeted with much skepticism and controversy among the majority of the village's Catholics, however, who viewed many of the priest's religious prac-tices as unconventional ("cultlike") and outside the realm of institutional-ized religion. They complained that his Focolare commitments divided the congregation[5] and detracted from his responsibilities as a priest to the com-munity, which, many parishioners felt, primarily entailed presiding over lo-cal masses and pilgrimages. Frustrated by his failure to garner widespread support for the movement within the village, Father Münster often con-fessed to his most devoted followers that he viewed many of his duties as a Catholic priest as secondary to his vision of the ideals of Focolare.

Local sentiment surrounding the priest and the Focolare movement was complicated by the changing role of the church—and by extension, of the priest—after the collapse of socialism. During the period of socialist rule, religion in this border village, as in other areas of the GDR and Poland, had been both a reason for and an expression of resistance to the regime (Berdahl 1999; see also Kubik 1994; and Nagengast 1991).[6] Having one's child baptized, sending a child to communion, and attending a local pilgrimage were both religious and overtly political acts. In a gesture of religious commitment, political opposition, and dedication to local tradition, for example, during the period of socialist rule village residents defiantly sent their children to the Catholic kindergarten housed in the Schwesternhaus, a church-owned facility staffed by three nuns who lived in the house, instead of the state-run day care located in the community center. Many of the pilgrimage sites in the surrounding regions, including the most sacred and popular one, were located in the highly restricted border zone of the GDR and were thus accessible only with special passes; yet pilgrimage attendance here was always high during the socialist period.

Since German reunification, however, the church has lost much of its appeal and interest as an alternative institution preaching against the official values of the socialist regime. As in the rest of the former GDR (as well as in many other postsocialist societies), there has been a dramatic decline in religious activity here. Church attendance has decreased, contributions to the collection plate on Sundays are half of what they were in the GDR, and participation in pilgrimages is far below what it used to be when special passes were required. Concomitantly, the priest's influence and role in the community have also declined. Villagers have increasingly sought out clergy in other churches for confession,[7] thus severely limiting Father Münster's access to and control of local and often privileged knowledge. People also have also begun attending Saturday evening masses in a nearby western German village, once inaccessible before the fall of the Wall, so that they can sleep late on Sundays. The priest's declining influence and involvement in community affairs, it should be noted, were also the product of the dramatic change in circumstances since the fall of the Wall, in which all community members have had less access to shared information.

These changes in circumstances include, above all, the end of the community's geographic isolation as a border village in the "high-security zone" (*Schutzstreifen*). Under socialism, villagers were able to keep track of one another's comings and goings as well as the occasional outside visitors because only residents and relatives with special passes were permitted to enter the village. Now, with the freedom to travel and receive visitors, keeping track of such details is impossible. This process of personal isolation was accelerated with the closing of regional factories in the early 1990s, where local information was exchanged and shared.

Father Münster responded to these challenges by attempting to cling to his control, occasionally through methods and strategies of manipulation. During the time of my fieldwork, for example, he would occasionally test the loyalty of his most dedicated followers (primarily women) by planning Bible study groups that conflicted with other scheduled public gatherings in the village. Similarly, viewing every stranger to the village as a possible recruit for the Focolare movement, he frequently attempted to schedule social events involving outside visitors at his own home. My husband and I both benefited from and were challenged by his actions. On the one hand, Father Münster had helped integrate us into village life by his introduction and stamp of approval during a Christmas Eve mass several weeks after our arrival (see Berdahl 1999). On the other hand, it was evident that he viewed us as a foreign and potentially disruptive presence in the village. We soon gathered that he was closely monitoring our activities, and we were often surprised, and dismayed, to hear him misrepresenting things we had said about the community, village residents, or the Focolare movement to promote his own perspective.[8] As educated outsiders, I believe he felt his association with us might grant his ideas a certain degree of legitimacy, and he often guarded that association jealously.

Johanna grew to be deeply troubled by what she, among others, viewed to be hypocritical and contradictory behavior on the part of the priest toward us and other members of the community. She was confused and alarmed by his comments about jettisoning friends who hadn't been persuaded "to believe,"[9] and she was particularly disturbed by what she knew to be misrepresentations of me and John, my husband. Johanna's ambivalence toward the priest did not affect her own deeply held religious convictions; as Riegelhaupt (1984) has noted, anticlericalism does not necessarily imply a rejection of religion. However, for Johanna it did entail a difficult and emotional personal struggle.

The amount of space in my fieldnotes devoted to this issue attests to its presence as a dilemma I found myself frequently negotiating throughout fieldwork. I felt a personal obligation to balance honesty about my own religious views and background with my professional needs as an anthropologist to observe the changing relationship between the priest and parishioners. Having been baptized in the Methodist church as a child but raised with little religious instruction in a family whose observances of Christmas and Easter were largely secular, I had developed my own sense of spirituality that had little connection to any organized religion. When asked by people in the village, however, I told them I came from a Protestant background. Although deeply skeptical of the charismatic, anti-intellectual nature of the Focolare movement and clear in my refusal to become involved, I also appreciated that its ecumenism was partly responsible for our warm welcome into the village's traditional Catholic church. I further recognized that, although Father Münster was a fairly controversial figure in the community, he still retained a certain measure of authority invested in him as a priest that needed to be acknowledged and respected if I were to remain in good standing in the community. So it was with delicate diplomacy, particularly in regard to Johanna, that I struggled to negotiate these contradictions, and I was not always successful.

Illness and Power

Johanna was diagnosed with an inoperable brain tumor the day I left Germany after a brief visit in 1994. She didn't tell me then, typically setting her own concerns aside to help me prepare for what promised to be a stressful drive to the Frankfurt airport with my feverish infant daughter. In fact, it was Father Münster who called me, once I was back in the United States, to break the news. "It's very serious," I remember him telling me, "[some of the doctors] can't believe she's even still alive." He went on to explain that he was calling because Johanna would be reluctant to convey the severity of her situation to me. Blaming the messenger for the message, perhaps, I hung up the phone angry at Father Münster and questioning his motivations for the call.

Without fully considering the implications or consequences of my actions, I immediately went to work to try to help Johanna. A friend who had visited me in the field and who had thus met Johanna put me in touch with a friend of hers with close contacts to leading neurologists throughout the United States and Europe. Assuring me he knew the best person in Germany to handle the case, he referred me to a brain specialist in Hamburg, who graciously agreed to take on Johanna as her primary doctor or to provide a second opinion. Johanna was a bit overwhelmed by all this attention, but agreed to send her test results to Hamburg, where the specialist confirmed the diagnosis and recommended against a biopsy until there was some indication of the tumor's growth. Much to everyone's relief, a second set of tests six months later revealed no significant change.

A year later, however, a CAT scan revealed that the tumor had grown, and Johanna's doctors in Göttingen were offering seemingly inconclusive advice about treatment. They informed Johanna that the risks of doing a biopsy of the tumor, a necessary precursor to treatment, included the slight possibility of total paralysis due to the tumor's location and size; yet allowing the tumor to go untreated, they said, could be fatal. On the other hand, there was the remote possibility that the tumor would stop growing and merely continue to be the source of Johanna's severely piercing headaches. At my request, she forwarded her test results to the Hamburg specialist, who, after consulting with several colleagues, quickly responded with a conclusive recommendation in favor of a biopsy followed by appropriate treatment. To me, Johanna's options, while painful and full of risk, seemed clear: the "leading specialists" had concurred that the danger of allowing the tumor to go untreated was greater than the risks of a biopsy. Johanna, however, fearing the risks of the biopsy more than death, opted to wait.

Concerned that she was making a potentially fatal mistake, I set out to ensure that her decision would be fully informed. I drafted a list of questions to ask of both the Hamburg specialist and her doctors in Göttingen. I talked to her husband about the importance of his presence during meetings with the doctors to relieve her of the burden of dealing with this alone. I initiated a series of phone calls and e-mails in order to convey to the doctor in Hamburg through my contact in the United States that Johanna was receiving mixed messages about treatment; I even discussed, but ultimately decided against, the possibility of a conference call with the German American contact of my friend in order to answer Johanna's questions and, possibly, to persuade her of the Hamburg doctor's expertise and experience.

I soon realized that I was also competing with the priest for a voice in providing Johanna with medical advice and personal support. I had easily sensed over the past year Johanna's growing closeness to Father Münster. The occasional criticism and ambivalence she had once felt comfortable sharing with me had ceased, and I began hearing through others in the village of her increased activity within the church. Father Münster, it appeared, had become Johanna's closest confidant. Knowing Johanna to be deeply faithful, I attributed this to a sense of spiritual security and companionship the priest was able to provide her as she faced a potentially imminent death. My experience of the priest, however, made me suspicious that he was acting out of both altruism and self-interest. I could imagine him genuinely wanting to help one of his most devout parishioners at the same time as I could imagine him striving to validate a religious authority and social identity as the village priest.

Father Münster, it turns out, had his own medical contact, an eastern German doctor actively involved in the Focolare movement, to whom Johanna was also sending her test results. According to this doctor, it was a "miracle" that she was still alive, which all three—the priest, the doctor, and Johanna—interpreted more literally, I believe, than the usual figure of speech. I knew Johanna to be a strong believer in destiny (she refused to wear a seatbelt for this very reason), and upon hearing her repeat the eastern German doctor's words (attributed in that first phone call by the priest to all "the doctors" caring for Johanna), I realized that she had decided to place her confidence in divine fate rather than in medical experts, at least for the time being. I had no choice but to accept her decision, albeit regretfully.

Implicit in my actions and reactions, but unrecognizable to me at the time, were the assumptions that my elite Western contacts were superior to the care and advice she was receiving from the less renowned doctors in Göttingen or especially in the former GDR and that I knew best how to negotiate the Western medical system. My efforts also revealed an unquestioned confidence that medical science was more likely to help Johanna in fighting the tumor than any religious faith or belief in miracles. In retrospect, I was surprisingly unconcerned about appearing and acting like a *Besser Wessi,* the term eastern Germans use to describe western Germans who act like "they know everything better." As De Soto points out (in this volume), the term also alludes to a more general power imbalance between East and West following the collapse of socialist rule in eastern Germany. Often described by eastern Germans as a process of "colonization," the hegemony of the West was reflected in nearly all realms of social and political life, ranging from the dismantling of the former East German legal and educational institutions, to the perceived victors' justice of the border guard trials, to the dominance of Western media. The power dynamics resulting from my positioning as an educated Westerner in this asymmetrical postsocialist context were of little concern to me; at the time, I was focused on trying to save my friend.

Distance and Displacements

An anthropologist's positioning, Jill Dubisch points out, is never static (1996: 107). Shortly before I returned to Germany for fieldwork in the spring of 1996, my mother was diagnosed with breast cancer. I had spent the month before my departure keeping her company during the awkward and frightening days before surgery, alternating nightly hospital shifts with my father after her double mastectomy and educating myself about the various forms and treatments of breast cancer. As an academic, perhaps I found particular comfort and refuge in the assortment of books and articles on breast cancer that I collected immediately upon learning of my mother's diagnosis. By the time I arrived in Germany, I was exhausted but also admittedly relieved by the opportunity to direct my energies elsewhere, at least for the moment. I soon discovered, however, that my own positioning as an anthropologist had been transformed by my experience of my mother's illness.

I also returned to the village as a mother. Although my daughter, Audrey, had accompanied me as an infant during a brief visit in 1994, this was the first time I would be doing fieldwork with offspring. Like many childless couples in the field, John and I had been the object of some curiosity and village gossip because of our decision to postpone childbearing; I was

Photographs of Audrey displayed in the priest's kitchen (Photograph by Daphne Berdahl)

curious to see how Audrey's presence would affect the dynamics of field research.

Finally, I returned to Germany knowing this might be my last visit with Johanna. Because I recognized the topic's potential divisiveness, I had resolved to avoid discussions with her about the priest. Indeed, although I intended to pursue the changing role of the church and religion in my research questions, I hoped to distance myself from the personal dynamics surrounding the priest and his relationship to parishioners, which had consumed so much time and energy during my initial research.

When I arrived to find photographs of Audrey prominently displayed across the priest's kitchen cupboard, however, I quickly discovered that this would be difficult. The pictures had been enclosed with Christmas cards that I had sent to Father Münster, along with many other villagers, since I had left the field; they were the only photographs in his kitchen. I was both amused and angered by what I perceived to be the use of my daughter in the priest's attempts to legitimate both his threatened position in the community and his religious views through an association with me and John. But I also sensed genuine affection for me and John and our child in the display of the photographs, and I was even slightly touched by the gesture and consequently embarrassed about my suspicion of his ulterior motives. The location of the pictures in the semiprivate space of the kitchen[10] rather than in the priest's more public office, I believed, was both an expression and a performance of a certain intimacy he felt toward us that was quite different from his relationship to parishioners.[11]

A conversation over lunch with Father Münster confirmed this perception. At his initiative, we began talking about Johanna's illness in a manner that would have been unusual with other members of the community. Just days before, she had received the results of her semiannual tests that revealed further growth in the tumor; her doctors in Göttingen, although astonished at Johanna's relatively good health considering the tumor's size and location, were now recommending a biopsy, as the Hamburg specialist had a year earlier. Father Münster, who had once reportedly told a dying villager that he envied him "for he would soon be with Christ," was deeply skeptical of any form of treatment. "I know two priests who have died of cancer," he told me, "and all they [the doctors] do is prolong your suffering." Growing increasingly passionate, he went on to castigate Johanna's husband and family, arguing that they failed to take seriously her illness or her religious faith. "[Johanna] has accepted and embraced this illness," he said, echoing the Focolare movement's glorification of suffering that encourages a passive and noninterventionist approach (Urquhart 1995: 62), "and her family must do the same."

During the course of this conversation, Johanna's recent behavior became increasingly understandable to me. If the priest was saying similar things to Johanna—and I had good reasons to believe he was and that she was listening—it was little wonder if she feared medical treatment more than death itself. In accusing her husband and family of indifference,[12] it appeared the priest had successfully positioned himself as Johanna's most trusted and caring confidant. It was also little wonder, then, that she was devoting much of her time and energy to the church. Johanna was one of several village women who had voluntarily assumed many of the duties and responsibilities once held by the three nuns who had lived in the community until 1993. These included, above all, preparing the sanctuary and ringing the church bells for services, keeping church records updated, and, frequently, cooking and cleaning for the priest. As elsewhere in Europe, women here are often regarded as "the guardians of their family's spiritual health," and their religious involvement is regarded as "religious activities on the family's behalf" rather than a "neglecting of their duties as wives and mothers" (Dubisch 1996: 210–211); however, several of these women, including Johanna, had crossed the boundary of appropriate behavior in the minds of many villagers.

I, too, began to view Johanna's religious activities as rather extreme and found myself growing increasingly irritated by her seemingly blind devotion to the priest. Her daily church attendance entailed arriving 30 minutes before services in order to ring the bells; afterwards she would frequently stay to clean up and talk with Father Münster. She regularly took over his religion classes for grade-school children and could frequently be found running an errand or taking care of something at the rectory on his behalf. What disturbed me, however, was her apparent uncritical acceptance of the priest's attitudes toward suffering, illness, and death. Indeed, I found myself at times enraged by this, angry at Johanna because I felt she wasn't fighting the disease, and furious at the priest, whom I (perhaps unjustly) blamed.

One Sunday that spring, while I was sitting among the congregation waiting for the morning mass to begin, I watched Johanna emerge from the sacristy, where she had been helping the priest and altar boys prepare for services. After gently closing the sacristy door, she proceeded to the base of the altar stairs and delicately genuflected to the ornate altar piece containing a dark oil painting of the Crucifixion. Johanna then carefully ascended the stairs to light several candles on the marble altar and place an open Bible on the wooden pulpit. At the bottom of the stairs she genuflected again, and then, with hands folded piously below her breast and eyes cast humbly to the ground, she tiptoed to her seat in order to avoid disturbing the silence of the waiting congregation. Upon reaching her seat she crossed herself, said a silent prayer, and sat down. Her actions and demeanor revealed an intensity of faith and purpose that I suddenly almost envied, and at that moment it occurred to me that her deep religious faith—and her devout practice, indeed embodiment, of it—just might be keeping her alive. Why hadn't I thought of this before? What was the source of my anger at Johanna? Would I have been so frustrated by her decision not to seek traditional medical treatment if I were doing research in a non-Western context—if she had been consulting a shaman, for example? Few experiences in fieldwork are perhaps as revealing of cultural differences as divergent understandings of health and illness are, for implicit in these understandings are deeply held cultural conceptions of the body, science, and religion. I knew that moral dilemmas surrounding conflicting cultural concepts of illness were nothing new for anthropologists; as Brown points out (in this volume), these kinds of dilemmas are variants of the old problem of "cultural relativism" in anthropology. However, I had not expected to encounter this in my own research in Europe.[13]

The complex and contradictory nature of my "halfie" status (Abu-Lughod 1991), "in which the 'other' is at least partly the 'self'" (Dubisch 1996: 15), thus became painfully clear. Of course, to some extent anthropologists are always halfies, positioned as insiders and outsiders in one sense or another. Indeed, as Narayan has pointed out, they are more than this, for "two halves cannot account for the complexity of an identity in

which multiple countries, regions, religions, and classes may come together" (1993: 673). Fieldwork in any society entails shifting identifications,
in which particular aspects of one's positioning become salient. Working in
a "less alien" society (see Jaffe 1993),[14] particularly within the context of a
similar religious tradition that I had chosen to accept only moderately, had
carried with it a set of expectations, theirs and my own, about my involvement, responsibilities, and behavior as an anthropologist in the field and as
a member of the community.[15] Further, the postsocialist context of my fieldwork, I later realized, had been almost dangerously deceptive: the apparent
cultural similarities between the new eastern Germany and my Western experience—capitalist market economy, democratic political structures, familiar consumer products, and common mass cultural references—had the
potential to conceal the profound cultural, political, and economic differences and life experiences that had separated us just years ago. Or, as Jill
Dubisch, drawing from an observation of Ernestine Friedl, has written
about ethnographic fieldwork in Europe in general: "Europe presents the
anthropologist with an anomaly, for it offers the unfamiliar in the deceptive
guise of the familiar" (1995: 35). Observing Johanna that day forced me to
acknowledge and respect both the distinct value of her experience and the
cultural distance between us.

   "Anthropology," Ruth Behar has written, "is frequently about displace-
ments" (1991: 351).[16] My anger at Johanna and the priest and the way they
were dealing with her illness was, I believe, also the product of displaced
emotions compounded by my "hybrid" positioning (Narayan 1993). To
some extent at least, I had displaced my rage at the cancer that had invaded
my mother's body, and displaced my fear over the possibility of losing her,
onto Johanna and her illness. I vehemently rejected the priest's insistence on
accepting death, because this was not an option I was willing to accept for
my mother. I needed for Johanna to fight the illness not only because I cared
deeply for her, but also because I wanted so desperately for my own mother
to survive. The fact that I had been asking Johanna to fight the illness in
terms that I understood—by educating herself about the illness and treatment options, by asking critical questions of her doctors, by seeking the best
medical advice and treatment available—highlighted for me my distance
and displacement.

   That Sunday after mass, with tears in my eyes and hands trembling, I lit
a votive candle for my mother.

Popular Faith, Institutionalized Religion, and Power

This revelatory moment of distancing and recognition of intercultural subjectivity, as well as Johanna's relationship to the priest, which had to some

extent prompted my reaction, all occurred within the context of transformations in religion, popular faith, and the Catholic church after the collapse of socialist rule.[17] The priest's involvement with Johanna's illness was in part, I believe, an attempt to sustain some sense of purpose and authority that had been diminished by divisions within the congregation surrounding the Focolare movement, as well as by the declining influence of the Catholic church and changes in religious practices since the fall of the Wall.

A week after this incident, on Easter, Father Münster announced to the congregation that the bishop had ordered his transfer out of the village. In three months he would take over a larger congregation located 30 kilometers away, Father Münster explained, and a new priest in a neighboring village would assume responsibility for this congregation in addition to two other nearby parishes. The village would thus not only be losing Father Münster but a resident priest as well; the future of the parish rectory, which had recently undergone extensive renovations, was yet to be determined. The news came as a surprise to everyone, even to Johanna and others among the priest's closest parishioners.

Although there was little visible reaction among the congregation that morning, villagers soon began expressing a range of opinions and speculations surrounding the reasons for and ramifications of Father Münster's departure. Many parishioners welcomed the change; others were indifferent. Many were saddened and angered over the loss of a resident priest, and several lamented a waste of time and money spent renovating the local rectory only to have it stand vacant two years later. Those parishioners close to Father Münster understandably felt a deep personal loss.

Further, having been given no concrete reason for the transfer by the priest or the bishop, particularly after Father Münster insisted to inquiring parishioners that he had not requested a change, people were left to speculate. For many, it was merely a normal course of events; 10 years was a normal tenure for a priest in any community, they argued, and this one had already exceeded his. Others pointed to the widespread shortage of priests in the Catholic church and explained the transfer as a product of diocese reorganization and consolidation. Soon, however, rumors began circulating that the bishop had received letters of complaint from several villagers. According to local gossip, one letter was critical of Father Münster's involvement in Focolare and claimed he was responsible for creating troublesome factions within the congregation. Another letter allegedly accused the priest of improper conduct in relation to several of his closest female parishioners. There were reportedly no charges of sexual involvement in the letter, nor were there rumors of them in the village; rather, the priest was blamed for having created divisions within families and between spouses as a result of his frequent activities and close relationships with several women in the village. Sensing a problematic and potentially disruptive situation, it was speculated, the bishop had determined it was time for the controversial priest to move on.

Most significant about the local gossip were the changes it reflected in perceptions and attitudes toward the church as an institution. The church had not merely lost the appeal it had under socialism as an alternative institution and forum for opposition to the regime; it had now itself become a power that had to be interpreted, negotiated, and contested. Echoing similar comments I heard from several villagers, a letter to the bishop protesting Father Münster's transfer stated: "Many [of us] working in the West have learned that those in power care little about the human effects of their decisions. . . . Is this true in this case as well?" Of the approximately four letters written to the bishop, three mentioned the painful loss of the Schwesternhaus, a visible landmark within the village because of its size, unusual yellow exterior, and hillside location. The building now stands empty, slowly showing signs of abandonment and decay with its crumbling facade and broken windows. The three nuns who once lived in the house, along with the elderly residents of its small nursing home, left in 1994 because of the financial pressures of their parent house, and its Catholic kindergarten is now housed in the former GDR day-care facility. What was once an important symbol of religious presence and resistance under socialism, particularly in the context of the community's status as a border village in the high-security zone (*Schutzstreifen*),[18] has now become for many residents a symbol of loss and betrayal. As one woman told me, "It makes me ill even to look up there at the Schwesternhaus." Similarly, a letter to the bishop protesting Father Münster's transfer wrote: "The Schwesternhaus overlooks [the village] like a memorial, empty and yawning. . . . Must our rectory also stand empty and unused?"

The priest's transfer and the villagers' reactions to it thus also reflected an increasing divergence between popular faith and institutionalized religion (e.g., Badone 1990), religious traditions whose interests had remained largely congruent during the period of socialist rule, when both popular religious expressions (local legends, superstitions, or religious symbols) and institutionally sanctioned practices (baptisms, communions, church marriages) united in opposition to the regime.[19] With the loss of a shared understanding of the meaning of religious survival after the collapse of socialism, the interests of unofficial and official religion have, to some extent, diverged, resulting in renegotiations and redefinitions of religious identities and practice. Whereas the clergy has been quick to preach about the dangers of consumerism and to deplore the decline in church attendance, parishioners have initiated new forms and expressions of religious devotion. Rather than attending Sunday mass in the village, for example—once an important means of social control and a measure of religious commitment because of the lack of alternatives to the village church during the period of socialist rule—villagers may now choose to go to Saturday evening mass in a neighboring village. Similarly, others may simply visit a famous pilgrimage site on a day trip in lieu of Sunday mass.

Reactions within the village to the priest's transfer reflect this increasing divergence. Recalling their allegiance to the church during socialism, for which many villagers paid a price through increased surveillance by the state or through being denied passes to visit western German relatives, for example,[20] parishioners described feeling abandoned and betrayed by the church. As one letter to the bishop argued: "We have defended our faith over the past years. . . . And what has it brought us? We feel abandoned, especially because, along with Father Münster, we are losing a permanent resident priest." Several parishioners, similarly reflecting a split between official and unofficial religion, threatened to leave the church, as conveyed in another letter to the bishop: "Some [people] have even indicated their intention to leave the church. They claim they don't need to pay church taxes in order to believe [in God]."

The bishop responded to parishioners' complaints with a single letter from a suffragan bishop addressed to Father Münster, which the priest shared with the congregation during a Sunday morning mass. Although the bishop appreciated the community's concerns, the letter read, "there are other points of view that must be considered." There was no explanation following this assertion, nor has one been forthcoming in response to an additional inquiry by a small group of parishioners. Many villagers were angered by the dismissive tone of the letter; for several, it confirmed their view of the ecclesiastical hierarchy as men in power indifferent to human and community concerns. "You'd think you could expect more compassion from the church," one woman told me, adding, "it's not necessarily the church that's bad but the individuals who are in power there."

Ethnographic Inversions, Attachments, and Positioning: Some Concluding Thoughts

Quite predictably, Johanna has been at the forefront of efforts to keep Father Münster in the community. Not only does she foresee the loss of a close confidant, but also with the absence of a resident priest and subsequent decline in religious activities in the village, Johanna anticipates no longer being able to partake in the many church activities and responsibilities through which she finds deep spiritual and personal meaning. After watching her before mass that Sunday, I, too, became concerned about the latter possibility. As a mutual friend said to me, "I'm concerned that with the priest gone it [her illness] could go rapidly downhill."

Johanna and I continued to be in telephone contact after my return from

Germany that spring.[21] During one conversation in which she shared her anger and frustration at the bishop's reply to parishioners, I expressed my curiosity about the reasons for the transfer and wondered aloud if a letter for my own research purposes would be answered similarly, if at all. Immediately upon uttering the thought I regretted it. "Oh Daphne!" Johanna exclaimed, "You would do that? I'm sure a letter from you, an outsider with some experience of living in the community, would help. The bishop wouldn't be able to dismiss it as being from us 'simple people,' as he has the other letters." Hoping to avoid becoming more involved than I suddenly already was, I explained that *if* I were to write such a letter, I would refrain from expressing any opinion about the transfer itself; my aim would be merely to learn the reasons behind the decision. I would think about it, I told her.

Johanna's enthusiasm and expectations for a letter from me revealed her own recognition and acknowledgment of my dual insider-outsider status; in her mind, I was also a hybrid. For me, this hybrid status in relation to Johanna was compounded by my recent experience with my mother's cancer: studying "the other" was, in this case, also a personal and emotional study of the self. My initial frustration with and subsequent compassion for Johanna, deriving in part from my experience with my mother, forced me to recognize and accept my own helplessness in relation to both women. Despite my attempts to secure the best medical advice for Johanna and despite all the books I could read about breast cancer for my mother, I was ultimately, and painfully, powerless. Our different approaches to a life-threatening illness—indeed, our different fears—had both bridged and highlighted a cultural distance; the coevality of the experiences made them mutually illuminating.[22] Lighting the candle for my mother that Sunday was thus a peace offering, a sign of hope, and a prayer. Together, the experiences have given me an unexpected awareness and understanding of what Ruth Behar has called "the paradoxes of attachment and displacement" (Behar 1991: 374), all reflected and united in the flame of a votive candle.

The conversation with Johanna and her argument in favor of my involvement, with its implications of her perception of the persuasiveness of my institutional letterhead and title, also reflected a shift in my professional status and positioning as an anthropologist. To my surprise, I would invoke that status several days later when Johanna called to suggest that if I did intend to write such a letter, it would be most helpful if I did it sooner rather than later while there was still time for the bishop to reverse his decision. In a gesture of inverted distancing, I chose to point to my own need as a researcher to avoid becoming entangled in local politics. "It might position me within the community in ways that I might find difficult later," I explained to Johanna, "and I doubt if I would get an answer from the bishop's office, anyway." Her obvious disappointment only complicated my conflicting emotions of guilt and responsibility. Had I invoked a notion of "objectivity" that I myself found highly questionable, indeed fictional, to protect my own (selfish) research interests? Was I putting those interests ahead of the needs and desires of my friend? Or was I being a "responsible anthropologist" by avoiding potentially troublesome partisanship? Or was it the reverse: was I being truly partisan because of my own suspicions of and, at times, difficult interactions with the priest?

My affirmative answers to all these questions reveals the "multiple and sometimes contradictory and inconsistent ways" in which all observers are positioned (Dubisch 1996: 107). This shifting and hybrid identification (Narayan 1993) may be especially highlighted by a distancing moment emerging out of the contexts and accidents of fieldwork or, as described above, by an inverted distancing initiated by the anthropologist; it may also be accompanied, and complicated, by conflicting allegiances and emotions. In this chapter, as in fieldwork, my positioning has included friend, Westerner, anthropologist, professional scholar, mother, daughter. My emotions surrounding Johanna, the priest, my role and identity as an anthropologist and friend, faith and illness, and the writing of this chapter have been similarly mixed and contradictory—feelings that were only compounded by eerily coincidental messages on my answering machine from both Johanna and Father Münster just days before completing an initial draft of this chapter. Although the specifics are unique to my situation, many of the issues raised here concerning the politics and practices of ethnography will be quite familiar to anthropologists. What is different, here, however, is the postsocialist context of my fieldwork, which at times appeared deceptively similar to historically capitalist Western societies. The transformations in and negotiations of local and extralocal power dynamics as well as changes in a dynamic interplay between organized and unorganized religion were products of the collapse of socialist rule; they were also processes that affected the social relations among, and my own relationships to, the people with whom I lived and worked. It was the convergence of these various processes around the specifics of a single distancing moment during fieldwork that highlighted for me particular dilemmas of research in a postsocialist context.

Anthropologists have long been committed to exploring the intersection of the large and the small; indeed, we may consider it one of the fundamental tasks of anthropology to explore how larger social, political, and economic processes are manifested and negotiated locally and specifically. More recently, anthropologists have devoted much attention to the separate issue of the poetics and politics of ethnography (e.g., Clifford and Marcus 1986), both through a reevaluation of anthropology and the colonial encounter (e.g., Asad 1973) and through more reflexive explications of the fieldwork encounter itself. My point here is simply that these are all related: the specific politics, struggles, and paradoxes of our ethnographic research and writing are situated within these larger contexts. Not only are the processes of production that shape the direction and outcome of our research the product of daily events, personal interactions, and even struggles in fieldwork;[23] they may also be the product of the very political, economic, and social processes that we intend to study. Indeed, there can be a dynamic interplay between the two. These dynamics are difficult but, I think, important to write about. For me, as an anthropologist and a friend, this particular attempt has been an exercise in mixed devotions.

Notes

This chapter is part of research that has been funded by the Fulbright Commission, the University of Chicago Division of Social Sciences, and a James Bryant Conant Fellowship in German and European Studies at the Center for European Studies, Harvard University. I am deeply grateful to these institutions for their support. Thanks as well to John N. Baldwin, Edward M. Bruner, Hermine De Soto, Nora Dudwick, Renate Lellep Fernandez, Kari Robinson, and Siegfried Weichlein for their helpful comments and insights. I dedicate this piece, with love and admiration, to the two strong women who inspired it.

1. Critiques of ethnography that have called these dichotomies (observer/observed, insider/outsider, self/other) into question have argued that they are products of a notion of ethnographic authority that has been used to perpetuate an ideal (and arguably a fiction) of objectivity. See Clifford 1983, 1986; Dubisch 1996; Handler 1993; as well as more general examinations of the fieldwork encounter (Crapanzano 1980; Dumont 1978; Myerhoff 1978; Rabinow 1977). Because feminist ethnography has often been particularly concerned with the implications and transgressions of "self" versus "other" or "West" versus "the Rest" dichotomies (Abu-Lughod 1990, 1991; Behar 1993; Behar and Gordon 1995; Tsing 1993), feminist ethnographers have more frequently described their relationships in the field as friendships (e.g., Abu-Lughod 1995; Behar 1993; McBeth 1993).

2. Anthropologists who have worked intensively with a particular individual, as in a life-history project, are also more likely to address issues of attachment, distance, and friendship in relation to a specific relationship and/or the fieldwork encounter in general. See, e.g., Behar 1993; Crapanzano 1980; Dwyer 1982; McBeth 1993. See also Silverman, this volume.

3. The village in which I conducted my fieldwork is located within the Eichsfeld region, for centuries a Catholic enclave in Protestant central Germany with its origins as an ecclesiastical territory. A large majority of village residents are practicing Catholics. See Berdahl 1999.

4. The Focolare movement, started in southern Italy in 1943 and officially sanctioned by Pope John Paul II, now exists in over 180 countries with several million "adherents" and 80,000 core members (Urquhart 1995: 6).

5. Complaints of the movement's divisiveness are not unique to this congregation (see Urquhart 1995).

6. The Catholic church, it should be noted, was a minority religion in the GDR. Whereas in 1986 the Protestant church claimed 6.5 million members (Ramet 1991), there were only 1 million Catholics, or approximately 6 percent of the population, in the GDR (Fischer 1991).

7. One of the principal reasons for this, I was told, is that Father Münster had an unfortunate tendency to ignore the confessional oath of secrecy; occasionally items discussed in confession were included in his sermons. Although the identities of the persons involved were never revealed, in a small community like this one, they didn't have to be.

8. My husband, John, was especially affected by this. Because the priest was often engaged in power struggles with several village husbands over the time commitments of their wives to the Focolare movement, for example, Father Münster often used John's support of me and my research as an example of the independence all men should give their wives. On the day John left Germany, the priest falsely told a community gathering about a glowing assessment John had given of the Focolare movement. It may be that Father Münster focused on John more frequently because their relationship was less problematic than the one between me and the priest (John was not the one asking probing questions of the priest and his parishioners), although I was not immune to similar misrepresentations.

9. I have since learned that the Focolare movement actively enjoins its members to rid themselves of all "attachments," including those to things, persons, ideas, work, and relatives, that interfere with fulfilling the movement's ideals (Urquhart 1995: 18). Father Münster was thus largely echoing instructions of the movement's leaders.

10. Although the kitchen was frequented primarily by villagers most actively involved in the church as members of the parish council, board of directors, or Focolare discussion group, Father Münster's efforts to create a relaxed atmosphere in which many people felt at home at his house made the kitchen more accessible than in many parish rectories.

11. From the beginning, Father Münster had addressed us with the informal pronoun *Du* rather than the formal *Sie,* which he used with all parishioners. It was a gesture of multiple, if not fully conscious, intentions that initiated our relationship as one of equals distinct and separate from others in the community, thereby extending to us a welcome approval from a visible authority figure as well as constructing an association with us that I believe the priest found useful.

12. While it was true that Johanna's husband rarely acknowledged or discussed her illness with her, I believe this was a product of his own fear, denial, and emotional capacities rather than indifference.

13. I recognize that a similar situation could easily occur in the context of research in the United States and am not attributing this dilemma to cultural differences among Europe, Germany, and the United States (a notion that implies a certain boundedness and homogeneity of "culture" that I reject), but to cultural differences in class, education, and religion, stemming in part from divergent life experiences under two different political economic systems as well as subsequent negotiations of change following the collapse of socialism described here.

14. For discussions of the particular challenges of doing fieldwork in Europe,

see, e.g., Herzfeld 1987; Jaffe 1993; de Pina-Cabral and Campbell 1992; Sheehan 1993.

15. For a compelling account of mutual expectations in fieldwork, see Kondo 1990.

16. I am indebted to Behar's (1991) discussion of displaced emotions in relation to her grandfather's death and her study of death and memory in a Spanish village for inspiring much of my perspective here.

17. For a more detailed analysis of these transformations, particularly in relation to a dynamic between popular faith and institutionalized religion, see Berdahl 1999.

18. As a border village in the high-security zone, this community was a special object of state efforts to root out religion in the GDR. The local pilgrimage chapel was enclosed by the border fence, for example, thus making it inaccessible for nearly 40 years, and church services were occasionally prohibited here during the 1950s.

19. "Popular religion," Caroline Brettell writes, "applies to any social situation where a conflict or dialectic emerges between official religious models proposed by the ecclesiastical hierarchy and 'unofficial' forms" (Brettell 1990: 55). Constraints of space prevent me from going into detail here about the changing dynamics of, and interplay between, popular faith and institutionalized religion before and after the collapse of socialism (see Berdahl 1999).

20. See Berdahl 1999.

21. Telephone ethnography, a relatively new phenomenon that is particularly pertinent for anthropologists working in Europe, has interesting implications for the changing dynamic between "ourselves" and "the field" by extending relationships beyond the ethnographer's departure from the field through the immediacy of telephone communication. In this sense, telephone ethnography arguably has contributed to the blurring of boundaries between these two traditionally opposed categories.

22. Renato Rosaldo (1984), in his poignant and well-known essay "Grief and a Headhunter's Rage," was one of the first anthropologists to reflect on how experiences of people and ideas in the field may shape an anthropologist's sense of self and life events. See also Abu-Lughod 1995; Kondo 1990; Riesman 1977; Dubisch 1996. For an illuminating discussion of the interplay between life experience and ethnographic interests, or "auto/ethnography," in the European context, see Herzfeld 1997.

23. From a personal letter to Edward M. Bruner.

References

Abu-Lughod, L. 1990. Can there be a feminist ethnography? *Women and Performance* 5 (1): 7–27.

Abu-Lughod, L. 1991. Writing against culture. In Richard G. Fox, ed., *Recapturing anthropology,* 17–43. Santa Fe, N.M.: School of American Research Press.

Abu-Lughod, L. 1995. A tale of two pregnancies. In Ruth Behar and Deborah Gordon, eds., *Women writing culture,* 339–349. Berkeley: University of California Press.

Asad, T., ed. 1973. *Anthropology and the colonial encounter.* London: Ithaca Press.

Badone, E., ed. 1990. *Religious orthodoxy and popular faith in European society.* Princeton, N.J.: Princeton University Press.

Behar, R. 1991. Death and memory: From Santa María del Monte to Miami Beach. *Cultural Anthropology* 6 (3): 346–384.

Behar, R. 1993. *Translated woman: Crossing the border with Esperanza's story.* Boston: Beacon Press.

Behar, R. 1995. Introduction: Out of exile. In R. Behar and D. Gordon, eds., *Women writing culture,* 1–32. Berkeley: University of California Press.

Behar, R., and D. Gordon, eds. 1995. *Women writing culture.* Berkeley: University of California Press.

Berdahl, D. 1999. *Where the world ended: Re-unification and identity in the German borderland.* Berkeley: University of California Press.

Brettell, Caroline B. 1990. The priest and his people: The contractual basis for religious practice in rural Portugal. In Ellen Badone, ed., *Religious orthodoxy and popular faith in European society,* 55–75. Princeton, N.J.: Princeton University Press.

Bruner, E. M. 1990. Introduction: The ethnographic self and the personal self. In P. Benson, ed., *Anthropology and literature,* 1–26. Urbana: University of Illinois Press.

Clifford, J. 1983. On ethnographic authority. *Representations* 1 (2): 118–146.

Clifford, J. 1986. Introduction: Partial truths. In J. Clifford and G. Marcus, eds., *Writing culture: The poetics and politics of ethnography,* 1–26. Berkeley: University of California Press.

Clifford, James, and George E. Marcus, eds. 1986. *Writing culture: The poetics and politics of ethnography.* Berkeley: University of California Press.

Crapanzano, V. 1980. *Tuhami: Portrait of a Moroccan.* Chicago: University of Chicago Press.

de Pina-Cabral, J., and J. Campbell, eds. 1992. *Europe observed.* London: Macmillan.

Dubisch, J. 1995. Lovers in the field: Sex, dominance, and the female anthropologist. In D. Kulick and M. Wilson, eds., *Taboo: Sex, identity, and erotic subjectivity in anthropological fieldwork,* 29–50. London and New York: Routledge.

Dubisch, J. 1996. *In a different place: Pilgrimage, gender, and politics at a Greek island shrine.* Princeton, N.J.: Princeton University Press.

Dumont, Jean Paul. 1978. *The headman and I: Ambiguity and ambivalence in the fieldworking experience.* Austin: University of Texas Press.

Dwyer, K. 1982. *Moroccan dialogues.* Baltimore: Johns Hopkins University Press.

Fernandez, J. 1986. *Persuasions and performances: The play of tropes in culture.* Bloomington: Indiana University Press.

Fischer, H. F. 1991. The Catholic church in the GDR: A look back in anger. *Religion in Communist Lands* 19 (3–4): 211–219.

Handler, R. 1993. Fieldwork in Quebec, scholarly reviews, and anthropological dialogues. In C. Brettell, ed., *When they read what we write: The politics of ethnography,* 67–74. Westport, Conn.: Bergin and Garvey.

Herzfeld, M. 1987. *Anthropology through the looking-glass: Critical ethnography in the margins of Europe.* Cambridge: Cambridge University Press.

Herzfeld, Michael. 1997. The taming of the revolution: Intense paradoxes of the self. In Deborah E. Reed-Danahay, ed., *Auto/ethnography: Rewriting the self and the social.* Oxford: Berg.

Jaffe, A. 1993. Involvement, detachment, and representation on Corsica. In C. Brettell, ed., *When they read what we write: The politics of ethnography,* 51–66. Westport, Conn.: Bergin and Garvey.

Kondo, D. 1990. *Crafting selves: Power, gender, and discourses of identity in a Japanese workplace.* Chicago: University of Chicago Press.

Kubik, J. 1994. *The power of symbols against the symbols of power.* University Park: Pennsylvania State University Press.

McBeth, S. 1993. Myths of objectivity and the collaborative process in life history research. In C. Brettell, ed., *When they read what we write: The politics of ethnography,* 145–162. Westport, Conn.: Bergin and Garvey.

Myerhoff, B. 1978. *Number our days.* New York: E. P. Dutton.

Nagengast, C. 1991. *Reluctant socialists, rural entrepreneurs: Class, culture, and the Polish state.* Boulder, Colo.: Westview Press.

Narayan, K. 1993. How native is a "native" anthropologist? *American Anthropologist* 95: 671–686.

Rabinow, Paul. 1977. *Reflections on fieldwork in Morocco.* Berkeley: University of California Press.

Ramet, S. P. 1991. Protestants in East Germany, 1949–89: A summing up. *Religion in Communist Lands* 19 (3–4): 160–194.

Riegelhaupt, Joyce. 1984. Popular anti-clericalism and religiosity in pre-1974 Portugal. In Eric R. Wolf, ed., *The northern shore of the Mediterranean,* 83–114. Berlin: Mouton.

Riesman, P. 1977. *Freedom in Fulani life: An introspective ethnography.* Chicago: University of Chicago Press.

Rosaldo, R. 1984. Grief and a headhunter's rage: On the cultural force of emotions. In E. M. Bruner, ed., *Text, play and story,* 178–198. Washington, D.C.: American Ethnological Society.

Sheehan, E. A. 1993. The student of culture and the ethnography of Irish intellectuals. In C. Brettell, ed., *When they read what we write: The politics of ethnography,* 75–90. Westport, Conn.: Bergin and Garvey.

Tsing, A. L. 1993. *In the realm of the diamond queen: Marginality in an out-of-the-way place.* Princeton, N.J.: Princeton University Press.

Urquhart, G. 1995. *The pope's armada.* London: Bantam Press.

10

Researcher, Advocate, Friend
An American Fieldworker
among Balkan Roma, 1980–1996

Carol Silverman

I began doing fieldwork with Balkan Roma during a 10-month trip to Bulgaria in 1979–1980 and continued research during one- to two-month summer trips in 1984, 1985, 1989, 1990, and 1994.[1] Research with Roma in Macedonia began in 1989 in Skopje and Prilep, after a month of fieldwork with Macedonian Roma in New York City. In 1990, I lived for five months in the Rom neighborhood Shuto Orizari, outside of Skopje. I returned in 1994 for a one-month visit. Many of my Balkan Rom friends now live in New York City, where I visit them frequently. The language of communication between us is usually Bulgarian or Macedonian, both of which I speak. Some Balkan Roma also speak various dialects of Romani, which I understand well; however, my speaking ability in Romani is limited.

This is a story of relationships built up over many years between myself, a Jewish American[2] anthropologist, and a group of Muslim Roma (Gypsies) from Bulgaria and Macedonia, who may have little in common except that they know me. The most striking thing about the transformation of our relationship is that many of these people are now part of my life in an emotional and tangible sense: I speak with them by telephone frequently, I grieve and celebrate with them, I ask favors of them, they ask favors of me, my father does their taxes, my mother looks for apartments for them, and I am expected to visit them if I am in the neighborhood, whether that is in the Balkans or in New York. Although this matter-of-fact description of growing closeness is the typical trajectory of fieldwork relationships according to anthropological textbooks, it obscures those very feelings and repercussions that make fieldwork a transformative experience for all parties.

Although I hope my Rom friends will write their own accounts of our relationship, I realize that most of them do not have the resources (or the desire) to do so. The majority of Balkan Roma are not academics, and writing is an activity they reserve for letters and documents. The men are employed as metalworkers, construction workers, delivery men, superintendants of apartment buildings, and musicians; the women are employed as cleaning ladies, baby-sitters, hospital and nursing home aides, and in sales; and both men and women work as traders and vendors and in factories. Trajko Petrovski (1993) is perhaps the only Rom ethnographer in Macedonia who has documented his own culture, and his path to higher education has been far from easy.³ This account is from my point of view and is surely only a "partial truth" (Clifford 1986); my greater access to resources, my outsider status, and my liberal upbringing have certainly affected my perceptions. Much of the postmodern discussion of ethnography rests on the acknowledgment of multiple views; my account, then, has become the occasion for my Rom collaborators to discuss their interpretations of my interpretations. Employing Elaine Lawless' concept of "reciprocal ethnography" (1992), I asked a number of Rom intellectuals and a few collaborators from the New York Macedonian Rom community to read this chapter. Comments from Rom collaborators were generally positive, although some contradicted each other: whereas one person wanted his real name used because he was "proud to be Rom," another person wanted her name and place of residence concealed because of her fear of discrimination. Taking the safest route, I decided to employ pseudonyms, except for well-known politicians and musicians. My collaborators' specific reactions and our discussions are the subject of an ongoing project on the issue of representation of Roma. One commentator, University of Texas professor Ian Hancock, who is Rom, reminds us that until recently all representations of Roma were constructed by non-Roma, and Roma exercised no control whatsoever over these descriptions and images, whether scientific, artistic, or literary (1997a: 2; 1997b: 39–40). Now this is finally changing, and the ethnographer either becomes obsolete or else must negotiate a delicate place for his or her interpretation as one of many interpretations.

This chapter seeks to explore my experiential level of fieldwork among Roma during the socialist and postsocialist periods. Studying an oppressed minority during the socialist and postsocialist periods highlights many major issues that have been raised in the fieldwork literature, namely, ethics, the role of the fieldworker, the power differential between fieldworker and informants, and the give-and-take in relationships.[4] As I accepted hospitality and knowledge from Roma, I continually asked myself: What is my relationship to these people? What am I doing for those who so generously taught me? How can I best discuss my own position in this research? As the Rom human rights movement emerged in eastern Europe in the 1990s, I struggled to combine activism and scholarship and was alternately accused of neglecting one for the other: Whereas a Rom activist said I should concentrate on documenting human rights abuses and forget about analyzing music and culture, some of my colleagues in academia said I was spending too much time documenting human rights abuses (which they regarded as "service," not scholarship). I interrogated myself about the role of a non-Rom scholar in the fields of education and human rights advocacy. What right do I have to speak about a group which is trying to define its own voice?[5] I believe I have an important role among non-Roma in education and advocacy. But Roma have their own organizing to do among themselves, and I learned to withdraw when a context required my exclusion. Among Roma, non-Roma such as myself can facilitate, mediate, and provide resources for various cultural, economic, and political projects while eschewing paternalistic and colonizing stances. As Kamala Visweswaran writes, "If we have learned anything about anthropology's encounter with colonialism, the question is not really whether anthropologists can represent people better, but whether we can be accountable to people's struggles for self-representation and self-determinism" (1988: 39). Because Roma are currently engaged in precisely the struggle for self-determinism, my research began to focus precisely on how Roma are constructing symbols and discourses in their self-representation. Music is an especially powerful currency in self-representation (Silverman 1996a, b). My roles, then, bridged analyst, documentor, advocate, and friend.

Embracing a feminist stance in ethnography,[6] I pursued the study of gender, first unconsciously, then more consciously through the last 15 years; this was not hard to do, since Rom society evinces much gender segregation, and, thus, I spent a great deal of time with women and often compared their perceptions and choices with those of men (Silverman 1996a). I spent time with men as well, but it was usually in the company of other women; the one exception to this pattern was my interviews with male political leaders, which were usually one on one. Gender issues were evident everywhere, in ritual, work, politics; also, people enjoyed talking about them. I tried to let the agenda of my research emerge in conjunction with my associates, taking cues from their comments and instructions. Finally, I tried to let myself be a person with emotions and feelings as well as a researcher; to me, part of feminism and activism is to encounter someone on human terms, not merely cross-cultural terms (also see Berdahl, this volume). Abu-Lughod makes a similar point in her chapter "Writing against Culture," where she advocates for "tactical humanism" (1991).

Why Roma?

My knowledge of Roma dates from my teenage years in New York when I began doing international Balkan folk dancing at clubs and universities. I learned that Roma are an ethnic group, originally from India, who number 10 million to 12 million people worldwide and that they have been hated by the majority populations but have been prominent as professional musicians in the Balkans (Crowe 1995). My first few trips to the Balkans (1972–1976) allowed me to observe Roma from afar, and I then began collecting records and tapes and learning to sing Bulgarian music. My commitment to understanding the contexts of Balkan music persuaded me to turn my hobby into my career: I enrolled in graduate school in the Department of Folklore at the University of Pennsylvania to acquire the analytical tools to analyze the music and ritual in which I was immersed.

When it came time to select a dissertation topic, I was sure it would be in Bulgaria, but in the mid-1970s there were horror stories about doing official research in Bulgaria (e.g., tapes being confiscated, prohibitions against fieldwork in rural areas), and I began to consider other options. Fortuitously, I became a volunteer teacher in a Rom alternative school in Philadelphia, and I decided to do my dissertation research with Roma in the United States. My research with the two largest Rom groups in the United States, Kalderash and Machwaya, dealt with ethnic identity, ethnic boundary maintenance, gender, and women's roles in the pollution and taboo systems (Silverman 1981, 1982, 1988). Having migrated to the United States from various parts of eastern Europe about a hundred years ago, many Kalderash and Machwaya know very little about their distant relatives in Europe. Among the few tangible things I was able to give to American Roma were historical information and cassette tapes of eastern European Rom music, and we had lively discussions about cultural differences.

Having immersed myself in American Kalderash and Machwaya culture for four years (1975–1979) and having gained some fluency in their Vlach dialects of Romani, I was anxious to pursue Rom fieldwork in Bulgaria, a country I had visited regularly since 1972. My husband, Mark Levy, an ethnomusicologist, received a grant to do dissertation fieldwork in Bulgaria during 1979–1980, and I accompanied him. At first I lamented that not having an academic affiliation would hinder my research, but the opposite was true; Mark had the hassle of obtaining official permission to do everything, while I, being "an accompanying spouse," was freer to pursue my research because I often went unnoticed.[7]

Socialist Bulgaria

The problems of doing fieldwork in Bulgaria in the 1970s and early 1980s among both majority and minority groups were myriad.[8] First, the government did not usually give permission to Westerners to live in villages, even if that stipulation had been specified in a grant proposal which the government accepted.[9] The state did not want foreigners wandering around rural areas seeing how people lived; there was less police supervision in villages, hence it would be harder to monitor our activities, which were suspicious, since we were surely spies. Mark and I waited and waited in Sofia for permission to live in a Rhodope Mountain village, and when a month went by and we realized we would never get permission, we compromised by agreeing to live in a hotel in Smolyan, the regional capital. We rarely slept in the hotel, however, and instead often slept in the homes of our friends, in violation of policy.

This brings up the second problem, namely, that Bulgarians were not supposed to socialize with or offer lodging to "the enemy," that is, people from the West. We would beg and plead with our friends to accept the fact that we could not sleep over, but their Balkan hospitality made us promise we would stay. If a knock was heard at midnight and a police officer entered and ordered us to leave, I do not know whose shame was greater, theirs or ours. Most of our nightly sojourns were undetected, but a few friends were fined a month's salary for hosting us, and when we offered to pay the fine, they would not accept our money. I felt unethical and guilty for causing these problems.

Third, we were told that fieldworkers had to be accompanied by a Bulgarian researcher; this unwritten rule was intermittently invoked to discourage us from going to isolated rural areas. Ostensibly Mark's assigned supervisor was to drive with us on each trip to the Rhodope Mountain region, but the first time he accompanied us, he saw that we knew the villagers already, so he turned around and headed home to Sofia! In 1979, we were also told that we could not film unless a Bulgarian camera person from the Institute of Music were next to us, filming the same thing at the same time. Since we were unaccompanied, this would have meant calling the institute a few days ahead and having its camera person drive six hours to the Rhodopes, just to stand next to us and film. We were too intimidated to film in the Rhodopes during Mark's initial grant period, but when we realized how ridiculous this agreement was and how unsupervised we really were, we ignored the agreement and filmed when we could.

Fourth, endless bureaucracy was required for every move. For example, instead of giving us our stipend for a few months at a time, the financial officer from the Academy of Sciences required us to drive back to Sofia every month; this, of course, was a tactic to disrupt our rural research. We surmounted this rule by living for a few months on one month's stipend. It also took two months to receive special permission to visit villages in the *granichna zona* (border zone) where Mark's key musician informants lived. Even Bulgarian villagers needed permission to visit these villages bordering Greece and Turkey, and inhabitants of these villages had a special pass. From the government's point of view, they didn't want to risk the possibility of Bulgarians escaping to the West over the mountains. For us, however, the rules made no sense, since we did not need to escape to Greece. On the other hand, the Rhodope border region is very isolated and is dotted with military installations, which we were not supposed to see; furthermore, many border villages are inhabited by Pomaks (Bulgarian-speaking Muslims), who were persecuted religiously and culturally during the socialist period.[10]

For me, the hardest thing about fieldwork in socialist Bulgaria was neither the hassle nor the surveillance I endured; rather, it was the suffering which I could have caused my informants: their surveillance, fines, interrogations, and emotional wrenching. I knew that if I were to do something wrong, I could always contact the American Embassy, but what could my friends do? When our passports were confiscated and we were questioned by the police for five hours after we took a hike into the border zone without the proper documentation, I knew that we would not be jailed. But when a friend was warned of dire consequences if she continued to associate with me, I was really worried for her. In later years, one Rhodope village woman cried when she confessed that in 1980 she had had to lock us out of the sleeping quarters we had rented on the orders of a superior who thought we were drug runners. She knew, of course, that we were innocent.

Working with Roma in socialist Bulgaria was especially challenging because by 1984 they did not officially exist. As part of the Bulgarization process, official policy claimed there were no ethnic minorities in the country; ethnic designations were removed from internal passports and from government documents.[11] Even earlier, scholars were discouraged from studying Roma; Bulgarian ethnographer Elena Marushiakova went to Czechoslovakia to do her dissertation research on Roma because it was impossible to do such research in Bulgaria; Bulgarian folklorist Lozanka Peicheva chose a different topic because her adviser dissuaded her from studying Rom music. Officials repeatedly told me (with an ironic smile) that I could not work with a people who do not exist. During 1979–1980 and in 1984 I took advantage of my unofficial status and tried not to draw attention to myself when I visited Rom settlements. In 1985 I invented a Sofia archive project as a cover for official status; in reality, I left Sofia for fieldwork among Roma every Thursday through Sunday.

Sonja

My first Bulgarian Rom friend was Sonja, who was 15 years old in 1979 and was a vocal student at the music high school in Shiroka Luka, a village in the Rhodope Mountains. Strikingly ironic is the fact that she was the only Rom pupil in a music school of hundreds of students. This was indicative of state discrimination; many Rom children are particularly talented musically because of continual exposure to live music from infancy (not because of genetic essentializing). I was also a vocal student, attending classes as well as studying music education in relation to state ideology. Sonja was very discreet about her ethnicity; she passed as a Bulgarian, and she told me not to speak about Roma in front of other students. She was interested in the tapes I had of Bulgarian Rom music from the 1950s, 1960s, and early 1970s. Because Rom music was banned from state recordings, my tapes were very valuable, and we often listened to music together. When she invited me to visit her home in a small Thracian town, I was thrilled. Her cousin Vela was to be married over spring vacation, and Mark and I were invited. This visit began a 15-year association with Sonja's family.

I already knew about discrimination against Roma in Balkan society from historical sources (Crowe 1995). But I could hardly miss the racist remarks Bulgarians (even intellectuals) regularly made about them, using the name "Tsiganin" (Gypsy) as an ethnic slur meaning "lazy, dirty, and untrustworthy." I was warned by many Bulgarian and Macedonian scholars that I would surely be robbed or even killed if I ventured into a Rom settlement. Evidence from a 1992 survey indicates that levels of prejudice against Roma in Bulgaria exceeded levels of prejudice against blacks in the American South in the 1950s. More specifically, 41 percent of Bulgarians polled (excluding Turks and Pomaks) indicated that they would not want to live in the same neighborhood as Roma; 27 percent indicated that they would prefer not to live in the same country as Roma (Kunev 1994, 1996). I always tried to argue with the racism of my Bulgarian friends, but I rarely succeeded. Often, in desperation, I merely concealed my involvement with Roma.

When I arrived for Sonja's cousin's wedding in April 1980, I immediately felt as if I were in another culture, closer to India than eastern Europe. The Rom settlement, which was on the outskirts of a small city, consisted of run-down houses and shacks, unpaved streets, outdoor sanitation, and a dense population of approximately 2,000 Roma, all of whom seemed to be in the streets and courtyards. The smells, sounds, and textures were vastly different from the Bulgarian and Pomak villages I had visited, and people were much poorer. Rom and Turkish music could be heard everywhere, children of all ages in various stages of undress played outdoors, and body distances were much closer. Street life was active, noisy, and multigenerational.

Sonja's family greeted us in true Balkan fashion; we were treated as royal guests and her father slaughtered a lamb for us. Her father was the *baro Rom* (big man) of the neighborhood, someone who was very respected by the Roma in their settlement and maintained good relations with state officials. Roma asked him to negotiate problems with the authorities for them. From Sonja and her family I learned about discrimination in school, tracking into classes for retarded children, housing shortages, employment discrimination, and regulations about the practice of Islam, including the closing of mosques, prohibitions against circumcisions, and prohibitions against wearing *shalvari* (the wide Turkish-style pants worn by Muslim women) (Silverman 1989, 1995a).

On repeated visits to Sonja's family I learned about Rom economic adaptations to socialism, especially in the second economy (Silverman 1986, 1996c). Sonja's parents, in addition to having state jobs, were involved in the sale of building materials, clothing, horses, brooms, and foodstuffs at various times during the nine years of socialism in which I knew them. I also learned about gender relations by seeing the choices Sonja had growing up, marrying, and having children. I compared women's choices with men's in relation to generational, class, and ethnic differences. After attending many Rom weddings, I realized the significant role of women in ritual, dance, and song. I noted similarities with and differences from Bulgarian Slavic weddings and Muslim Pomak weddings, and I began to flesh out the patterns and the symbols in Rom ritual. And finally, from Sonja and many others, I learned about the tremendous importance of wedding music in the lives of Roma, both as musicians and as active patrons. Despite its prohibition, or perhaps because of it, wedding music became a countercultural expression.[12] Sonja patiently helped me with Romani song texts, some of which I now sing.

As I engaged in more intimate conversations, I decided not to do formal interviews, with either Sonja's family or other Rom families. A tape recorder would have been too formal and intrusive and would have disrupted the conversational flow. Instead, I took notes during conversations, especially noting new Romani phrases, and I wrote up more extensive fieldnotes whenever I could. Finding fieldnote writing time, however, was sometimes difficult, since I often had no privacy during most visits. I might be with my hosts continuously for a three- or four-day wedding, except for sleeping a few hours at night. In Macedonia in 1990 this problem of lack of privacy was solved by my renting my own room in a Rom settlement (see below). Obviously, I could not do the same in socialist Bulgaria. In post-socialist Bulgaria and in socialist Macedonia, I did formal interviews with Rom political leaders. These men were used to being recorded and wanted their exact words to be disseminated.

I tape-recorded, photographed, and videotaped many Rom ritual events, such as weddings, circumcisions, baptisms, soldier send-off celebrations, and house warmings, making sure to procure permission from the sponsors. Ritual events lent themselves to documentation by electronic media; everyone was very interested in seeing the products, and I regularly sent videos, tapes, and hundreds of pictures to the families. At first I thought my camera would be conspicuous, but I observed that the sponsoring family usually hired a local cameraman to videotape.[13] My photographs and videos were useful in helping me write up fieldnotes and analyze performance. Families often viewed videotapes with me and offered valuable interpretations. Often their interpretations of their events centered around the "Rom way of doing things," in the light of being both Bulgarian and Rom. Discussions always turned on the role of the state in their lives. I realized that the state was also a defining feature of my fieldwork.

Shutka, 1990

My experiences living in Shuto Orizari (locally known as Shutka), a Rom neighborhood outside Skopje, Macedonia, sharply contrasted with my Bulgarian socialist experiences in that I had neither supervision nor bureaucratic hassles. The Macedonian Institute of Folklore let me arrange my own affairs,[14] and I checked in with them only once a month. Arranging my accommodations, however, was not an easy task. Without prior Rom contacts, it would have been impossible to walk into Shutka and look for a room to rent. Roma would have been too suspicious of my being either a government official or an unexplained entity. I seemed even more suspicious because I was a woman apart from my family. I knew I wanted to live with a Muslim family (the majority religion among Shutka Roma), but Shutka is a formidable community of 40,000 Roma (perhaps the largest Rom neighborhood in the world), covering several square miles, with many Rom dialect groups, occupational groups, and economic classes. I had to learn the lay of the land.

I was brought into the community by Zoja, a Rom woman whom I had met in New York when she was visiting her brother, Kadri, for a few months. I had met Kadri at a conference of the Gypsy Lore Society held in Staten Island in 1987. When he found out my parents lived in his neighborhood in the Bronx, he invited me to meet his wife, Rabija, his sister Zoja, and the rest of the family. I attended Kadri and Rabija's two sons' circum-

cision party a few months later and began research with the community of
Macedonian Roma in the Bronx, which dates from the 1960s. I began attending Rom ritual events in the same rented halls in which I had attended
bar mitzvahs as a child. I discovered my old neighborhood was Albanian
and Rom.

When Zoja invited me to visit her in Skopje, I began to plan a longer research trip to Shutka for 1990. But I still wanted to check out the situation
in Shutka myself before arriving for a five-month trip. During summer
1989, Mark and I and our three-year-old daughter, Nesa, spent the summer
improving our Macedonian language skills at the Ohrid seminar, visiting
Zoja's mother in Prilep, and checking out possible living arrangements in
Shutka. The three brothers of Zoja's husband, Ekrem, lived in Shutka, in a
recently divided *zaednica,*[15] the compound of a multigenerational extended
patrilineal-patrilocal family; unfortunately, there were no empty rooms to
rent in the compound. Zoja introduced me to their neighbor, Ahmed, a
fairly well-to-do[16] merchant and taxi-driver living with his five sons and
their families in a few adjacent houses. Zoja was very concerned that I live
with a respectable family close to her husband's brothers because she felt responsible for me. She even tried to convince me to live with one of Ekrem's
brothers who lived in a new apartment complex far from Shutka near the
airport. When she realized how determined I was to live in Shutka, she sent
Ekrem to talk seriously to Ahmed about which room might be available and
how much it would cost.

When I arrived alone in March 1990, Zoja and Ekrem helped me negotiate rent and utilities for my two rooms, plus use of the telephone and hot
water in Ahmed's house. I had minimal furniture, a stove, no water, and no
heat. I explained that I didn't need furniture except for a bed and a crib, and
I would prefer a "Turkish style" house with cushions lining the walls for sitting and learning. The women in Ahmed's family heartily approved of my
taste and proceeded to outfit my sitting room. For the first month I used water from the central courtyard, which I shared with three daughters-in-law;
I also used the courtyard outhouse. When I informed Ahmed that my parents would be arriving in a month with my three-year-old, he immediately
began planning the construction of a bathroom (toilet and sink) on my balcony. He wasn't concerned about my convenience, but when he heard my
parents were over 70 years old and would be traveling over 24 hours from
New York, he became concerned about their well-being. In Macedonia,
most Roma do not live into their 70s; a 60-year-old person is considered
very old. Although construction proceeded slowly, by the time my parents
arrived I had a cold-water faucet and a toilet installed in a makeshift room
on the balcony. I was very thankful.

Having my parents visit for three weeks made me more human in everyone's eyes: I was a person connected to a family, not a free floating researcher.[17] My parents were invited to visit the families I knew, and their presence introduced important topics of conversation such as generational differences, economics, and religion. My daughter's presence taught me much about the socialization of values and behaviors. I believe three-year-old Nesa knew more about wedding rituals than I did because she played "wedding" every day with the Rom kids; for example, she imitated perfectly the modest stance of the bride and knew exactly how brides are supposed to fold their hands.

When Mark arrived in July, I was relieved, because being a single parent left little time for long conversations and journal writing (my parents had left in May). As a single parent, most of my time was taken up by cooking, washing clothes (heating water on the stove, washing by hand), and keeping an eye on Nesa. She was actually rarely alone, for the neighborhood kids quickly adopted her into their play groups. Even though Mark had his own fieldwork project learning to play the *surla*,[18] he was ready and willing to help me with domestic chores so I could have more time for research. I, on the other hand, wanted to conform to the gender division of domestic labor in the region, namely, that men do not clean and wash (they do cook occasionally and shop regularly). So Mark and I worked out a system whereby I would carry the dirty dishes outside and then into the bathroom; I would wait there a few minutes and leave the dirty dishes there; later, Mark would go into the bathroom, wash the dishes, and leave them there; then I would go into the bathroom and carry out the clean dishes, hopefully giving the impression that I had actually washed them. We did the same for dirty clothes, with me always doing the public task of hanging them on the line in the courtyard. We managed to maintain a superficial appearance of conventional gender roles while subverting them for our own needs. I always wondered if anyone suspected the truth. No one ever mentioned it to me in later visits, but a few people remarked that I never wore pants (a positive trait in their eyes), unlike many American women.

Was I abandoning my feminist principles? Of course, I could have chosen the path of my setting a different example, that is, demonstrating that men wash dishes and hang clothes in America; I could have helped women and men realize that roles can change. But at that point in my fieldwork I was too worried about my own reputation and acceptance. When my parents came to visit, my mother was also ready to do the domestic chores so I could concentrate on research and writing. But elderly women in Rom society are supposed to be served by daughters and daughters-in-law, so I refused my mother's help. This brings up the question of how much a fieldworker's behavior should or does influence the people of the community. In my case, I tried to show respect by conforming to local behavior; on the

Macedonian Rom bride at her henna party in Skopje, May 1990 (Photograph by Carol Silverman)

Female relatives of a Macedonian Rom bride bringing presents of clothing when visiting her for the first time at the groom's house in Skopje, 1990 (Photograph by Carol Silverman)

other hand, I freely initiated conversations about gender roles and willingly offered comparisons with and opinions of my own society, explaining the history of American feminism. I was, perhaps, a conduit of new ideas. I chose to be more conservative in my behavior than in my words because my reputation had to be impeccable: I now represented Zoja's family. Any breach in my behavior would reflect their bad judgment in placing me in the community.

In the first few weeks when I was alone, for example, the question arose about the appropriateness of my having male visitors; Rom political activists (alone or in groups) came to visit me, and my landlord, Ahmed, was upset. He said that I was setting a bad example for his daughters-in-law, daughters, and granddaughters. Inside, I certainly resented his assumption of improper activities, but I realized that it didn't matter to him whether we were discussing politics or kissing. What mattered to him was that people saw men entering the home of a woman alone. I politely explained to him that part of my work, my reason for being in Shutka, was to understand the politicization process (Silverman 1995b), and that I might occasionally need to have male visitors in my home. But after that, I did avoid male visitors and arranged visits in their homes and offices rather than in my own.[19]

I also had the problem of being taken seriously as a woman by some male politicians.

This brings up the issue of giving and taking in any fieldwork encounter or any friendship. I always arrived in the Balkans with a suitcase or two of beautiful gifts to be distributed among all the persons I visited, for example, sweatshirts from the University of Oregon. I felt this was the least I could do to assuage my guilt over being richer than my Balkan friends; I did not consider payment, since there is virtually no precedent for monetary compensation in Balkan ethnographic research. One might say I gave such things as my time, my attention to any topics they wanted to discuss, and my efforts to bring their problems of persecution to the attention of Americans. But I always felt I was taking more than I was giving. Especially in Bulgaria, where material conditions were worse than in Macedonia, I felt guilty about taking food, hospitality, and presents from people hardly able to provide for themselves. Of course, there are always the few people in any group who ask for your car or your tape recorder as a present! And indeed, I would have liked to give everyone a car or a tape recorder. Surely the precise nature of my finances always remained a bit of a mystery to my Rom friends, no matter how many times I explained my salary, stipend, rent, living expenses, and so on. I am sure I must have seemed rich to them. The ease of my financial situation has motivated me to utilize my knowledge in activist projects, and this has been easier to do in the postsocialist period.

Postsocialism and Coming Over to Dinner: Balkan Roma in the United States

The most dramatic changes for Roma in the Balkans during the postsocialist period are the drastic decline in the economic situation, the threat of violence against them, and (for Bulgarian Roma) the new possibility of emigrating. In Macedonia and Bulgaria, rates of Rom unemployment have increased up to 90 percent in some regions (Human Rights Watch 1996: 2; Cahn 1997), because Roma are fired from failing state enterprises and not hired into private ones. In Shutka in 1994, people complained about increased prices, increased hostility between Macedonians and Roma, police harassment of street vendors (Cahn 1997), and increased harassment in the trading niche, which was one of the few viable occupations (Silverman 1995a, b). In 1998, the European Roma Rights Center issued a country report on Macedonian Roma, documenting legal and judicial abuses, destruction of property, discrimination in allocation of welfare payments, discrimination in education, and service bans on Roma in public establishments. It seemed as if every Rom wanted to emigrate, and I was asked frequently to sponsor families. In Bulgaria the situation for Roma is even worse; in addition to a dire economic situation for Roma, over a hundred incidents of individual, mob, and police violence have been documented against Roma by Human Rights Watch (1991) and the Human Rights Project (1994, 1995). The economic and psychological situation in some settlements is very grim, and media stereotypes abound; I began to focus my research on the political and cultural terms of the human rights struggle (Silverman 1995a, 1996c).

Wherever I went in the Balkans, I was now considered a link to the West (also see Dudwick; Kuehnast; and Zanca, all in this volume). I was asked to arrange emigration, university education, concert tours, CD production, book publication, and invitations to conferences. The last item is the only thing I could easily do (except for finding the airfare to get to the conferences). It was difficult saying no so often, especially because I wanted to reciprocate for all the years of hospitality. I ended up doing some of the latter on American soil. Mark and I sponsored a Bulgarian student who lived with us for one year and lived with my parents for over a year. I am currently investigating how my Macedonian Rom tutor in Shutka, a young woman, can study nursing in the United States.

As I mentioned earlier, Macedonian Roma began coming to the United States in the 1960s (some for short visits), but since 1991 many more have arrived, and, more significant, many more want to remain. During the years 1991–1995, Zoja and Ekrem's nephew arrived, then came their eldest son, then Zoja, then their youngest son, then finally Ekrem. In fact, a double wedding for the two sons was planned in New York for many months, but it had to be delayed until Ekrem could obtain a visa. Viewing this situation from both Old World and New World viewpoints helped me understand how the Rom diaspora works and how Roma negotiate across distances. Whereas Zoja hadn't seen her husband in over a year, I saw them both in my going back and forth, bringing gifts to her relatives and providing each side with pictures and videotapes I had made. I realized I was a link in a large communication network consisting of relatives traveling back and forth visiting, working temporarily, and looking for brides and grooms. I became closest with Rabija, the wife of Zoja's brother Kadri, because she was open and honest in assessing traditional values. We often had long conversations about marriage choices and gender conflict. Being kin-oriented, these Roma always invited my parents along with me to visit, and my parents and I extended invitations and warmth to them. My mother began to look for vacant apartments on our street for them, and my father, an accountant, began doing the taxes for Rom families.

Unlike the situation with Macedonian Roma, there are virtually no Bulgarian Roma in the United States, since most do not have the money to travel and there are no kin networks to sponsor them. My field sites of Rom research, Bulgaria and Macedonia, were, then, very separate and distinct in my mind until a Turkish Rom musician from Bulgaria, named Yuri Yunakov, immigrated to the Bronx in 1994. I met Yuri in Bulgaria in the 1980s when I was researching contemporary wedding music; he was the saxophone player in the band Trakija, the foremost Rom wedding band, headed by Ivo Papazov. In Bulgaria, Yuri was a legendary musician who was in great demand for Rom and Bulgarian celebrations, concerts, and festivals; he had also toured western Europe and North America. I met Yuri again in 1991 when Trakija did a concert in Portland, Oregon. Mark and I brought gifts and Balkan food to their motel rooms, and we took them shopping and relaxed together. When Trakija was on tour in New York City, some of the Macedonian Roma went to their concert, and they were so enamored of each other that the Macedonian Roma invited them to the Bronx for an impromptu dance party. As legend goes, the dancers went wild and $2,000 was collected in tips. (The band had agreed to play for no salary, only tips.) On the approach of the following New Year's, a Macedonian Rom who lived in New York sent Yuri airplane tickets and an invitation to play at a New Year's party; Yuri decided to stay, and his wife soon followed. Amazingly, my two separate worlds of Macedonian Roma and Bulgarian Roma had suddenly merged in the Bronx.

In August 1994, Yuri, his wife, Lidija, my family, and I found ourselves together teaching at the Balkan Music and Dance Workshop in Maryland, sponsored by the East European Folklife Center.[20] As I got to know Yuri and Lidija better, I began to understand better the world of Bulgarian Rom music of the 1980s and 1990s through Yuri's family history and his training and through Lidija's recollections of their meeting (she is a Pomak). In New York, I saw how Yuri adjusted his previous musical repertoire and learned a new repertoire for the demands of new audiences, because he was now playing not only for Macedonian Roma, but for Macedonians, Albanians, Albanian Roma, Turks, Armenians, Arabs, and occasionally for American folk dancers. When he asked me to help him apply for a work permit, I was happy to oblige. When I started helping him prepare his asylum case, I began to document the arrests and fines he had endured during the socialist period (because he was playing Rom music, which was outlawed by the state) and the harassment and discrimination he had suffered (simply because he is a Rom) during the postsocialist period.[21] As a translator for his asylum case in August 1995, I was able to show, with the aid of documents from Human Rights Watch (1991), Amnesty International, and the Human Rights Project (1994), a systematic pattern of abuse of the human rights of Roma in Bulgaria, in his town specifically and involving him personally. Two weeks later he found out that he had been granted asylum; I believe this was one of the first cases in the United States in which political asylum was

The author (*right*) with Macedonian Rom singer Esma Redzhepova at the Balkan Music and Dance Workshop in Mendocino, California, in June 1997 (Photograph by Jennifer Blecha)

awarded to a Bulgarian Rom. I was thrilled that I had applied my knowledge in a practical, tangible task. But Yuri and Lidija were even more ecstatic because they felt safe and could then apply to bring their two young children, whom they had not seen in over a year, to the United States (they arrived a few months later). Through the next year, I helped Yuri and Lidija navigate through much paperwork, a task only an English speaker could do (he and his wife did not yet speak English).

Even before receiving asylum, Yuri decided to form another band in New York, the Yuri Yunakov Ensemble, one that would play a combination of Bulgarian wedding music and Macedonian Rom music, which overlap in the area of Rom repertoire.[22] The band members included a Macedonian Rom drummer, a Bulgarian bass player, a Bulgarian accordionist, an American clarinetist (who was Yuri's student), and an American guitarist. When he called me to ask me to perform with the band as a singer, I was flabbergasted. At first I thought he was trying to repay me for help I was giving him in preparing his immigration documents. I told him so, saying that I lived too far away (in Oregon), that he could ask singers from Bulgaria who now live in New York, and that I was just a beginner. He laughed and insisted that he wanted me as a member of the band, and that I could rehearse and perform on trips to New York. I realized he was serious, accepted, gulped, and realized that he had offered me a big musical challenge. Yuri's invitation caused me to evaluate and sort out the different roles of music in my life. I had sung Balkan music for over 20 years and Rom music for about 5 years, but mostly in American contexts; I had studied Balkan village music and was now studying Rom music, but my Rom friends in Bulgaria and Macedonia and in the Bronx had never even heard me sing, although they had occasionally helped me with lyrics. Being in the band has given me more visibility in the Bronx Rom community, and this has been helpful in making contacts.[23] Also, my explanatory introductions to our perform-ances have provided opportunities to counteract stereotypes of Roma among non-Roma and to provide historical and cultural information. An-other educational conduit has been the release of the first CD of the Yuri Yunakov Ensemble, *New Colors in Bulgarian Wedding Music* (1997), for which I wrote the liner booklet. After being in the band for over two years, I now see that it has united many aspects of my involvement with Roma: politics and music; performing and studying performance; and education and advocacy.

A cursory overview of the fieldwork trajectory from socialist to postsocial-ist settings reveals a movement from a focus on informant and fieldworker problems in relation to the state to a focus on dealing with the profound transformations in economics, politics, and personal life. Rather than cop-ing with and resisting the centralized state as during socialism (with the ethnographer as witness), citizens of eastern Europe must now refashion their lives and negotiate new choices (with the ethnographer as accom-plice). Their choices often involve the ethnographer-friend in an active role as contact, conduit, or advocate (also see Zanca, this volume). And this can now sometimes be done on American soil, in one's own living room.

Through my fieldwork encounters, advocacy and cultural analysis have become two sides of the same project. In the fall of 1995, for example, I hosted three people from the Human Rights Project in Sofia (two Roma and one Bulgarian) for a "democracy training" program. They were shown how and where affirmative action works and doesn't work in Eugene, Ore-gon, including police sensitivity training, the human rights commission, and multicultural education in the elementary schools. I also took them to meet our local Kalderash Roma. One of the Bulgarian Roma was a music arranger for a popular Rom band, and, while we listened to new tapes, we discussed how recent trends in music relate to the politicization of Roma.

Perhaps this case illustrates how politics can lead to music. The converse also occurs: When I saw Sonja in Bulgaria in 1994, we went to visit her cousin Vela, whose wedding in 1980 was my entrée into Rom culture. Vela's husband had become an official in the Rom regional union and was helping to lobby for food subsidies for the poor. I recently received a letter from him from London; he had to flee from Bulgaria after losing his job because of his political organizing activities and because he was being harassed by the police. I am trying to figure out what I can do to help his asylum case. The different threads of my involvement with Roma are thus interwoven in complex ways: education, research, performance, and advocacy all impact each other. Above all, I try to be alert and aware of the ethical and global implications of my changing roles.

Notes

1. Fieldwork took place in the cities of Sofia, Septemvri, Razlog, Smolyan, and Straldzha and in various villages.

2. American Rom activist-intellectual Ian Hancock (personal communication) encouraged me to reflect on my involvement with Roma in terms of my eastern European Jewish upbringing. I see that what we have shared—the warmth of and respect for the extended family, as well as a history of suffering (notably the Holocaust)—has helped in establishing rapport.

3. There are a growing number of Balkan Rom intellectuals, including Rajko Djuric from Serbia (writer and activist), Nicolae Gheorge from Romania (sociologist and activist), Andrzej Mirga from Poland (sociologist and activist), and Hristo Kyuchukov from Bulgaria (linguist and activist). Trajko Petrovski is the only member of his family to receive a higher education. Employed at the Institute of Folklore in Skopje, Macedonia, Petrovski recently completed his dissertation on Macedonian Rom customs. In 1990 he was one of my mentors at the institute, and I wish to thank him for his valuable contacts.

4. The literature about roles and ethics in ethnographic fieldwork is vast, encompassing such works as Jackson 1987; Fluehr-Loban 1991; and Wolcott 1995.

5. Although I saw myself speaking about Roma in the cause of advocacy, would I be seen as speaking for Roma at a time that they were seeking their own voice? This issue has been raised in the debates over representation as in Marcus and Fischer 1986; Roof and Wiegman 1995; and Wolf 1996. For the Rom case, see Hancock 1997b.

6. A specifically feminist ethnography has been discussed widely in the literature; see Abu-Lughod 1990; Behar and Gordon 1995; Visweswaran 1988; Wolf 1992; Wolf 1996; also De Soto, this volume.

7. The accompanying female spouse as a writer of ethnography is a common pattern (e.g., Margery Wolf, Elizabeth Fernea, and Marjorie Shostak). In my case, I was already a trained folklorist.

8. Note that the problems I describe below are related more to totalitarianism

than to socialism; these problems would likely be encountered in any repressive society, capitalist or socialist.

9. To my knowledge, Gerald Creed was the first American to be allowed to live in a village during socialism (1988–1989). His circumstances were somewhat special in that his mentor was the wife of an official highly placed in the Communist Party.

10. I was also doing unofficial research among Pomaks during this 1979–1980 research trip.

11. The government policy of Bulgarization intended to turn all minorities into proper socialists. The policy began in the 1970s with the Pomaks and Roma and was extended in 1984–1985 to the ethnic Turks, attracting international attention (see Poulton 1994).

12. See Rice 1996: 187–194; Buchanan 1996: 200–212; Silverman 1989, 1996b.

13. The videotapes made by the local cameramen usually differed from mine in that they focused on the most public moments of the rituals; mine included more private ceremonies and preparations for events. One reason for this is that the cameramen were males and thus lacked access to these female-centered events. Their videotapes also depicted the sponsoring family as the "patron-stars" of the video; after all, they were paying the cameramen. My videotapes depict a wider array of performers, including crowd scenes, uninvited onlookers, and so on.

14. This pattern was not typical of the institute in the 1980s. A few years earlier, a music researcher working with the Albanian minority was hassled frequently. My research was probably less threatening, since Macedonians perceive Albanians, not Roma, as the main ethnic threat to their security. Also, the International Research and Exchanges Board (IREX, which provided my funding) had not negotiated an official contract with the Macedonian Academy that year; instead, there was an informal agreement. Thus, my money came directly from IREX and avoided the academy bureaucracy. Finally, I strategically divided my mentorship at the institute between two people—one senior folklorist, whom I chose for legitimacy, and one younger scholar, Trajko Petrovski, the only Rom ethnographer in Skopje. Both let me supervise my own research, which I preferred.

15. *Zaednica* is the local word for *zadruga.*

16. In Shutka, markers of a well-to-do family included such amenities as a paved courtyard, a water heater in the bathroom, and a television.

17. Lila Abu-Lughod (1988) also mentions that having her father accompany her to her field site in Egypt was his way of showing the community that she was loved and protected by her family.

18. A surla, or *zurla,* is a double-reed pipe played exclusively by Roma.

19. Another conflict with Ahmed was about the rather mundane topic of telephone bills. In the end, my sponsor Ekrem intervened and told me that unless I agreed to pay what Ahmed wanted, Ekrem himself would have to pay it, to preserve neighborly relations. At this point I realized I had endangered relationships between friends, and I paid my landlord. The line between standing up for one's own principles and being flexible and generous is often hard to negotiate.

20. Yuri was teaching Americans to play the Bulgarian-style clarinet and saxophone; I was teaching Balkan singing. The East European Folklife Center (EEFC),

founded in the 1970s by my husband, Mark Levy, sponsors two week-long residential seminars every summer on Balkan music and dance.

21. Even before preparing his asylum case, I spent months preparing Yuri's application for a green card on the basis of his status as an extraordinary artist. This involved consulting with lawyers, eliciting from him an oral account of his musical résumé, tour history, training, and so on (since he had no documents), and gathering over 10 letters from scholars attesting to his ability and fame in Bulgaria.

22. The other bands in which Yuri played did not perform Bulgarian music at all. Yuri was motivated to form the new band as a result of an invitation to perform at Folk Parks 1995, a festival sponsored by the Ethnic Folk Arts Center.

23. Another thing which gave me more visibility in the Bronx Rom community is helping to win Yuri's asylum case. I have heard that my name is somewhat legendary as someone who can help to "get Roma green cards." Although I would like to help my Macedonian Rom friends receive asylum, I cannot fill the role of lawyer; the laws have become so complicated in the last few years that only a lawyer can prepare a viable set of documents. I do, however, support viable cases with letters.

References

Abu-Lughod, L. 1988. Fieldwork of a dutiful daughter. In S. Altorki and C. El-Sohl, eds., *Arab women in the field: Studying your own society,* 139–161. Syracuse, N.Y.: Syracuse University Press.

Abu-Lughod, L. 1990. Can there be a feminist ethnography? *Women and Performance: A Journal of Feminist Theory* 5 (1): 7–27.

Abu-Lughod, L. 1991. Writing against Culture. In R. Fox, ed., *Recapturing anthropology,* 137–162. Santa Fe, N.M.: American School of Research Press.

Behar, R., and D. Gordon. 1995. *Women writing culture.* Berkeley: University of California Press.

Buchanan, D. 1996. Wedding musicians, political transition, and national consciousness in Bulgaria. In M. Slobin, ed., *Returning culture: Musical changes in central and eastern Europe,* 200–230. Durham, N.C.: Duke University Press.

Cahn, Claude. 1997. Legislating ruin: Macedonia's law on commerce and the ensuing police violence. *Roma Rights* (Newsletter of the European Roma Rights Center) (autumn): 25–34.

Clifford, J. 1986. Introduction: Partial truths. In J. Clifford and G. Marcus, eds., *Writing culture: The poetics and politics of ethnography,* 1–26. Berkeley: University of California Press.

Crowe, D. 1995. *A history of the Gypsies of eastern Europe and Russia.* Armonk, N.Y.: M. E. Sharpe.

European Roma Rights Center. 1998. *A pleasant fiction: The human rights situation of Roma in Macedonia.* Country Reports Series No. 7. Budapest.

Fluehr-Loban, C. 1991. *Ethics and the profession of anthropology.* Philadelphia: University of Pennsylvania Press.

Hancock, I. 1997a. Introduction. In I. Hancock, ed., *The media and the Roma in contemporary Europe: Facts and fictions,* 2–3. Princeton, N.J.: Project on Ethnic Relations Report.

Hancock, I. 1997b. The struggle for the control of identity. *Transitions* 4 (4): 36–44.

Human Rights Project. 1994. Annual report. Sofia, Bulgaria: S. Danova.

Human Rights Project. 1995. Quarterly progress report. April 15–July 15, 1995. Sofia, Bulgaria: S. Danova.

Human Rights Watch. 1991. *Destroying ethnic identity: The Gypsies of Bulgaria.* New York: T. Zang.

Human Rights Watch. 1996. *Children of Bulgaria: Police violence and arbitrary confinement.* New York: Y. Thonden.

Jackson, B. 1987. *Fieldwork.* Urbana: University of Illinois Press.

Kunev, K. 1994. *Etnokulturnata situatsija v Bulgaria.* Sofia, Bulgaria: Center for the Study of Democracy.

Kunev, K. 1996. Dynamics of interethnic tensions in Bulgaria and the Balkans. *Balkan Forum* 4 (2): 213–252.

Lawless, E. 1992. "I was afraid someone like you . . . an outsider . . . would misunderstand": Negotiating interpretive differences between ethnographers and subjects. *Journal of American Folklore* 105 (417): 302–314.

Marcus, G., and M. Fischer. 1986. *Anthropology as culture critique.* Chicago: University of Chicago Press.

Petrovski, T. 1993. *Kalendarski obicaj kaj Romite vo Skopje i okolina.* Skopje, Macedonia: Feniks.

Poulton, H. 1994. *The Balkans: Minorities and states in conflict.* London: Minority Rights Publications.

Rice, T. 1996. The dialectic of economics and aesthetics in Bulgarian music. In M. Slobin, ed., *Retuning culture: Musical changes in central and eastern Europe,* 176–199. Durham, N.C.: Duke University Press.

Roof, J., and R. Wiegman. 1995. *Who can speak? Authority and critical identity.* Urbana: University of Illinois Press.

Silverman, C. 1981. Pollution and power: Gypsy women in America. In M. Salo, ed., *The American Kalderash: Gypsies in the New World,* 55–70. Centenary College, N.J.: Gypsy Lore Society.

Silverman, C. 1982. Everyday drama: Impression management of urban Gypsies. *Urban Anthropology* 11 (3–4): 377–398.

Silverman, C. 1986. Bulgarian Gypsies: Adaptation in a socialist context. *Nomadic Peoples,* nos. 21–22: 51–62.

Silverman, C. 1988. Negotiating Gypsiness: Strategy in context. *Journal of American Folklore* 101 (401): 261–275.

Silverman, C. 1989. Reconstructing folklore: Media and cultural policy in eastern Europe. *Communication* 11 (2): 141–160.

Silverman, C. 1995a. Persecution and politicization: Roma (Gypsies) of eastern Europe. *Cultural Survival* 19 (2): 43–49.

Silverman, C. 1995b. Roma of Shuto Orizari, Macedonia: Class, politics, and community. In D. Kideckel, ed., *East-central European communities: The struggle for balance in turbulent times,* 197–216. Boulder, Colo.: Westview Press.

Silverman, C. 1996a. Music and power: Gender and performance among Roma (Gypsies) of Skopje, Macedonia. *The World of Music, Journal of the International Institute for Traditional Music* 38 (1): 1–15.

Silverman, C. 1996b. Music and marginality: Roma (Gypsies) of Bulgaria and Macedonia. In M. Slobin, ed., *Retuning culture: Musical changes in central and eastern Europe,* 231–253. Durham, N.C.: Duke University Press.

Silverman, C. 1996c. State, market, and gender relationships among Bulgarian Roma, 1970's–1990's. *East European Anthropology Review* 14 (2): 4–15.

Visweswaran, K. 1988. Defining feminist ethnography. *Inscriptions,* nos. 3–4: 27–46.

Wolcott, H. 1995. *The art of fieldwork.* Walnut Creek, Calif.: Altimira Press.

Wolf, D. 1996. *Feminist dilemmas in fieldwork.* Boulder, Colo.: Westview Press.

Wolf, M. 1992. *A thrice-told tale: Feminism, postmodernism and ethnographic responsibility.* Stanford, Calif.: Stanford University Press.

Yuri Yunakov Ensemble. 1997. *New colors in Bulgarian wedding music* (with liner notes by Carol Silverman). Traditional Crossroads CD 4283.

Afterword
Intimations from an Uncertain Place

Michael Herzfeld

For an ethnographer in Greece there is something of an embarrassment in being asked to comment on a set of ethnographic accounts of eastern Europe. In Greece—geographically in eastern Europe but politically once more clearly "Western" than some of its citizens would now claim— ethnography has generally proved to be a relatively risk-free activity: the police (even during the nastier years of junta rule) have not usually interfered except under conditions of real crisis, the locals are (by their own assessment) talkative, and intimacy is offered with sometimes surprising generosity. In the years of Soviet domination north of the Greek border, I could carp about the relative lack of ethnographic specificity in less fortunate colleagues' work, but then I did not have to cope with rules prohibiting hospitality to anyone further removed than a first cousin (Kligman 1990: 399) in a state that had taken the official co-optation of kinship to its logical but absurd extreme. True, I was often seen as a spy; true, too, I was kicked out of Greece by the colonels' police during the height of the Cyprus crisis that also precipitated their own ignominious exit. But the difficulties of my situation paled by comparison with the consequences my colleagues' informants would have suffered as the result of any indiscretion on the part of the anthropologists—as we see from Silverman's dismay when her Bulgarian informants insisted on defying the law to give her lodging in their homes

219

and from her concern at the inescapably real punishments her visits occasionally caused her hosts.

Reading most of the accounts then available of life under actually existing socialism, I missed the intimacy that, I felt from my own relatively safe haven, should grace every ethnography. Some whole countries were missing; as Kuehnast notes here, contact was often close to impossible. The resulting absence from the majority of ethnographic descriptions of immediate, living, passionate selves was itself an ethnographic marker, had I only been able to appreciate it as such, although a few notable (if partial) exceptions gave the lie to the stereotype of an undifferentiated, uniformly inhuman socialist bloc. But Greece was not unlike Yugoslavia as described here by Živković: the terror was there, perhaps all the more damaging for its benign appearance, but it was not so pervasive that one had to be alert to it at every turn (unless, ironically, one had a communist past). Some of the early ethnographies of Yugoslav villages are redolent with telling detail. But by and large, as Silverman notes, the really big change has been "a movement from a focus on . . . problems in relation to the state to a focus on dealing with the profound transformations in economics, politics, *and personal life*" (emphasis added).

Many of the otherwise excellent early studies of socialist countries indeed seemed studiously impersonal, while virtually nothing was heard from the citizens of the Soviet Union itself. As I came to hear about the difficulties of doing fieldwork in the Soviet Bloc, the reasons for this became more obvious, and the silences took on meaning. But it was all very frustrating nonetheless, for one wanted to know what social life, not the Five-Year Plan, was really like for those living under the East Bloc regimes. Did everyone there live in a Le Carré novel? Certainly the people there thought the visiting anthropologists were spies (that was true in Greece as well), but were we for our part able to garner a picture of their existence that was any more realistic? Today we are beginning to do so, although the sweet mist of nostalgia—one of the many versions of the "postsocialist syndrome" described here by Živković—makes some of the hard edges difficult to discern for those informants who have become disenchanted with their new version of "our" system.

To be sure, some things have changed radically. My colleagues work, in one sense, in a virtual space—the *former* East Bloc—to much of which Greece, former home of the colonels' cultivated paranoia about "red fascism," looks for new partnerships in capitalist adventure and Eastern Orthodox purism alike. In 1984 it was socialist Bulgaria, as Silverman relates, that refused to recognize the Roma as an ethnic entity; today, it is Greece that is internationally castigated for refusing to recognize any ethnic minorities at all. Not all the shifts are thus what one would have expected from the vantage point of self-congratulatory capitalism. But some changes are less surprising. Thus, people in the former East Bloc, previously cowed, often now want to talk. Yet here again their resentment is often no less bitter toward the West than it is toward their former masters (and sometimes a great deal more so, as they find the welfare state receding in the merciless heat of post-Thatcherite venture capitalism). (The Greeks also want to talk, and they, too, are furious with the Western powers for what they see as systematic betrayal of Greek interests in the unending state of near-war with Turkey.) Relatively speaking, eastern Europeans now have the freedom to talk, but they also have the freedom to starve (as the Albanians who voted with their feet and fled to a hostile reception in Greece and Italy can well attest). There may even, conceivably, now be more to talk *about,* since the evident uncertainties have multiplied. But that is not necessarily a cause for local contentment, however nicely it enriches the anthropologists' collection of new data, for it probably means that there is more to complain about as well.

In any event, talk they do, and that is one reason for which the set of accounts presented here is especially welcome at this juncture. Conversations create intimacy, and intimacy is the key to successful ethnography. If, as several of the contributors to this volume attest, anthropologists have an alternative to offer to the formal explanatory models promulgated by elites, it is because they do field research of an often intensely intimate nature, and, like their informants, they are now (relatively) free to reveal what lies within those intimate spaces. Our informants, Berdahl reminds us, are often also our friends, and she teaches us that we would be dishonest if we did not recognize that friendship was what made possible the intimate perspective that is our distinguishing stock-in-trade. That recognition has sometimes been regarded as a professional transgression in the past, as she notes. But this is no reason to deny it from now on.

All these ethnographers are still working in countries whose citizens, collectively and individually, recently experienced wrenching insecurity in the so-called transition—a term challenged by the authors represented here (and see Verdery 1996). As Zanca points out for Uzbekistan, it has not been clear what the transition was *to:* it seems more like a movement away from something, a fall, as he says, from socialist grace.

The resulting sense of an unstable and unpredictable engagement with both past and future makes the ethnographic approach all the more urgent. People's understandings of what is happening to them cannot be captured by any of the top-down methods that once dominated, for better or for worse, the analysis of Soviet and Soviet-controlled society. The very fact that, as Anderson observes, the so-called transition has brought both temporal and social readjustments of its own into the actual conduct of relations between ethnographer and informant is itself a valuable datum, and it furnishes insights that would almost certainly escape more formal modes of analysis.

While there is no absolute guarantee that ethnographers can do better than their colleagues in other social sciences, there is, I would argue, one aspect of their work that is radically different from that of those colleagues. It is one that is specifically advantageous in situations where nothing is certain, but where people appeal to the supposedly certain resources of "culture" to deal with the uncertainties of "society." I have qualified these terms with quotation marks in order to emphasize that they, like the various entities (from communism to national identity) that they are used to justify and explain, are reifications of experience. There are endless spin-offs of these terms, which are models for a pattern of generalization that the ethnographer does not—or, rather, should not—use as analytic tools but should keep under critical inspection. Thus, for example, the crude essentialism of "starving Armenians" is nicely ironized in Barsegian's rueful account: Can one be a post–Soviet Armenian if one is well fed? What practices of everyday getting by and muddling through (see de Certeau 1984; Reed-Danahay 1996) do such essentializing devices conceal or ignore? The intensity of the ethnographer's intimacy with the messy but sociable domain of coping from day to day makes nonsense of such stereotypes. Against the pernicious stereotypes generated by what Kuehnast calls the "visual imperialism" of Western media, again, we can set the close observation of who watches, how these individuals are related to each other, and how they interpret what they see—an important and specifically ethnographic alternative (see, e.g., Mankekar 1993) to the self-fulfilling and culturally hermetic analyses offered by armchair experts. Some informants, like De Soto's *Mitfrauen,* might actually find the visiting ethnographers quite congenial in contrast with other social scientists; and indeed, establishing such rapport is essential to genuine intimacy. As De Soto notes, and as Živković elaborates methodologically, telling stories—what anthropologists then turn into written text (Geertz 1973: 19)—is conducive to intimate relations, unlike most formal survey research.

However, the problem is that, as a formal discipline in the wider geopolitical and academic arenas, anthropology may be expected to contribute (and in the past has contributed) to the production of the sweeping generalizations that some associate with "science," usually for the purposes of enumerating a set of bounded, definable "cultures." *Pace* Barsegian, it was not only foreign observers who engaged in this kind of "cleansing," nor do I think Soviet ethnologists were different from their Western colleagues—or, for that matter, from virtually any other community of human beings—in claiming positive value for their imposition of classificatory tidiness, intended in this case to eliminate all conceptual pollution (and giving rise, in its worst excesses, to ideas about racial purity and ethnic cleansing). What, after all, are the "detached descriptions" for which Barsegian calls, if not another form of conceptual purity? And are the intimate descriptions offered by one's informants detached? Yet intimacy seems to be what the latter often want: De Soto's friend Carola actually tells De Soto that she prefers being asked about her subjective experience of real-life situations.

Local actors nevertheless do not necessarily resent being categorized if it suits their pragmatic purposes, and they may have assimilated that classification to the point where they understand that only harm can come from challenging it. As we see in Anderson's account of the effects of earlier Soviet ethnographers who literally gave the Siberian Taimyr and Dolgan their *raison d'être,* the production of ethnic categories and stereotypical descriptions has immediate utility both for state bureaucrats and for those attempting to consolidate an identity that will relieve some of the immense collective burdens of state oppression. For that reason, a visiting ethnographer's refusal to answer questions about which group is "more cultured"— like my own evasion of the question of whether Greeks are European— simply provoked annoyance. As several of the authors point out, moreover, some notion of anthropology still appears to offer some inhabitants of the former Soviet Bloc a useful source of validation, and they become distinctly irritated by the visiting anthropologists' evasion of such politically motivated projects of self-definition. The legacy of the Soviet state, Anderson reminds us, has made many informants not only more aware of the political character of ethnographic research but also more insistent that the research should have a political character—a benignly, from their standpoint, proactive one.

The confluence of anthropology and national policy is not, in itself, surprising. Anthropology and nationalism historically share a common conceptual base, of which the terms *culture* and *society* are fundamental components (see also Handler 1985; Herzfeld 1987). This burden—perhaps reflected in the search for origin myths that De Soto exposes in some of the social science methodologies that preceded her own more informal intervention—is both historically embarrassing and practically awkward today. But it is also a potential source of reflexive insight, especially under the intense light shed on such processes by the rapid renationalization of the former East Bloc lands. Ethnographers working in this region, beset by uses of "their" concepts with which they feel distinctly ill at ease, are now, for precisely this discomfiting reason, in a uniquely privileged position. They can hold up a new looking glass to their discipline—their fieldwork to their academic field, as it were—in order to recontextualize these concepts and terms in an empirically grounded form of critique. (De Soto's insight into the production of origin myths, for example, was in part generated by the immediacy with which her research followed that of the more superficial survey analysts.)

If the reasons for attempting such a comparison in Greece permitted a simultaneous reflection back on the self-constitution of "Western civilization" and the role of both "Greece" and "anthropology" in that project, moreover, the present set of accounts permits us to examine the relationship between a somewhat differently constituted West–Rest relationship. It also allows us to consider critically both the past role of anthropology in generating reified notions of society and culture and its present engagement in trying to undo the damage (as many practitioners now see it) done by the alleged misuse of these same concepts. And so the turn to deeper ethnography is opportune for this region, while the intensified ethnographic engagement with the region is clearly beneficial for the discipline. Moreover, the resulting intimacy—revealing what Barsegian calls "the private or social lives of the local people"—is not simply more recognizably ethnographic than much of the earlier work; it also permits a more analytic examination of the politics of culture at the national and supranational levels.

It is not often that states are viewed as intimate apparatuses; their external formality seems to forbid such a perspective. But that formality is a form of collective defense. In any country there are many things that the leadership would prefer not to see exposed to the gaze of the international community but without which it knows the *Volk* would not manage to exist. Some of these things—political corruption is a familiar example—are locally recognized as most extensively practiced by the representatives of the state itself. This potentially disreputable but familiar cultural matter, as I have argued elsewhere (Herzfeld 1997a), is the very substance of what holds people together; paradoxically, because illegitimately, it provides the state with the internal solidarity it needs in order not only to justify but also to maintain its very existence. Some of that substance even includes resistance to the state itself; Americans nurtured on a national historiography of rebellion against authority will especially recognize the linkage between their national myths and their own rebellious attitude to the levying of taxes, for example.

Moments of sudden, radical change have a tendency to reveal such previously hidden and still rather embarrassing qualities. So when the "prosperous" Armenians reappear as "starving" reincarnations of their former selves, the adaptation on the part of the state to new circumstances suggests that neither discourse represents the actual experiences of citizens. The *intimate* realities may have changed far less than the surface images—people muddled through then, and they muddle through now—but the government, responding to a new external audience, shows itself as being no less adept than its citizens at dissembling and, yes, muddling through. But it would never announce muddling through as policy, and it would probably deny that muddling through was appropriate statecraft for the sovereign authority of a newly proud and independent nation. Still less would the state admit to maintaining negative traits as a means of control, yet I could not help wondering whether De Soto's friend Anna (her fretful fear of negotiating traffic in the West has a tragic intimacy that lingers in the memory) was perhaps the victim of a subtle form of economic and class discrimination against eastern Germans that is capable of reproducing itself in this palpably embodied form for many generations to come.

Can the government keep this ethnographic insight under wraps? Battered by the violence of the recent upheavals and subject to newly exigent demands for freedom of expression, the states of the former Soviet Bloc no longer control access to such cultural secrets. Their citizens are free to complain and to vilify both the authorities and themselves, and they are not slow to do so, for the gags have come off with a vengeance. But the crucial complaints are also no longer generalizations about the political system alone. They are comments drawn from an everyday life that has itself become much more directly accessible to foreign observers (or that can be more freely discussed abroad by indigenous commentators). To be sure, even in their weakened condition the states of this region have not ceased to be *internally* hegemonic institutions, so that the visiting anthropologists' sometimes censorious inspection may be not only a side effect of Western hegemony but also, on occasion, a comfort as much as an irritation for dissatisfied citizens. But in that case the observers' gaze opens up the nation's hitherto secluded intimacy even more relentlessly, for people apparently want to talk and there are few consistent reasons not to do so.

It is this underside of official discourse that I have called *cultural intimacy* and that is especially accessible to the *social intimacy* that marks good ethnographic fieldwork. It becomes clear in at least two of these accounts, moreover, that intimacy may serve to replace the older fieldwork requirement of bounded residence (see Gupta and Ferguson 1997); both Berdahl and Silverman conduct some of their research by telephone, and this, it transpires, marks intimacy rather than its absence. The remarkable feature of fieldwork emerging from a region hitherto noted more for the absence of such immediacy is that work in the area now, if these accounts are any indication, seems to be characterized by an exemplary commitment to diversifying the forms and locations of an intimacy that is richly and undeniably ethnographic.

Anthropologists often endure uncomprehending disdain for the small scale on which they investigate. But their statistical counterpart to the comprehensiveness of the survey-oriented methodologies of economics and political science is, if a positivistic measure be needed, the sheer intensity of their engagement. It is, in a word, the intimacy of their encounters. Frequently, moreover, what that intimacy reveals is strikingly different from what the more grandiose, top-down approaches produce and find, suggesting that the latter may, for all their vaunted objectivity, be more uncritically complicit with the official discourse than their proponents realize.

Sometimes, we should also remember, citizens share the state's distaste for self-exposure. Here, levels of embodiment may reinforce each other: were the Kyrgyz women's objections to Kuehnast's photographic representation of them really about the defense of a Soviet image? or fear of being thought "primitive"? or even a distant echo of Muslim concerns with the sacred privacy of female space? Yet even the women's objections were a (presumably unintentional) disclosure of some intimate concern, however inchoate, as is Kuehnast's own irritation at the incident of the "nightgown" photograph, for, as she says, both sides had something to "cover up." And the constant invocation of gendered, familial images in nostalgia for the paternalistic Soviet regime certainly reinforces this sense of homology between home and homeland, itself further emphasized for the Kyrgyz by the disciplined presence of the state media in their lives. In respect to another of the Muslim republics, Zanca's sensitive main title, "Intruder in Uzbekistan," signals the potential for the violation by every ethnographer of an intimacy that is as much national as it is domestic in the more literal sense. And here, too, there is an appeal to nostalgia for a time when the state and therefore the people were less subject to embarrassment by intimations of economic infirmity than they are today. Less clear is whether this kind of longing for the past is unique to the post-Soviet sense of lost directions or whether it is truly a *structural* nostalgia in the sense of a cliché repeated in successive generations and claiming to recall a sense of order in a time now just out of reach because "we" have become corrupt (see Herzfeld 1997a: 22)—an idiom of collective self-criticism that is one of the hallmarks of cultural intimacy. That remains an open question for further research.

When Silverman reports that officials told her, "with an ironic smile," that she was studying a nonexistent phenomenon, she is providing us with a European version of the Geertzian wink—that trademark of "thick description" (see Geertz 1973: 6–7). But again I prefer to emphasize the intimacy of the encounter rather than the thickness of the description, since thickness is possible only when intimacy precedes it: for a brief instant we see even the official representatives of state ideology as human beings capable of wincing at the absurdity of what they must nevertheless proclaim. Given the repetitive nature of such experiences in Silverman's fieldwork, this awareness of absurdity would appear to have been widespread. The ironic smiles were truly intimate: they were intimations for any fieldworker

receptive enough to understand them. But they were also the index of a usually well-masked collective intimacy rather than of a purely local or personal one.

The analysis of cultural intimacy reveals a curious collusion between the
self-presentation of weaker (and not only post-Soviet) states and Western
media discourse. The collusion lies in the denial of the intrinsic importance
of what is contained in those intimate spaces; it is denied by the local state
as an embarrassing aberration and ignored by powerful Western commentators as too trivial for comment. It suggests convergence among the international media, state authorities, and those social science disciplines that
play to the dictates of policy rather than to the interests of people. As
Kapferer (1988) has cogently observed, the "myths of state" often distort
and even conceal what really matters to ordinary folks—the "legends of
people"—even though official myths usually purport to draw on those legends. The intimacy of the ethnographic encounter offers an antidote to this
co-optation. But is that antidote perhaps unwelcome? Indeed, a suggestive
irony of the present situation is that it is perhaps only now, when Soviet
power has collapsed, that ethnographers can really get inside its intimate
spaces, at least retrospectively, and more or less freely tell others what they
have seen.

The United States has not withdrawn altogether from the region, as witness its willingness to varying degrees of engagement in Bosnia, Kosovo,
and Macedonia. But there seems to be less eagerness to seek informed advice, and when advice is asked, it is usually not that of anthropologists,
whose reporting on the inconveniently untidy details of ethnography in the
post-Soviet countries has become less like straightforward political analysis
and therefore of much less obvious import for policy-makers. It seems that
no one wants to know how understanding kinship and gender configura-
tions might complicate the miseries of Bosnia in a manner that would make
it much harder to generalize about Balkan "tendencies" and "hatreds" (see
Herzfeld 1997b: 126–127)—a pattern that seems confirmed by the ethno-
nationalism of almost all the new eastern European constitutions (until anthropologists again most inconveniently discover that the models for these
are locally not at all old but represent a novel though pervasive development of largely imported models of identity) (see Hayden 1996). That these
models now threaten the domestic tranquillity of families (Brown offers a
fine example from Macedonia) is the existential horror that discourses of
geopolitics suppress but that good ethnography can still recover.

Other aspects of the "transition" similarly become clear in the light of
seemingly insignificant detail. The refusal of Berdahl's friend Johanna ever
to wear a seatbelt in her car can illuminate the play of state authority, religious commitment, and the conceptual basis of habitual practices shared

by a large segment of a country's population, yet there seems little awareness in the media that this configuration might help to explain both the passivity of life under the old regime and the weary skepticism evoked by the new order of things. There seems little public interest in recovering such connections. A cynic might remark that if ever evidence was needed of the rapid marginalization of the former East Bloc countries from the focus of Western interest, it is to be found in the sudden burgeoning of first-rate ethnography.

To varying degrees, however, these countries have not uncritically joined the capitalist world, and it is not clear that they will do so in the foreseeable future. Doing fieldwork in the still volatile and embattled atmosphere of Armenia or Serbia continues to pose risks, for informants as much as for ethnographers. And it is here that the thorniest ethical issues arise. Is one to speak out about the dirty laundry one finds in one's hosts' national backyard? What harm or good might this do, and to whom? Can an anthropologist ever hope to control the effects of such risky interventions? And is this "problem of choice" worse, as Barsegian suggests, for those who might plausibly be accounted native observers?

In these accounts it becomes clear that the anthropologist is almost always most alone precisely at the moment when such questions demand responses. Already rendered "unscientific" in the eyes of many because fieldwork is conducted by a single researcher who engages often on a casual basis with informants whom he or she renders anonymous, ethnography also suffers by comparison with survey research done by those who put their faith in huge samples. I would again argue that the intense intimacy of the ethnographic encounter can be justified as no less rich a form of statistical sampling than the most exhaustive survey; with ethnography there is also no collective responsibility behind which to hide when things go horribly wrong—when, for example, one's work becomes the basis for a police action or for some new act of ethnic discrimination.

Now, I do not mean here to heroize the anthropologists in some simpleminded fashion. The authors of these accounts have adopted a largely antiheroic view of their ethnographic calling, one that reflects the self-deflation of an anthropology embarrassed by the revelation of its past complicity in such hegemonic structures as colonialism. That embarrassment has done us no harm; indeed, it has generated ethnography of vastly increased sensitivity and reflectiveness, ironically revitalizing the practice of ethnography at the very moment in which gloomy experts on both sides, for *and* against "postmodernism," were predicting its demise. But it would be a great pity were the real hardships of much fieldwork to drown in a downpour of penitential self-abnegation. I read the work of those who ventured into Soviet-dominated territory, especially, with the respect due colleagues

who have braved numbing discomfort: bureaucratic harassment, dull work-
places and duller food, petty restrictions at every turn, deep suspicion of
one's motives from all around one, and substantial risks to those who had
become one's friends.

The piranhas of this Amazon are not excitingly exotic. To be sure, a spell
in a Soviet jail might well have made for some good heroics. But most of the
time the downside of this ethnographic setting has mostly offered poor material for dramatic narration. Yet that is precisely what should give us pause.
Should we not see in this drab banality itself a reason to respect those who
have endured it? There is in the accounts collected here a tale no less heroic
for being modestly told. It is also a tale of productive self-awareness, as in
Dudwick's use of her and her informants' parallel irritations with bureaucratic pettiness to explore, after her return home, the experiential differences underlying the shared outrage.

Perhaps, indeed, these accounts will help to reinstate respect for research
undertaken under conditions of hardship but, because of the very drabness
in question, without reviving all the pretentiousness against which our rejection of field heroics was a reaction. Anger at being scolded by a small-
town bureaucrat cannot as easily be dressed in the smugness of imperial
ethnography as disdainful tales of "Nuerosis" (Evans-Pritchard 1940: 13).

The image of the lone ethnographer as a heroic figure has become part of
a heritage that embarrasses our postmodern sensibilities. Yet I believe that
we should not abandon that figure so easily. We should instead contextual-
ize it, turning it, as the authors of these accounts do, to analytic advantage.
Thus, for example, Zanca's challenging observations about the almost
stereotypically Western anthropological insistence on the individualistic
character of field research nicely suggest one way of reinserting our own activity into the comparative perspective that, together with the fieldwork itself, constitutes the core of the discipline. Without such practical heroics,
moreover, the intimate spaces of cultural and political action would remain
hidden. One irony of the anthropological turn to Europe, that zone once
considered off limits to anthropologists, is that through such reflexive and
personal engagement it has helped to clarify and preserve what is distinctive about anthropology among the social sciences.

Most dramatic among these individualistic concerns is the loneliness of
ethical decision-making. Having experienced this in a very minor way under the Greek junta, I must express profound respect for those who have
braved doubt (professional identity in conflict with the desire to protect
those who are, as Berdahl points out, our friends) under a system that was
often comprehensively vicious. Some of these ethnographers have continued to be circumspect, and we must, I think, continue to respect their decision: it is not we, their readers, who must live with the consequences to their

informants of the choices they have made about what to include in published work.

The emergence in these pages of a closely observed social reality is also,
after all those years of repression, a courageous move and one that is complicated by the nostalgia that many report hearing their informants express
for the harsh security of the old days. If the present insecurity should bring
back the old repressions, or if the militant far Right should now seek to exact revenge from those who still mourn the passing of the discredited Left,
the intimacies revealed here could still have the power to harm those who
volunteered them. Then again, one might argue that the new transparency
is the best means of forging an alliance against a return to the brutality of
either extreme. But what if that were simply too idealistic? These are choices
fraught with menacing consequentiality.

For some years, indeed, it was not clear that those working in the East
Bloc were doing much ethnography at all. What might have lent dramatic
luster to their work actually became a reason for disguise. These ethnographers had to be so careful: a revelation even of some innocuous piece of
folklore locally read as an allegory of resistance could land an informant (or
someone suspected of having furnished the information) in jail, or worse.
Heroism here lay in *not* dramatizing one's work but rather in risking an appearance of dullness in a discipline that was already decidedly inhospitable
to Europeanists of any kind. Much, although not all, of the anthropological writing that came out of the East Bloc at that time had the feel of political science or folklore whose authors wanted it to be something else—and
that, in a sense, is what it was. Viewed across the frontier from Greece or the
other side of the Berlin Wall, it looked dispiriting. And yet these scholars
persevered and produced much that has, in fact, contributed significantly to
current theoretical realignments in social and cultural anthropology.

My task is not to comment on socialism or what passed for it. That task
has been addressed by those who worked "in" it (see especially Verdery
1996). It is, rather, to ask what we can now learn about ethnography by
reading what has emerged in the work on the former East Bloc since the collapse of the socialist regimes. Does postsocialist ethnography simply reproduce the principled confusions embraced by postmodernism? How does the
work collected here provide us with a new set of ideas about the ethnographer's task in an age when, as everyone seems to be admitting, the isolated
community has ceased even to be a hypothetical possibility?

I suggest that it is the before-and-after quality of these accounts, sometimes largely implicit, sometimes foregrounded, that generates their distinctive novelty. This perspective is not simply a reversion to positivistic
dreams of longitudinality. But they return us to an empirically grounded
awareness that the ethnographer with this kind of long-term perspective

holds a looking glass to the local narration of social change that constitutes one of the major sources of data in this collection—an example of what Deborah Reed-Danahay (1997) has labeled "auto/ethnography." In this genre, people's accounts of their own society are treated as a variety of ethnography in their own right, sometimes permitting an especially fruitful exploration of intersections and parallels between anthropologists' professional trajectories and informants' autobiographies. David A. Kideckel's (1997) chapter in the Reed-Danahay volume gives us an especially vivid retrospective picture of what was suppressed for so long—and of how it was nevertheless preserved.

Berdahl shows us, for example, with an appealing mixture of embarrassment and courage, how the pervasive recognition of her personal predicaments provided an insistently intimate mode of what we might call practical comparativism—a direct and highly informative translation of the personal experience of fieldwork into one of the discipline's defining intellectual commitments. Barsegian and Živković both give us a sense of how this can be complicated when the two roles merge in a single person and the issues of responsibility discussed above come to a head. Some of these tales are familiar to many anthropologists (Barsegian's double *déracinement* as a Ukrainian-born Armenian anthropologist reproduces an almost archetypical *Bildungsroman*), but they entail a more vital engagement than most with the consequences of choices made. For Barsegian even the commitment to ideals of Western academic freedom and detachment eventually risks becoming a betrayal of interests he cannot escape to the extent that he still identifies with aspects of his family's history. From the "other" side, that of the nonnative, Dudwick also perceives the risk that the locally embedded ethnographer faces of being regarded as a traitor to a self-evidently noble cause. And this is where the issue of cultural intimacy—the embodiment of state ideology in domestic experience—becomes most exigent. One's choices are embedded in the familiar and the familial, as in Brown's arresting example of the Macedonian woman with the Vlach husband whose marriage and family were at perpetual risk from particular readings of mutually antagonistic national pasts.

Each anthropologist, alone and unaided, must confront the encompassing ethical dilemma: there are no easy escapes through the paths offered by the new global moralism, even when one fundamentally subscribes to its principles. Berdahl's evocation of her mixed reactions to the officious (but well-meaning?) priest and to the advice he gave her desperately ill friend, like her agonizing over whether her scientifically informed advice might undermine the good that the priest had perhaps achieved, illustrates key dilemmas of choice intensified by the desire to avoid condescension (of which moralism is often merely a variant). (Berdahl notes the "intimacy" of her and her husband's relationship with the priest, an intimacy that was all the more real for both sides because it was qualified by negative sentiments: it induced feelings of guilt in Berdahl over her censorious reactions while it was also a theme of the priest's self-serving public performance.)

Even recognizing with one's informants, as De Soto does, that the West entered as a "colonizing" force is not a sufficient antidote to the risks of condescension when one's very presence in the community originated in the wake of that hegemony. Yet to say nothing, to pretend to agree, is also condescending, as Brown notes of discourses on nationalism and as Anderson, in an illuminatingly revelatory vignette, discovered when he praised a snowmobile that would have been better described as "a pile of junk." For this is the minefield the foreign ethnographer walks, in Dudwick's apt metaphor, and a loss of credibility may also entail a destruction of trust. On the other hand, there are also situations in which conformity and acquiescence may, as for Silverman, simply be a form of discretion maintained out of consideration for one's hosts' social position. The ethnographer must forever be making those lonely choices. They carry considerable risks for immediate relationships, for, as Dudwick notes, trust may sometimes be incompatible with one's own cherished sense of what is right. Informants may set ironic traps for unwary ethnographers (see Chock 1987): our polite disagreements with their scathing self-deprecation may be heard as an implicit confirmation that this is indeed our real opinion of them. Anderson's portrayal especially suggests these pitfalls and shows how we can learn from them.

The choice of how much of the embarrassing aspects of local life one should explicitly acknowledge must depend on each ethnographer's own assessment of what is appropriate, tempered with the recognition that the positioning of *all* social actors, including ethnographers, does not so much determine what is ethically right as it sets the pragmatic compromises people will be forced to make. One's censure should not be silenced, but it should be tempered by a sober assessment of how one's own cultural status may affect the discussion. Conversely, whatever one says will in turn receive censure somewhere. I think of the reaction I often hear whenever I try to make sense of the official Greek policy of not recognizing ethnic minorities. I do in fact strongly disagree with that policy, but it is easy for critics from Western countries to denounce it when it rests in part on a view of the Greeks' own identity largely fabricated by the leaders of those same powerful Western states. And until the latter can also come to terms with their own historical responsibility, they can do little good by blithely casting it onto other, weaker shoulders, for that tactic breeds only deep resentment. In this regard we should do well to heed Dudwick's timely warning. She acknowledges that skepticism about our informants' "sacred narratives" may be quite damaging to people's lives and self-esteem. When local scholars do, remarkably, recognize that "the past . . . keeps time with the present" (in Brown's happy phrase), we should respect the political and social risks they are taking and think twice about propelling them further into potential danger. Indeed, Brown's sensitive account of his encounter with such an individual shows that the image of a nation of madcap chauvinists is itself a self-serving Western distortion, but the problem remains: do we extol those who work against the political establishment and put them at increased risk, or do we reinforce the caricature through our silence? I have encountered the same dilemma in Greece. Indeed, Brown is right—and what an irony this is—that his nonnationalist Macedonian colleagues force us to rethink our essentialized images of all the Balkan scholarly establishments, including the Greek.

However, even when the narratives we hear do provoke our anger by their chauvinism, should we not also recognize that the prefabricated moralism of our own comfortable academic environment may be irresponsible and that the task is less to condemn than to engage our informants in a discussion of why we think their positions may be harmful to them as well as to their alleged foes? After all, if our reasoning is so well-grounded, should it not prevail? Or do we subscribe to the nasty doctrine that only we are capable of understanding logic? Those moments in the field when we think we have irrevocably alienated our friends can be terrifyingly lonely—but what *pragmatically ethical* alternative do we have?

Moreover, some of our colleagues face an intensified version of this terror. For those who have no links of familial identity with the country they are studying, moralism comes cheap, but Barsegian's chapter shows that it is much harder for those with ties of kinship there. And for the truly local ethnographer the conflicts of obligation and multiple ethical codes must often be overwhelming.

Ultimately, all ethnographers, even those who are considered native in any sense, are guests. They are, moreover, guests on several levels: their immediate hosts are also representatives of a host country. Each encounter is, in Victor Turner's (1974) terms, a social drama in which the participants act out, sometimes quite ritualistically, the dynamics of a geopolitical relationship. Unlike Turnerian social dramas, however, these may be rites of inversion, turning a perceived inequality on its head through irony or even generosity (as in acts of hospitality). One of the most vivid images I have encountered of the symbolic inversion of power entailed in such moments is Zanca's account of how informants would turn his information-seeking "into their own entertainment"—a valuable object lesson for all ethnographers.

Like the provision of information, the proffering of food and drink inverts relationships of clientage and dependence. But when those commodities grow embarrassingly scarce, as Kuehnast found, people may no longer be able to sustain their dramas of symbolic reversal. At that juncture, does tact require the ethnographer to withdraw? When it becomes more humiliating for informants to invite an ethnographer into the home than to fail to offer hospitality, when (as in Zanca's account) the erstwhile beneficiaries of a national health care system once far more comprehensive than that of the United States must beg aspirin from the visiting ethnographer, we are close to the breaking point. The deep embarrassment of which Zanca writes is the personal and cultural response to disaster; economic collapse has intruded into symbolic performance. Yet there is also a new opportunity to understand what these disasters mean in practical, everyday terms: the hitherto sheltered ethnographer is drawn into directly experiencing a terrifying indeterminacy that, as Kuehnast and Zanca evocatively describe it, is unlikely to correspond to anything experienced at home.

With uncertainty comes fear. A telling metaphor of this condition is the hovering suspicion that one is a spy, so nicely detailed here by Zanca and Silverman. It would be easy to dismiss this as paranoia and to attribute it to the Soviet legacy, but that temptation—mercifully avoided here—would be unfortunate for two reasons. First, it would miss the significance of such charges for evaluating the international power dynamics of entertaining someone who is a guest in another land. The ambivalence of the stranger, long ago remarked by Simmel ([1908] 1971) and Pitt-Rivers (1968), has taken on a modernist guise, but it has not lost its sometimes painful ambivalence. And second, precisely because such an interpretation overlooks the fact that anthropologists face such charges in many lands (it has certainly happened to me in Greece), it occludes useful comparative implications. A comparative study of ethnographic embarrassments would indeed be no bad thing. It would further the aim of situating ethnographic practice within the complex geopolitical dynamics of which it inevitably partakes. In studies such as the ones in this volume, those dynamics, through access to the intimate spaces of a country rather than through the formal analysis of its political institutions, constitute one of the most important topics that anthropology can and should illuminate from its productively peculiar angle of vision.

References

Certeau, Michel de. 1984. *The practice of everyday life.* Trans. Steven F. Rendall. Berkeley: University of California Press.

Chock, Phyllis Pease. 1987. The irony of stereotypes: Toward an anthropology of ethnicity. *Cultural Anthropology* 3: 347–368.

Evans-Pritchard, E. E. 1940. *The Nuer: A description of the modes of livelihood and political institutions of a Nilotic people.* Oxford: Clarendon Press.

Geertz, Clifford. 1973. *The interpretation of cultures.* New York: Basic Books.

Gupta, Akhil, and James Ferguson, eds. 1997. *Anthropological locations: Boundaries and grounds of a field.* Berkeley: University of California Press.

Handler, Richard. 1985. On dialogue and destructive analysis: Problems in narrating nationalism and ethnicity. *Journal of Anthropological Research* 41: 171–182.

Hayden, Robert M. 1996. Imagined communities and real victims: Self-determination and ethnic cleansing in Yugoslavia. *American Ethnologist* 23: 783–801.

Herzfeld, Michael. 1987. *Anthropology through the looking-glass: Critical ethnography in the margins of Europe.* Cambridge: Cambridge University Press.

Herzfeld, Michael. 1997a. *Cultural intimacy: Social poetics in the nation-state.* New York: Routledge.

Herzfeld, Michael. 1997b. Anthropology and the politics of significance. *Social Analysis* 41: 107–138.

Kapferer, Bruce. 1988. *Legends of people, myths of state: Violence, intolerance and political culture in Sri Lanka and Australia.* Washington, D.C.: Smithsonian Institution Press.

Kideckel, David A. 1997. Autobiography as political resistance: A case from socialist Romania. In D. E. Reed-Danahay, ed., *Autoethnography: Rewriting the self and the social,* 47–70. Oxford: Berg.

Kligman, Gail. 1990. Reclaiming the public: A reflection on creating civil society in Romania. *East European Politics and Societies* 4: 393–438.

Mankekar, Purnima. 1993. National texts and gendered lives: An ethnography of television viewers in a north Indian city. *American Ethnologist* 20: 554–563.

Pitt-Rivers, Julian. 1968. The stranger, the guest, and the hostile host: Introduction to the study of the laws of hospitality. In J. G. Peristiany, ed., *Contributions to Mediterranean sociology,* 13–30. Paris: Mouton.

Reed-Danahay, Deborah. 1996. *Education and identity in rural France: The politics of schooling.* Cambridge: Cambridge University Press.

Reed-Danahay, Deborah E., ed. 1997. *Autoethnography: Rewriting the self and the social.* Oxford: Berg.

Simmel, Georg. [1908] 1971. The stranger. In Donald L. Levine, ed., *Georg Simmel, on individuality and social forms,* 143–149. Chicago: University of Chicago Press.

Turner, Victor. 1974. *Dramas, fields, and metaphors: Symbolic action in human society.* Ithaca, N.Y.: Cornell University Press.

Verdery, Katherine. 1996. *What was socialism, and what comes next?* Princeton, N.J.: Princeton University Press.

Contributors
Index

Contributors

David G. Anderson is assistant professor of anthropology at the University of Alberta. He lectures on circumpolar ethnology, aboriginal rights, and ecological anthropology and has coedited *The Curtain Rises: Rethinking Culture, Ideology, and the State in Eastern Europe* (Humanities Press, 1993). His current research is focused upon comparing the culture and identity of two circumpolar indigenous nations in Siberia and northern Canada.

Igor Barsegian is a research associate at the Institute for European, Russian, and Eurasian Studies of George Washington University. He carried out extensive fieldwork in Soviet Armenia, beginning in 1982–1983, on a joint research project on Armenian rural culture. In 1989 he began research on ethnic minorities and nationalism, and from 1991 through 1993 worked among the so-called dispersed groups in Armenia. In 1994, he carried out research in Armenian and Jewish communities in New York and Washington, D.C., looking at the role of ethnic stereotypes in identity-building and nationalism. His recent publications are: "War and Peace: International Involvement in Nagorno-Karabagh," in Michael Szaz and Edith Laszlo, eds., *United States Geostrategic Interests in the Transcaucasian Region* (1997); and "Armenian Nationalism Past and Present," in Ole Hoiris and Sefa Martin Yurukel, eds., *Contrasts and Solutions in the Caucasus* (1998).

Daphne Berdahl is assistant professor of anthropology at the University of Minnesota. She is the author of *Where the World Ended: Re-unification and Identity in the German Borderland* (University of California Press, 1999), and she is coeditor of *Altering States: Ethnographies of Transition in Eastern Europe and the Former Soviet Union* (University of Michigan Press, forthcoming). Her present research focuses on the relationship between consumption and the changing definitions, understandings, and practices of citizenship and nation-building in reunified Germany.

K. S. Brown is currently a lecturer in anthropology at the University of Wales, Lampeter. Between April 1992 and October 1993, he conducted dissertation fieldwork in what was then the Yugoslav Republic of Macedonia. His main research interests are nationalism and the politics of identity; foci of study include jokes, cinema, monuments, and historiography. He is currently researching early twentieth-century Macedonian labor migration to the United States. His publications include: "Seeing Stars: Character and Identity in the Landscapes of Modern Macedonia," *Antiquity* (1994); "Cultural Specificities and Political Realities in Macedonian Jokes," *Western Folklore* (1995); and "Macedonian Culture and Its Audiences: An Analysis of Before the Rain," in F. Hughes-Freeland, ed., *Ritual, Performance, Media* (1998).

Hermine G. De Soto taught anthropology in the Department of Anthropology at the University of Wisconsin–Madison and was a research fellow in sociocultural anthropology at the Women's Studies Program and Women's Studies Research Center at the University of Wisconsin–Madison, and the Center for Eastern Europe, Russia and Central Asia. She is the editor of *Culture and Contradiction: Dialectics of Wealth, Power and Symbol* (Mellen Research University Press, 1992) and the coeditor of *The Curtain Rises: Rethinking Culture, Ideology, and the State in Eastern Europe* (Humanities Press, 1993). De Soto conducted fieldwork in western Germany in 1993 and 1994, in postsocialist eastern Berlin in 1991 and 1992, and in Saxony-Anhalt, eastern Germany in 1995, focusing on comparative postsocialist ethnography; ritual and identity; gender, urban anthropology, political economy, poverty, the politics of culture, and ecology and the environment. In 1997 and fall 1998 she participated in an ethnographic poverty study in the new country of Moldova (former Soviet Union). In spring 1999 she was invited by the World Bank to conduct a social assessment of rural and economic development in Kyrgyzstan. She has now joined the World Bank, where she will continue her comparative ethnographic research interests and the anthropology of development in Europe, Russia, and Central Asia. Among her recent articles are: "In the Name of the Folk: Women and Nation in the New Germany," *UCLA Women's Law Journal* (1994); "Citizenship and Minorities in the Process of Nation Rebuilding in Germany," *Political and Legal Anthropology Review* (1995); "From Decollectivization to Poverty and Beyond: Women in Rural East Germany before and after Unification," in David Kideckel, ed., *East European Communities: The Struggle for Balance in Turbulent Times* (1995); "(Re)Inventing Berlin: Dialectics of Power, Symbols and Pasts, 1990–1995," *City and Society* (1996); "Reading the Fools' Mirror: Reconstituting Identity against National and Transnational Political Practices," *American Ethnologist* (1998); and "Contested Landscapes: Reconstructing Environment and Community in Postsocialist Saxony-Anhalt," in Martha Lapland, Daphne Berdahl, and Matti Bunzl, eds., *Altering States: Ethnographies of Transition from Russia and East-Central Europe* (1999).

Nora Dudwick began conducting fieldwork in Soviet Armenia during the 1987–1988 academic year, the very period in which mass nationalist demonstrations took place throughout the Soviet Union. She has since returned many times to Armenia, both Soviet and post-Soviet, to conduct research on nationalism, ethnicity, and conflict. Since joining the World Bank, she has organized and carried out studies of transition and poverty in Armenia, Georgia, Moldova, Ukraine, Albania, Latvia, and Macedonia. Current interests include the impact of poverty on social structure and on ideologies in transition economies and the role of social networks in shaping post-socialist class structures. Among her recent articles are: "Political Structures in Post-Communist Armenia: Images and Realities," in Karen Dawisha and Bruce Parrott, eds., *Conflict, Cleavage and Change in Central Asia and the Caucasus* (1997); "Out of the Kitchen, Into the Crossfire," in Mary Buckley, ed., *Post-Soviet Women: From Central Asia to the Baltic* (1997); and "Independent Armenia: Paradise Regained or Lost?" in Ian Bremmer and Raymond Taras, eds., *New Politics, New States: Building the Post-Soviet Nations* (1997).

Michael Herzfeld is professor of anthropology at Harvard University, where he has taught since 1991, and curator of European ethnology in the Peabody Museum. A past president of the Modern Greek Studies Association and the Society for the Anthropology of Europe, he currently edits *American Ethnologist.* He is the author of *Ours Once More: Folklore, Ideology, and the Making of Modern Greece* (University of Texas Press, 1982); *The Poetics of Manhood: Contest and Identity in a Cretan Mountain Village* (Princeton University Press, 1985); *Anthropology through the Looking-Glass: Critical Ethnography in the Margins of Europe* (Cambridge University Press, 1987); *A Place in History: Social and Monumental Time in a Cretan Town* (Princeton University Press, 1991); *The Social Production of Indifference* (Berg, 1992); *Cultural Intimacy: Social Poetics in the Nation-State* (Routledge, 1997); and *Portrait of a Greek Imagination: An Ethnographic Biography of Andreas Nenedakis* (University of Chicago Press, 1997). He is also currently at work on a general survey of social and cultural anthropology for UNESCO and Basil Blackwell and is doing research on apprenticeship and historic conservation in Greece and Italy. His major general research interest is currently the comparison of the forms of historical experience in these two countries. He has written extensively on anthropological and semiotic theory, narrative, metaphor and symbolism, the ethnography of southern Europe, local politics, and nationalism. Winner of the Chicago Folklore Prize for 1981, the J. B. Donne Prize on the Anthropology of Art (1989), and the Rivers Memorial Medal (1994) (both from the Royal Anthropological Institute, London), and the J. I. Staley Prize (School of American Research, 1994), he was elected a fellow of the American Academy of Arts and Sciences in 1997.

Kathleen Kuehnast is currently a research associate at the Institute of European, Russian and Eurasian Studies at George Washington University. She received her Ph.D. in cultural anthropology from the University of Minnesota in 1997. From 1990 to 1996, she spent 20 months conducting field research in Central Asia, investigating the social ramifications of rapid political and economic transformation underway in the former Kirgiz Soviet Socialist Republic, which is now Kyrgyzstan, an independent republic. She is interested in illuminating the intersection of several theoretical problems: the issue of how the category of woman becomes an ideological site for economic, political, and religious projects in society, especially the ways in which gender ideologies are transformed during political upheaval. Current research interests include the impact of international development efforts, nation-building activities, global market and consumerism, and ethnic revival upon women. She has also led several research projects on women and poverty in Kyrgyzstan for the World Bank and the Asian Development Bank. Her 1993 World Bank report on women's coping strategies in Kyrgyzstan, as well as her two recently published co-authored studies for the ADB—*A Generation at Risk: Children in the Central Asia Republics of Kazakstan and Kyrgyzstan* (1998); and *Women and Gender Relations: The Kyrgyz Republic in Transition* (1997)—demonstrated the importance of ethnography as a tool for uncovering widespread problems of poverty and social upheaval in transitional economies. She is currently investigating problems of poverty, conflicting gender ideologies, and transitional economies in Central Asia.

Nancy Ries is associate professor of anthropology at Colgate University. She is the author of *Russian Talk: Culture and Conversation during Perestroika* (Cornell University Press, 1997), which won the Barbara Heldt Prize in 1997. Other publications include "The Burden of Mythic Identity: Russian Women at Odds with Themselves," in Susan Weisser and Jennifer Fleischner, eds., *Feminist Nightmares: Women at Odds* (1994); and "The Power of Negative Thinking: Russian Talk and the Reproduction of Mindset, Worldview, and Society," *Anthropology of East Europe Review* (1991). She is coeditor of *The Anthropology of East Europe Review.* She has conducted extensive fieldwork in Russia in the past several years, focusing particularly on popular conceptions of wealth, poverty, class stratification, and the mafia.

Carol Silverman has been involved with Balkan music and culture for over 20 years as a researcher, teacher, and performer. She is currently associate professor of anthropology and folklore at the University of Oregon, where she teaches classes on eastern European culture, feminism, and ethnographic theory. In spring 1999 she served as educational coordinator for the North American tour of "The Gypsy Caravan." Focusing on Bulgaria and Macedonia, she has investigated the relationship among music, politics, ethnicity, ritual, and gender. She has written numerous articles and book chapters about Balkan folklore and Roma (see references cited), including: "Who's Gypsy Here? Reflections at a Rom Burial," in Bruce Jackson and Edward Ives, eds., *The World Observed: Reflections on the Fieldwork Process* (1996); "Persecution and Politicization: Roma (Gypsies) of Eastern Europe," *Cultural Survival Quarterly* (1996); and "Rom (Gypsy) Music," in T. Rice, C. Goertzen, and J. Porter, eds., *Garland Encyclopedia of World Music,* Europe vol. (1999). Forthcoming is "'Move over Madonna': Gender, Representation, and the 'Mystery' of Bulgarian Voices," in M. Zaborowska and S. Forrester, eds., *The Change (Mis)Interpreted: East–West Cultural Criticism since the Cold War.*

Russell Zanca received his Ph.D. in anthropology from the University of Illinois at Urbana-Champaign in 1997. He is assistant professor at Northeastern Illinois University. In 1998 he conducted research outside Samarkand among pastoralist, seminomadic Uzbeks.

Marko Živković is currently a doctoral candidate in anthropology at the University of Chicago. He is writing his dissertation, entitled "The Stories Serbs Tell Themselves (and Others) about Themselves." When he tells stories about himself, he usually mentions his more than 20-year fascination with Japan, explaining that it was the war in his former country, Serbia, that prompted him to make it the focus of his research rather than Japan.

Index

abortion rights, 75, 83
Abzug, Bella, 80, 95*n14*
advocacy roles, 15, 197, 213
anthropologists. *See* foreign anthropologists; halfie anthropologists; native anthropologists or ethnographers
Arctic identity, 132–33
Armenia: Armenian diaspora, 16, 24; Azerbaijan conflict, 120, 125; continuities in transition, 119–20; documentation of historical claims, 18–19; Nagorno-Karabagh movement, 16–21; self-representations, 18, 126; "starving" stereotype, 124–26; Yerablur Cemetery, 19; Yerevan State University, 13, 17
asylum, 210–11, 213, 215*nn21, 23*
audience: subjects as, 24–25, 39–41; world as, 44
authoritative roles: authoritative voice, 173; competing authorities, 179; interpreter of West, 15; of outsiders, 40–41; researcher empowered by state, 123
auto/ethnography, 231
Azerbaijan: Armenian conflict, 120, 125; Karabagh movement in, 17; Shushi/Shusha, 21–22
Azerbaijani Popular Front, 19

Baku, Azerbaijan, 19
"bearable evil" thesis, 57–60
Berlin, Germany, 76–79, 81
Berlin Wall, 79, 81, 92–93, 173
Besser Wessi behavior, 77–78, 180
Bishkek, Kyrgyzstan, 100, 108, 115
Bitoski, Krste, 35–36, 38–39, 41, 43
borders. *See* boundaries
boundaries: as administrative tool, 135; as arbitrary separations, 16–17; Berlin Wall, 79, 92–93; Bulgarian border zone, 200; defining and mapping, 133, 136–37, 141; dissolution of Soviet Union and, 155; ethnic distinction and, 135; fixed by state ethnography, 141; fluidity of ethnic identity, 141; Macedonian, 37; renegotiation during transition, 11–12; subjectivity and, 173

Brettell, Caroline, 5, 39–41
bribery, 161
broker role, 50, 114–15, 162–64
Bulgaria: obstacles to research in, 199–200; Roma of, 209–10
bureaucracies: ethnographers as bureaucrats, 137; as obstacles to research, 154, 157, 199–200; petty regulation by, 16, 229

Canada: Quebecois culture, 40; subarctic, 132–33; as Western example, 138–40
capitalism: as anthropological subject, 4; attractiveness to postsocialist peoples, 164; as Cold War victor, 155–56; gender and, 111; information sources about, 108–9, 162–63; trade opportunities sought, 114–15, 156, 162–64
Catholic church, 175–77, 191*n6*
Central Asia: dissolution of Soviet Union, 168*n3*. *See also* Kyrgyzstan; Uzbekistan
children: death of, 161; play as research, 205; religious education of, 176; of researchers, 180–82, 204; social programs for family, 111–12; subjects' stake in history, 43; survival of Evenki identity, 142–43; Uzbek, 165, 167
Clifford, James, 40–41
Cold War: binary logic as legacy of, 138–39; capitalism as victor, 155–56; as cognitive organization, 102–7; as context, 100; ideo-

244

logical persistence of, 82, 101, 131,
    145–46; as obstacle to research, 120–21;
    othering and, 5, 104; reflexivity and, 115
collaboration, between researcher and sub-
    ject, 82–83, 86–87, 196
colonization: German reunification as, 76,
    94*n7,* 232; research as, 77–78, 232
communism: control and unresolved issues,
    59–60; corruption in Serbia, 60; Nagorno-
    Karabagh movement and Communist
    Party, 17; research during Cold War, 103;
    shortages under, 55; Yugoslav Communist
    Party, 59
"communitas," 17
confidentiality, 25–26, 35, 127
conspiracy theories: KGB and ethnic vio-
    lence, 18; Serbian, 52
corruption: bribery, 161; communism as
    influence, 58; political, 224; reform target,
    16–17; routine practice, 16, 55–56
cultural criticism, 61–62, 138–41; critical re-
    sponsibility, 124; cultural relativism, 33
cultural intimacy, 225–27, 231
curiosity, 16, 87, 89–90, 131
Cyprus, Greek/Turkish conflict, 26, 219,
    221

Danojlić, Milovan, 58–61
deconstruction of ethnic/national beliefs, 15
demystification, 61–62, 124, 138–40
deportations, 21
diagnostic roles, 142–44
diaspora: Armenian, 16, 24; Rom, 208–9
dichotomies: army *vs.* people paradigm, 23;
    Cold War logic and, 120–21, 138–39;
    East/West, 63*n2,* 119–20; object/subject
    constructions, 86; polarizations in field,
    14; of research, 90–91, 190*n1;* truth *vs.*
    lies, 58–59; USSR *vs.* United States,
    155–56; us/them, 58, 120–21, 140
differences: denial of, 121–22; within
    "them," 27
discourse: conversations, 221; postsocialist,
    166–67; public *vs.* private accounts, 23,
    126–27; socialist rhetoric, 153. *See also*
    narratives; stories
discrimination, ethnic: existence denied,
    200–201, 220–21, 226–27, 232; in
    Nagorno-Karabakh, 17; against Roma,
    200–201, 208–9

Dolgans, 134–36, 140
Donev, Jovance, 35–36, 38
dualisms: binary logic of Cold War, 138–39;
    in research, 90–91. *See also* dichotomies

economic disruption: as context for re-
    search, 155–56; in Kyrgyzstan, 101,
    105–6, 111–14, 116*n1;* in Macedonia,
    31–32; privatization, 105–6; public health
    system and, 160–61; Roma and, 208; in
    Taimyr Autonomous District, 132; in
    Uzbekistan, 159–64
economies: capitalism emergent in, 108–9,
    114–15, 156, 162–64; dual economies,
    114; "gray" or "shadow," 120–21, 169*n8*
educator roles, 165, 169*n9,* 197–98, 213
elders, Roma attitude toward, 204–5
employment: German reunification and,
    79–80; in Kyrgyzstan, 101; of Roma,
    208–9; socioeconomic networks and,
    112–13; women and, 79–80, 101, 112–13
Enola Gay exhibit, 39, 45*n6*
espionage, 154–55, 169*n5,* 199, 219
ethics, 26–27, 93; of advocacy, 144–46; of
    challenging behavioral norms, 205–6;
    confidentiality of subjects, 25–26, 35, 127;
    of cultural criticism, 61–62, 138–41; of
    eliminating "dirt," 127–28; of feminist
    practice, 93; of fieldwork, 26–27, 228–29;
    of generalizing, 127–28; of gift exchange,
    208; nationalism and, 233; policy viola-
    tions and, 199–200; in politically charged
    situations, 131; of practical service,
    165–68; pragmatic, 233
ethnic cleansing: Armenian genocide, 124–
    25; in Azerbaijan, 19–20; deportations,
    21
ethnic conflicts: Armenian/Azerbaijani, 120,
    124–25; Dolgan/Evenki in Siberia, 140;
    Greek/Turkish in Cyprus, 26, 219, 221;
    historical roots for, 18; Nagorno-
    Karabagh movement, 16–21; Uzbek/Kyr-
    gyz conflicts, 156–57; violence against
    Roma, 208
ethnic minorities, recognition denied, 137,
    200–201, 220–21, 226–27, 232
ethnography, as state function, 135–38
Evenkis, 133–35; conflicts with Dolgans,
    134–35, 140; survival as people, 142–43
exogamy, 43, 142–43

families: ethnic conflicts impact on, 43; Evenki survival and, 142–43; field identities and, 180–82, 204–5; Roma kin orientation, 209
favors, 163–64, 195
feminism: epistemology, 76; feminist critiques of, 90–91; gender issues as study, 197–98; German reunification and, 77, 84–85, 87–88; as research stance, 86–87, 89, 93
fieldnotes, 202–3; intrusive quality of, 88; subjects' opinions of, 139
fieldwork: dynamic nature of, 114; ethical choices inherent in, 26–27; intrusive nature of, 151; map of countries, 2; narrating, 122; rapid change as context for, 115–16; as transformative experience, 195–96
Focolare movement, 175–77, 185, 190nn4, 5, 191nn8, 9
folklore: Gypsy Lore Society, 203; Macedonian Institute of Folklore, 203; Serbian urban tales, 51–52
foreign anthropologists: dissolution of the Soviet Union and, 155–56; fieldwork identities of, 130–31; freedom of the outsider, 123–24; as guest, 166; *vs.* native anthropologists, 26. *See also* outsider status
friendships, 26, 82–83, 91, 171–90, 195–213, 221

gender: bias in language, 77; domestic chores and, 205; feminist ethnography and, 197–98; gendered objectivity, 86; in Kyrgyzstan, 100–101; media portrayals of, 101–2, 109–10; among Roma, 205, 207–8
generalizations, to be avoided, 222; differences within "them," 27; "dirt," 127–28, 222–23; ethics of, 127–28. *See also* stereotypes
genocide, Armenian identity and, 124–25. *See also* ethnic cleansing
Germany. *See* reunification, German
gifts, 208
globalism: media and, 101–2, 107–10; national identity in world community, 44
Gorbachev, Mikhail: postsocialist attitudes about, 155; reforms and Armenian activism, 16–17

gossip: priest's reassignment and, 185–86; problems aired in, 126. *See also* rumors
graffiti, 82
"Grandma's cupboards," 54–55
Greece, 153, 219–21, 224
guest anthropologists. *See* foreign anthropologists
Guli, Pitu, 37
gypsies. *See* Roma
Gypsy Lore Society, 203

halfie anthropologists: friendships and fieldwork, 172–90; identity of, 74–75, 123, 183–84, 188
Handler, Richard, 40, 61–62
Hável, Vaclev, 58–59
health care: abortion rights, 75; access to care, 160–62; cultural understandings of health and illness, 183; friendship dilemmas and, 178–80; public systems collapse, 160–62
history: construction of, 17, 28n3; denied by researchers, 85; destructive research and, 43; documenting claims, 17–18; Evenki "forgotten" history, 140–41; fictionalized accounts of, 125; historical truth, 32–33; historiography, 62; Institute for National History (Skopje), 31; oral *vs.* written sources, 42; orientation and, 79; priorities of popular history, 39; subject's stake in, 43, 79, 85
hospitality: economic collapse and, 234; information provision as, 233–34; reciprocity norms, 113; research relationships and, 14–15, 16, 233–34; scarcity and, 113–14; state control of, 199–200, 219
human rights: asylum issues, 210–11, 213, 215nn21, 23; atrocities, 28n6; cultural criticism and, 33; in Guatemala, 23; Sofia Human Rights Project, 212

identities: of east German women, 79–80, 90; family and, 180–82, 204–5; fieldwork identities, 78, 116, 130–31, 203–5, 207–8; "forgotten" history and, 140–41; halfie, 74–75, 123, 183–84, 188; interpretive roles of, 15; negotiating, 115; pop culture and, 116; as subjectivities, 79. *See also* national identities ideologies: Cold War, 82, 101, 131, 145; loss as cultural vacuum, 109; nationalism and, 43–44; othering and, 102; research defined by state, 154; violence and, 21. *See also* capitalism; Cold War; nationalism

Ilinden revolution (1903), 34, 36–37

illness, cultural understandings of, 183. *See also* health care

images: Armenian stereotypes, 124–26; mud and slush in Serbia, 56–58; as representation of other, 104–7, 226; of women, 100

individualist-communalist divide, 80, 95*n14*, 158–59

Institute for National History (Skopje): dispute between historians at, 35–39; establishment and mandate of, 36, 38

Internal Macedonian Revolutionary Organization, 36–37

International Research and Exchanges Board (IREX), 13, 214*n14*

interpersonal spaces, 151–52

interview practices: conversations as interviews, 202–3; formal interviews, 203; journalistic, 88–89; patient deference in, 158; public *vs.* private self-representations, 126–27; subjects frustrated by naive questions, 85–86, 88. *See also* fieldnotes

intimacy: cultural, 225–27, 231; life story approach, 82–83; social, 225–27

Islam: in Kyrgyzstan, 100–101; Pomaks, 200, 202, religious persecution, 21, 200, 202

journalism, 33, 34, 88–89, 104. *See also* television

Karabagh movement, 16–21

Karev, Nikola, 37

KGB, 18

Khantaiskoe Ozero, 130–44; children of, 142–43

Kirghizia, Republic of. *See* Kyrgyzstan

Kosovo, battle of, 33–34

Kruševo, Macedonia, 34; Ilinden revolution and, 36–37

Kruševo Manifesto, 37, 42

Kul'tura, 140

Kyrgyzstan, 100–116; economic disruption, 101, 111–14, 116*n1;* Uzbek/Kyrgyz conflicts, 156–57

land disputes. *See* boundaries

leadership: cynical nationalism of, 57; Western notions of rejected, 80–81

life-story approach, 86

Macedonia: Bulgars (Slav-speaking minority) in, 36; economic disruption, 31–32; Ilinden revolution, 34, 36–37; international recognition of, 31–32, 41, 43; Kruševo, 34; as *narod,* 41; Roma of, 196, 209; Vlachs in, 36, 43

Macedonian Institute of Folklore, 203

maps: of fieldwork countries, 2; national identity and, 133, 141

marginality: critique of privilege, 90; transition construct and, 119–20; Yugoslav self-perception, 56

marriage: exogamy, 43, 142–43; weddings, 202, 205–6

Mashpee identity, 40–41

media: coverage of war in Serbia, 60–61; film as documentation, 199; misinformation source about West, 52, 138; and outsider identities, 115; ritual events documented with, 203; visual imperialism of Western media, 222; Western pop culture, 101, 107–10. *See also* television

medical care. *See* health care

Milošević, Slobodan, 51; ode to, 57; slogans, 59; in urban folklore, 51–52; use of battle of Kosovo, 34

Mitfrauen, 77

mud, 56–57

music, 198; Roma identity, 197, 202, 212–13; Uzbek women, 159; Yuri Yunakov, 210–12

mystifications, 61–62, 65*n8*

Nagorno-Karabagh movement, 16–21

narod, 41, 46*n7*

narratives: battle of Kosovo, 33–34; destructive narration, 38; "Grandma's cupboards" theme, 54–55; Macedonian history, 31–44; nationalism and, 233; public *vs.* private accounts, 23; Serbian self-representation genres, 53–60; skepticism as destructive of, 232; of victimization, 20–21. *See also* stories

national identities: Armenia and imagined communities, 124–26; consolidating

national identities (*continued*)
native peoples, 134–36; denied ethnic minorities, 200–201, 220–21, 226–27; Macedonian recognition, 31–32, 41, 43; manipulation by state ethnographers, 134–37;
maps and, 133, 141; Popov on, 134,
136–37; reconstructed through speech,
17; Roma, 197, 202, 212–13; Serbian self-
representations, 53–60; Siberian, 130–46;
survival issues of Evenki, 142–44; world
community requirement, 44
nationalism: anthropology and, 223; authentic *vs.* cynical, 57; deconstructing,
62–63; double standard and power, 61–62;
historical contexts for, 44; and historical
truth, 33–34; in Macedonia, 31–44; myths
of, 124; Nagorno-Karabagh movement,
16–21; Serbian, 51, 58–61
native anthropologists or ethnographers: as
broker with West, 50; choosing sides, 123,
127; *vs.* foreign anthropologists, 26; nationalism and, 49–63; perceived as biased,
26, 33; Trajko Petrovski, 196; in socialist
societies, 121
neutrality, 15
nostalgias: as postsocialist syndrome, 220;
in Serbian narratives, 54–56; structural
nostalgia, 226

objectification, 85–86
objectivity: anthropology as "unscientific,"
228; as excuse, 188–89; as exploitative
stance, 14, 165, 225–26; Faustian contract
and, 14–15, 21, 27; friendships as threat
to, 173; gendered objectivity, 86; of native
anthropologists, 127–28; object/subject
constructions, 86; other and, 74; positionality of researcher, 74, 123
observers: positioning of, 188–89; subjects
as, 81–83
Olympics (1996), 41
origin myths, pursuit of, 85–86, 88, 223
othering: Cold War ideologies and, 102; of
east German women, 81, 85–86; Evenki/
Dolgan dynamics, 140; friendship and objectivity, 173; halfie status and, 183–84,
188; socialist societies and, 121; us/them
dichotomies, 58, 120–21; visual representation and, 104–7

Ottoman Empire: battle of Kosovo and,
33–34, 37; as oppressive regime, 18
outsider status: authority rejected by subjects, 40; friendship and, 24; identities
and, 114–15; *vs.* native status 123–24; perceived power of, 188; as resource for subjects, 156. *See also* foreign anthropologists

parents of researchers, 204–5
participant-observation method, 24; native
vs. foreign researchers and, 123
perestroika: fieldwork during, 15–16;
Nagorno-Karabagh conflict and, 16–17
Petrovski, Trajko, 196
photographs: power relationships and, 181–
82; as representation of other, 104–7, 226
play: in research relationships, 90; rituals
learned through, 205
politics: avoiding entanglements, 50, 124,
140, 188; ethnography as political task,
136–37; during German reunification, 77,
81–85; religious resistance, 176
Pomaks, 200, 202
Popov, Andrei Aleksandrovich, 134, 135–37
positioning: hybrid, 184, 188; objectivity, 74;
as observer, 188–89; of researcher, 73–76,
151
postsocialism: as context for fieldwork,
13–27; discontents of, 54, 159–62, 166;
source for anthropological understandings, 166–67
poverty: absent under socialism, 166; in
Kyrgyzstan, 102, 111–14, 117*n3*; starving
Armenian stereotype, 124–26
power relationships: ambivalence toward
foreign "guest," 234; *Besser Wessi* behavior, 77–78, 180; nationalism and, 62; political violence and, 21, 23; priest's role in
community, 176–80; between researcher
and subject, 6, 153; researcher empowered by state, 123
practical service to subjects, 197
processual paradox, 36, 155
protest: affective bonds formed during, 17;
culture of, 16

reciprocity: hospitality norms, 113; reciprocal ethnography, 151–52, 196; in research
relationships, 27, 87

reflexivity: Cold War ideologies and, 115; distancing moments and, 172, 184; ethnography and, 230–31; negotiated identities and, 115; Nietzsche on, 115; of researcher, 35, 74, 84, 188–90, 196–97; sequestration as research obstacle, 158–59
reindeer herding, 131–32, 134, 138
religion: Catholicism, 175–77; ethnic cleansing and, 21; Focolare movement, 175–77; Islam, 21, 100–101, 202–3; Macedonian religious communities, 36–37; nationalism and, 34; negotiating during fieldwork, 177–78; popular faith vs. institutionalized, 186–87, 192n19; resistance to socialism, 186–87
"Remembering the Wall: Before and After" (poem), 92
research: audiences for, 24–25; intrusive nature of, 88, 167–68; obstacles to, 120–21, 157–59, 199–200; positionalities of, 73–76, 151; trust and loyalty issues, 14; as voyeurism, 14, 26. See also research relationships
research relationships: adversarial, 39–41, 85; friendships, 82–83, 91, 172–90; as negotiation, 100; reciprocity in, 27, 87, 196; research bargain, 24–26; subjective and objective, 75; visual images effect on, 110
resettlements, 136
reunification, German: as colonization, 76, 94n7; as context for research, 75; cultural losses after, 80, 91; decline of religious involvement, 176; feminism and, 77, 84–85; political changes during, 81–82
revelatory incidents, 172
rituals: attending as fieldwork, 203–4; demonstrations as, 17; learned through play, 205; media for documentation, 203; religious, 176
Roma: asylum issues, 210–11, 213, 215nn21, 23; diaspora, 208–9; discrimination against, 201, 208–9; Islam, 202–3; Kalderash, 198, 212; kin orientation of, 209; Machwaya, 198–99; music and identity, 197, 202, 212–13; recognition of, 220; unemployment of, 208–9
rumors: about KGB, 18; Serbian, 52. See also gossip

scarcity: "Grandma's cupboards" stories, 54–55; hospitality norms and, 113–14; public vs. private discourse, 126–27; research bargains and, 233–34; in rural Armenia, 123; in Uzbekistan, 160–62, 164
self-reflection. See reflexivity
self-representations: accountability to, 197; Armenian, 18, 126; "jeremiads," 57–58; mud and slush images in, 56–58; public vs. private, 126–27; Serbian, 49–63; socialism's legacy, 153
Serbia: battle of Kosovo, 33–34; disintegration of Yugoslavia, 50–52; narratives of self-representation, 49–63; opposition movements in, 51–52
shamans, 134
Shushi/Shusha, Azerbaijan, 21–22
Shuta Orizari (Shutka), 203–8
Siberia, 130–46
similarities: apparent/deceptive, 183–84; similarity hunting, 121–22
Skopje, Macedonia, 31
socialism: advantages for women, 79–80, 111–12; as bearable evil, 57–60; control of media, 108–10; interdependency, 112–13; legacy of, 54–56, 153; nostalgia for, 54–56, 220, 226; parallel worlds of, 54; positive perceptions of, 103; poverty absent under, 166; religious resistance to, 186–87; rhetoric of, 153
social reality, opacity of, 50–53
solidarity, 93
Soviet Union: dissolution of, 120, 155–56; state ethnography in, 135–38; USSR vs. United States dichotomy, 155–56
Stefanović, Nenad, 57
stereotypes: of Armenians, 124–26; Cold War, 120–21; of victims, 22–23. See also images; photographs
stories: east German women, 82–91, 171–73; life stories, 82–91, 159–62; resentment stories, 54–56; revival during transition, 53; as sense making activity, 53; truth in fictions, 51–52; urban folklore, 51–52; Uzbek, 159–62
subjectivity: bonds of understanding and, 17. See also friendships; objectivity
subjects: amusement value of researcher, 157–58; as audience for research, 24–25,

subjects (*continued*)
39–41; collaborative research, 86–87, 196;
confidentiality for, 25–26, 35, 127; in control of research situations, 15, 166; curiosity of, 16; information controlled by, 15;
negativity toward researcher, 85; objectified by researchers, 73, 87–89; as observers, 81–83; punished for researcher's
behaviors, 199–200; respect for, 32, 144;
understanding of ethnography, 130–31,
135–41
Sumgait, Azerbaijan, 17–18

Taimyr Autonomous District: demographics, 132; fieldwork in, 130–35, 137; Soviet
control of, 135–37. *See also* Evenkis
Tashkent, 155, 157, 164
telephone ethnography, 192*n21*
television: capitalism via, 108–9; content of
programs, 109; gender relationships and,
109–10; globalism, 107–8; in Kyrgyzstan,
107–10; as policy supplement, 108; source
of information, 101–2, 160–61
"thick description," 226–27
Tito, Josip Broz, 32, 36, 64*n7*
trade, 114–15, 156, 162–64
train travel, 158–59
transition, 227–28; ethnographic gaze during, 132; opacity of social reality, 50–53;
postsocialist ethnography and, 230; self-
representation and, 224–25; stories revived during, 53. *See also* transition construct
transition construct: continuities and,
119–20; criticisms of, 71; meaning and
continuum, 122–23
trust relationships, 14, 24–26, 89; credibility
and, 232
truth: in fictions, 51–52; historical truth,
32–33; journalistic accounts and, 33; *vs.*
lies (dichotomy), 58–59; "partial" truth
and point of view, 196

unemployment. *See* employment

us/them dichotomies, 58, 121, 140
Uzbekistan, 153–68

victimhood: aggressors and, 18, 23; Armenian stereotypes, 124–25; of Azerbaijanis,
20–21; of non-Western women, 87; real
vs. stereotyped, 23
violence: interethnic, 17–21; political, 21, 23;
ritual killings, 21; against Roma, 208; in
Sumgait, Azerbaijan, 17–18; against
women, 82, 109; writing about, 19–23. *See
also* ethnic conflicts; wars
Vlachs, 36–37, 43, 198–99

wars: as context for fieldwork, 6, 13–27, 124;
Ilinden revolution, 34, 36–37; media coverage of, 60–61. *See also* ethnic conflicts
wealth: gift exchange ethics, 208; of West,
114–15, 156, 162–64
weddings, 202, 205–6
women: east German, 80–91, 171–73; emancipated by Soviet system, 103; employment, 79–80, 101, 112–13; Evenki survival
issues, 142–44; poverty and, 111–14;
Power Women of Germany, 84; propaganda images of, 100; religious dedication
of, 175–77, 182–83; Roma gender roles,
205, 207–8; socialism as advantage for,
79–80, 103, 111–12; as victims, 87; violence against, 82, 109. *See also* feminism
writing: adversarial potential of, 40; audiences for research, 24–25, 39–41, 44; authoritative voice and distancing, 173; historiography, 62; political nature of, 72; of
state ethnographers, 136–37; subjects' relationship to, 196; about violence, 19–23.
See also fieldnotes

Yerevan, Armenia, 13, 17
Yugoslavia: compared with Greece, 220; disintegration of, 50–52; Macedonian autonomy, 31–44
Yunakov, Yuri (musician), 210–12,
215*nn21–23*